Inlander Histories

Volume 2

EDITED BY TED S. McGREGOR JR.

INLAND NORTHWEST HISTORY, SPOKANE HISTORY,
WASHINGTON STATE HISTORY, IDAHO HISTORY

COVER DESIGN: CHRIS BOVEY
COPY EDITOR: ANNE McGREGOR

EXCERPT: "THE PATSY CLARK MANSION," PAGE 60;
FROM HENRY C. MATTHEWS; *KIRTLAND CUTTER: ARCHITECT IN THE LAND
OF PROMISE*; PP. 112-113, 124-132 AND 157; © 1998; REPRINTED BY PERMISSION
OF THE UNIVERSITY OF WASHINGTON PRESS.

INLANDER BOOKS
1227 W. SUMMIT PARKWAY
SPOKANE, WASHINGTON 99201
INLANDER.COM/BOOKS

ISBN-13: 978-0692568279 / ISBN-10: 0692568271

PEOPLE WHO SHAPED THE INLAND NORTHWEST

INLANDER

HISTORIES, VOL. 2

inlanderbooks

SPOKANE, WASHINGTON
INLANDER.COM/BOOKS

TABLE OF CONTENTS

INTRODUCTION
Chasing History
BY JACOB H. FRIES   PAGE 9

CHAPTER ONE
The Prodigious Son: Bing Crosby
BY SHERI BOGGS AND ROBERT CARRIKER   PAGE 11

CHAPTER TWO
The Detective and the Davenport: Dashiell Hammett
BY JESS WALTER   PAGE 21

CHAPTER THREE
Wobblies on the Corner: Elizabeth Gurley Flynn
BY RONALD A. MYERS   PAGE 29

CHAPTER FOUR
The Prince of Prohibition: Albert Commellini
BY PATRICK HEALD   PAGE 43

CHAPTER FIVE
Frontier Dreambuilder: Kirtland Cutter
BY TED S. McGREGOR JR. AND HENRY MATTHEWS   PAGE 53

CHAPTER SIX
The Ringmasters of Nat Park: Louis and Emma Vogel
BY ROBERT M. WITTER   PAGE 67

CHAPTER SEVEN
Captain Coeur d'Alene: Peter Sorensen
BY E. J. IANNELLI   PAGE 75

CHAPTER EIGHT

People of the Century: 1900 - 2000

BY TED S. McGREGOR JR., IVAN MUNK,
JACK NISBET AND J. WILLIAM T. YOUNGS PAGE 91

CHAPTER NINE

Healing Pioneers: The Sisters of Providence

BY WILLIAM STIMSON PAGE 111

CHAPTER TEN

The Speaker from Spokane: Tom Foley

BY TED S. McGREGOR JR. PAGE 117

CHAPTER ELEVEN

Blending In, Standing Out: Ed Tsutakawa

BY DAN RICHARDSON PAGE 125

CHAPTER TWELVE

Father's Footsteps: Carl Maxey

BY LUKE BAUMGARTEN PAGE 135

CHAPTER THIRTEEN

A Tangled Legacy: James Glover

BY LISA WAANANEN JONES PAGE 147

CHAPTER FOURTEEN

The Wanderer: Jaco Finlay

BY JACK NISBET PAGE 161

CHAPTER FIFTEEN

Into the Unknown: Lewis and Clark

BY ROBERT CARRIKER PAGE 173

ABOUT THE AUTHORS PAGE 236

Chasing History

I t's been said that journalism is the first rough draft of history. At the *Inlander*, with the benefit of a little time and reflection, we aspire to that elusive second draft, the one that reaches beyond initial impressions for the *whole* story, warts and all. The drive to dig deeper has propelled the paper since its founding in 1993, and it's felt throughout this second volume of *Inlander Histories* in the stories of people who helped shape the Inland Northwest.

There's Bing Crosby in all his complicated glory: the American icon, Gonzaga law student, tough kid prone to shoplifting and hard drinking, the much-misunderstood musical pioneer who keeps us dreaming of a "White Christmas."

There's Elizabeth Gurley Flynn, the so-called "East Side Joan of Arc," one of the radical labor organizers known as the Wobblies who, in 1909, turned the eyes of America on Spokane for its prohibition on speaking in public.

And there are Bill and Bevan Maxey — sons of Carl Maxey, the man the *New York Times* credited "with virtually singlehandedly desegregating much of the Inland Northwest" — whose own modern-day stories remind us that history is very much alive.

That's the thing about history: So much of the past informs the present. And inevitably our understanding of historical figures changes over time and is enriched by a closer, second reading. Even James Glover, the reputed father of Spokane, has enjoyed (or suffered, rather) a reexamination in recent years.

In the end, *Inlander Histories, Volume 2* is not a ranking of influential people, but a collection of fascinating local characters who grabbed our attention once and simply won't let go.

JACOB H. FRIES
Inlander Editor
November 4, 2015

9

Bing Crosby back in the old neighborhood for Homecoming in 1951.

The Prodigious Son: Bing Crosby

BY SHERI BOGGS

First published in the *Inlander* on February 8, 2001

B ing Crosby, with his boyish face and penetrating gaze, has one of those instantly recognizable faces of the 20th century. Like other icons of American pop culture, he represents as much about a time and place as he does his own body of work. For instance, Joan Crawford's arched eyebrows and flying buttress shoulder pads evoked the newfound power of the first generation of career girls. Marilyn Monroe's half-lidded eyes still suggest both the sex-goddess allure of Hollywood and its inevitable failure to sustain life on any real level. And Humphrey Bogart's world-weary stance will always mirror the nation's postwar loss of innocence. But what does Crosby represent? Was he the nattily dressed poster boy for white American optimism? A regular Joe from a provincial Northwest background who made good in Hollywood? The face of Irish Catholic holiday goodwill as the voice of a "White Christmas"? Or a tired old crooner around whom allegations of child abuse swirled like stale tobacco smoke?

Crosby is the subject of an ambitious new biography by music critic Gary Giddins, who, in addition to writing for the *Village Voice*, won the National Book Critics Circle Award for his book *Visions of Jazz* in 1998. Most recently, Giddins collaborated with Ken Burns on his jazz series for PBS, and, prior to *Bing Crosby: A Pocketful of Dreams, The Early Years 1903-1940*, has written biographies on Louis Armstrong and Charlie Parker.

As someone who could write about any musical giant of the past century, the question he is asked most often by interviewers is the most inevitable.

"For the last 10 years, when I would tell people that I was working on this book, the first question I'd get was why," says Giddins from his home in New York City. "To begin with, he was a very great singer and a great musical figure. And I felt that his reputation was being buried and misunderstood. I wanted him to reclaim his position at the epicenter of popular American music in the years before the advent of rock and roll."

After all, as Giddins points out, Crosby amassed more than 400 hit records over his career – a feat unmatched by Elvis Presley, the Beatles and Frank Sinatra. But of most interest to local readers will be the fact that *A Pocketful of Dreams* chronicles Crosby's early years in Spokane. The years when his nights were spent as a budding musician in local watering holes and his days were spent as a law student at Gonzaga University. In fact, some of the book's liveliest passages come from accounts of Crosby's hijinks as a young musician prone to shoplifting and drinking binges (and other running-wild type escapades) in the rough but growing city. Still, Spokane helped Bing become the man he would eventually be.

"Certainly, I think that he grew up on the wrong side of the tracks, and he had to learn to fend for himself to a degree," says Giddins. "The family wasn't well off, so he held job after job, and he was harshly disciplined by his mother. And then there was his experience at Gonzaga University. He received a very good education, he learned enunciation, he was a voracious reader, and he learned to debate. I think all of these things contributed to the intellectual interpretation of music he made popular in American music. He was the first one who thought about, 'What do these lyrics mean?' So I think his background was crucial."

❖ ❖ ❖

While the chapters on Spokane are a must-read for anyone interested in local history, the book is garnering significant critical praise for its amazing depth and scope. It's in this area that Giddins shines as a writer – his 10 years of exhaustive research is equally matched by his incisive-yet-affectionate prose. Part of his enthusiasm for Crosby lies in what the man was able to accomplish in his lifetime, and also, for the person Crosby was underneath the often mystifying persona.

"One of things that was paramount for me in writing a book on Bing Crosby was to use his story to trace the development of technology in the recording industry. He was a pioneer in radio, in sound and with the microphone," Giddins explains. "And then I wanted to get into the growth of Paramount Studios and how he was a big part of that. I also wanted to look at the growth of Decca Records and the technological advances he helped further there, which peaked in 1946 when he put up a lot of his own money to finance the development of tape."

While we take audio tape for granted, at the time Crosby's excitement about the new recording medium was considered a nervy gamble. "It was a very courageous move at that time. Radio was a live medium, and nobody wanted to change that," says Giddins. Crosby's popularity with American audiences – a national poll taken in the late 1940s had him declared the most admired man alive, ahead of Bob Hope, Jackie Robinson, General MacArthur and Harry Truman, Giddins points out – was largely due to his insouciant sense of individualism. "You couldn't sway him," says Giddins. "Paramount wanted him to be in this picture, *Alice in Wonderland.* Gary Cooper – well all those guys, they just knuckled to the studio and said, 'Whatever you want.' Not Crosby. He opened up negotiations and threatened to walk if he didn't get what he wanted. And walk he did."

As for Crosby, the person, Giddins hoped to provide a more balanced picture than had previously been offered. The most recent book on Crosby that Giddins knew of was Gary Crosby's tell-all biography, written after Bing's death in 1977, which damned the elder Crosby as the source behind the younger Crosby's persistent alcoholism. "With Crosby, I wanted to show how he can be one way, how he could be a performer that projected this almost universal warmth, and then be a real bastard in real life. But as I got into the research, I found myself liking him more and more." While Giddins admits that there is a grain of truth to what Gary Crosby wrote – Bing was a firm believer in corporal punishment – it wasn't the horrific "Daddy Dearest" childhood many imagined. "I went looking for the dirt, I really did, but it simply wasn't documented," says Giddins. "[Later] things get a little ugly because that was when his marriage to [first wife] Dixie began to fall apart and the kids were getting older and more difficult. But there was a reason I stopped... in 1940. This book is about Bing Crosby's rise. This is the man he was then."

The man Giddins discovered over the course of more than 300 interviews with as many as 250 sources was a far cry from the aloof tyrant he half-expected. "As a human being, he was constantly surprising me. A colleague of mine was doing a documentary on Bing for Disney, and I called him one night and asked him, 'Am I talking to the wrong people?' Everyone I'm talking to says, 'He's the most generous man I ever knew, he's the friendliest man I ever knew.' [He] laughed and said, 'You know, I've been thinking the same thing.'"

So where did Der Bingle's reputation for chilly reserve come from? "He was a really generous guy," says Robert Carriker, history department chair at Gonzaga University. "His life was kind of shattered by the fact of having two families, the old family and the new one, and it was the sort of situation in which the right arm didn't know what the left arm was doing. Bing didn't really get a chance to become a musical movie hero who transcends generations. Some, like Frank Sinatra, are passed on from generation to generation, but that never happened with Bing."

Still, Crosby continued to donate to his old alma mater and hometown causes throughout his life. Crosby also gained a reputation for his fairness to people of different races and nationalities during a period when it wasn't particularly fashionable to do so. Electrified by Al Jolson while still a schoolboy in Spokane, Crosby was eager to work with Louis Armstrong, Bessie Smith and countless other African American musicians. One of the first whites to include blacks in his band, Crosby was definitely ahead of his time. "He really had no sense of prejudice at all," says Giddins. "Anthony Quinn said he was treated horribly as a Mexican American until he met Bing. Of course, he had all the prejudices of his generation; he said the kinds of things in private that white Irish guys say when they get together. But in his public life, racism simply wasn't there."

❖ ❖ ❖

While Harry Lillis Crosby wasn't born in Spokane – he was born in Tacoma in 1903 – it wouldn't be long before his family would make the smallish mining and logging town its home. "There's that quote from Bing's father early in the book about how Spokane looked good because it was a place where people, 'Don't care who you are, what you've been or what your reputation was before they met you,'" says Giddins. "He was in a bit of trouble in Tacoma apparently."

While the book talks about the little yellow house on Sinto and about young Harry going to school at Webster Elementary, the most interesting stuff comes after Crosby is renamed Bing (the nickname came from *The Bingville Bugle*, a full-page hillbilly newspaper parody that ran in the *Spokesman-Review* in 1910). As a high school student, Crosby discovered sports and proved to be an adept swimmer, golfer and baseball player.

Gonzaga University was small but nevertheless beguiling to someone of Crosby's wit and intelligence. While there, he developed his oratory skills, studied law, played football, performed in school plays and discovered music. It was these last two interests that would prove to be prophetic in Crosby's later life. In 1924, he was taking his fourth year of law school classes when he joined the Musicaladers, a group of young musicians whose fresh faces and loudly striped suits were in direct contrast to the speakeasies, pool halls and other establishments of ill repute where they played. That year, Crosby dropped out of school and hit the road to Los Angeles with fellow Musicalader, Al Rinker, in a shaky Model T with the words "Eight Million Miles and Still Enthusiastic" emblazoned on the back. The morning of that drive – October 15, 1924 – is a key moment in *A Pocketful of Dreams*:

"Bing and Al pooled about fifty dollars each," Giddins writes, "all they had from their savings [earned playing at the Clemmer Theater]. Al suffered a nervous, restless night, but he was up with the dawn that wintry Thursday morning. He had decided to postpone his good-byes until he picked up Bing, since they had to pass the Rinker house on the way out of town anyway. He pulled up to Sharp Avenue at nine, only to learn from [Bing's mother] that the habitual early riser was dead asleep. She told Al to go upstairs and wake him. He did, annoyed by Bing's seeming nonchalance. Bing finally came downstairs with his suitcase, and he and Al carried his drums and golf clubs to the car. As they emerged from the house, a small crowd began to congregate and quickly grew as the two young men packed everything into the back seat.

"One neighborhood girl recalled the scene: 'It was early in the morning and all of us kids were around. Mrs. Crosby brought out a sack lunch for the boys and when the Ford wouldn't start, Al and Bing borrowed a screwdriver from Mrs. Crosby's sewing kit to fix it.'

"After driving to retrieve Al's suitcase and saying good-bye to Mr. Rinker and his wife, they made one last stop at a service station at Boone and Division, where the attendant, an old friend, provided them with a free tank of gasoline. They continued down Division, then turned west toward Seattle... In a short while, they were up to speed: thirty miles per hour and still enthusiastic."

❖ ❖ ❖

While Crosby never returned to Spokane to live, he never severed his ties either. In addition to his philanthropic donations to the city, he continued to make public appearances in Spokane right up until his last at Expo '74, with his second wife Kathryn.

"I think there was a certain nostalgia for Bing in coming back. The first time he returned for Gonzaga's homecoming, he had not been back for 12 years," says Giddins. "Of course, there was the football game, he was extremely nostalgic about that and in the spirit of the moment, he said, 'I might broadcast the radio show from there.' Well of course the whole town went nuts, everyone was talking about how Bing might broadcast from here. It was a huge event, and then he was performing at the orphanage, at convents, at hospitals, he became the hero of the week while he was here."

As anybody who's lived here for any length of time knows, Gonzaga is proud to claim Crosby. While researching the book, Giddins spent several weeks at the Foley Library at Gonzaga University going through box after box of Crosby memorabilia ranging from photographs and album covers to a rare Bing Crosby board game and a pair of Der Bingle's own pajamas. One of the first people he thanks in the book is Stephanie Edwards Plowman, chair of special collections at GU.

"I was the first person ever to see [the collection]," says Giddins. "They had just hired Stephanie Plowman to inventory it, and we spent days and weeks just going through all of these boxes. I was discovering it at the same time she was."

Not surprisingly, Plowman is among the many Crosby enthusiasts who are glad to see an old friend get his due. "I think it's great that he's finally getting a fair assessment by someone as good as Gary," says Plowman. "It will help to dissolve some of those negative public opinions that are out there about Crosby."

What Giddins hopes is that readers of *Bing Crosby: A Pocketful of*

Dreams will see Crosby for his mastery of popular music, his verve for technology and for the fun-loving, everyman that existed below his cool exterior. "I think readers of my generation will be surprised by his politics and by how hip and far ahead of his time he was," says Giddins, "that he wasn't just this effortless crooner, whose songs went down like mother's milk. He really was an innovator whose work became a part of the modern musical American vernacular."

Home Sweet Home

BY ROBERT CARRIKER

First published in the *Inlander* on October 6, 1999

When Bing Crosby died of a heart attack on the 17th green of a Spanish golf course in mid-October 1977, the mayor of Spokane pronounced him "by far Spokane's most renowned and favorite son." And it was a two-way relationship, for Bing genuinely loved Spokane and his friends who resided here. Dozens of celebrities offered the same sentiment when informed of the death of their friend. Spokane and Crosby were intertwined in a personal and public relationship that was truly sincere.

While attending local elementary and high schools, Crosby built up quite a reputation as a dramatist and athlete. As a freshman at Gonzaga University, conveniently located across the street from the family home, the young man joined five other men in the Musicaladers, and a singing career began to take shape. So much so that in 1924 he quit a pre-law course in his senior year and drove to Los Angeles, where bandleader Paul Whiteman signed Crosby to a contract with the Rhythm Boys. The public seized upon their rendition of the jazz tune "Mississippi Mud," and the rest, as they say, is Hollywood history.

After a brief stopover in Spokane in 1926, Crosby was unable to return again for more than a decade. But when he did, he made the occasion grand. For five days during the third week of October, 1937, Crosby – by then an acclaimed veteran of both stage and screen performances – brought Hollywood to Spokane. Bing Crosby Week included the live performance of his weekly radio show from the Spokane Armory and a charity dance at Natatorium Park with the Jimmy Dorsey Orchestra. In between, the Athletic Round Table initiated Crosby into their esteemed company, and Gonzaga made him an official alumnus by awarding him an honorary doctorate in music.

Then Bing made some presentations. He gave a one-of-a-kind galvanized steel and chrome water wagon to the Gonzaga football team, and he unveiled a new marching song for the school, "The Game Is On," for which he commissioned the lyrics and music. He also formed a committee to bring the Gonzaga football team to Southern California for a game. He also promised, and delivered, bit parts in movies for some of his Spokane classmates.

But that wasn't the end of the association; Bing kept in contact with the city and helped some dreams to come true. There was another blow-out in 1948, when he brought his weekly Philco Hour radio show to Spokane and raised $10,000 toward the building of Albi Stadium, . The Gonzaga Glee Club sang on Crosby's radio show, making them virtually a household name across the country. Between 1949 and 1957, Crosby donated more than $680,000 toward the building of a new library at his alma mater (later the student center, with his likeness cast in bronze out front to greet visitors). But he made other gifts as well to the school's engineering building and Jesuit House residence. All of Crosby's gold records and his 1944 Oscar for *Going My Way* now reside at Gonzaga.

The singer's famous Pro-Am Golf Tournament donated all proceeds to fund scholarships at more than 100 colleges, including several Spokane-area institutions. Certainly by the mid-1950s, when Crosby bought a Hayden Lake home as a getaway, he enjoyed public receptions less and less. But he kept on giving. A clever businessman, he found ways to make donations. He consigned, for example, the receipts for his 1955 film *Anything Goes* to tax-exempt Gonzaga and did likewise for *The Edsel Show* on television two years later.

Bing Crosby's last appearance in Spokane came during Expo '74, and the city welcomed him as if he had been a lifelong resident. In a way, he had been just that. ∎

THE MALTESE FALCON

BY
DASHIELL HAMMETT

AUTHOR OF
THE DAIN CURSE

Dashiell Hammett's 1930 classic, *The Maltese Falcon*, takes a literary detour through Spokane.

The Detective and the Davenport: Dashiell Hammett

BY JESS WALTER

First published in the *Inlander* on February 14, 2008

For a literary manifesto, it's not much to look at — a thousand words spread over 13 paragraphs on three pages, an odd philosophical detour in Dashiell Hammett's otherwise insistent masterpiece, *The Maltese Falcon*. But the story of "a man named Flitcraft," who one day disappears from his life and then must explain himself in a room at the Davenport Hotel, has become a landmark, not only in noir, hard-boiled mystery writing and 20th-century existentialist fiction, but in the literature of Spokane as well.

Since its release in 1930, *The Maltese Falcon* has been called a lot of things — "the best detective story ever written" for one — but no one has ever called it boring. And watching the 1941 Humphrey Bogart movie version instead isn't cheating because *The Maltese Falcon* is one of the few works to earn places in both the Modern Library's 100 Best Novels and the American Film Institute's 100 Best Films.

The Maltese Falcon tells the story of Sam Spade, a private detective in San Francisco whose partner is murdered while working a bogus case for a beautiful dame named Brigid O'Shaughnessy. As Spade sticks his V-shaped nose deeper into the case (which revolves around the jewel-encrusted statue of the title), there is no shortage of plot. But plot is hardly the point. The genius of Hammett's book lies in its cool, clear-eyed prose, which mirrors its amoral outlook: People lie. Life is tough. Big deal.

The Flitcraft Parable, as it has been called, really has nothing to do with the falcon or the dame or the dead partner, which is why it calls so much attention to itself in Hammett's economical book. At the beginning of Chapter Seven, with the story in full bloom, the stoical Spade inexplicably pauses the action to tell Miss O'Shaughnessy "about a thing that had happened some years before in the Northwest."

The story: In 1922, a Tacoma real-estate agent named Flitcraft disappeared, leaving behind an inheritance, a loving wife, two boys, "a new Packard and the rest of the appurtenances of successful American living ... 'He went like that,' Spade said, 'like a fist when you open your hand.'"

Five years later, Flitcraft is spotted in Spokane and Mrs. Flitcraft hires Spade to track him down. In Spade's room at the Davenport, Flitcraft explains that he was walking to lunch one day when he passed a construction site and a beam fell. The beam barely missed him, shaking him from his prosaic existence. Flitcraft felt:

> *like somebody had taken the lid off life and let him look at the works. ...*
> *The life he knew was a clean orderly sane responsible affair. Now a falling*
> *beam had shown him that life was fundamentally none of these things ... He*
> *knew then that men died at haphazard like that, and lived only while blind*
> *chance spared them.*

After that Flitcraft simply walked away from his life, without telling a soul. For a while he drifted around the Northwest, but eventually he settled down in "a Spokane suburb," where Spade finds him remarried to a woman much like his first wife:

> *You know, the kind of women that play fair games of golf and bridge and*
> *like new salad-recipes ... I don't think he even knew he had settled back into*
> *the same groove he had jumped out of in Tacoma. But that's the part of it I*
> *always liked. He adjusted himself to beams falling, and then no more of them*
> *fell, and he adjusted himself to them not falling.*

❖ ❖ ❖

Dashiell Hammett's time in Spokane was as brief an episode in his life as the Flitcraft story was in his novel. Born in Maryland in 1894, Samuel Dashiell Hammett went to work in 1915 for the Pinkerton Agency, the largest private detective agency in the United States. After a brief stint as a soldier in World War I, Hammett returned to Pinkerton and was sent to the Spokane office. He lived here from May to November of 1920, at which point he went to a Tacoma hospital for tuberculosis treatment. He got married, had a couple of kids and moved to San Francisco.

He quit Pinkerton in 1922 to write. Most mystery authors learn about detective work to write crime fiction. Hammett was a detective who learned to write. Between 1929 and 1934, he published all five of his novels – *Red Harvest, The Dain Curse, The Maltese Falcon, The Glass Key* and *The Thin Man*. As literary outputs go, it's a slender library, but its effect was profound. Calling himself "one of the few people … who take the detective story seriously," Hammett hoped to "some day … make 'literature' of it."

That's just what he did. Part of the holy noir trinity – along with Raymond Chandler and James M. Cain – Hammett took Ernest Hemingway's carved sentences and post-World War I cynicism and put a fresh coat of paint on the disrespected mystery novel. *The Maltese Falcon* made him famous, and writing for Hollywood in the '30s and '40s made him rich. He got involved in liberal politics, became a Marxist, served in World War II, got smeared by Joseph McCarthy and spent the years before his 1961 death indulging those two staples of a writer's life: drinking and not writing.

So what did Hammett do during his six months in Spokane? It's intriguing to imagine one of his wise-ass detectives skulking around Spokane during its rough-and-tumble heyday, following cheating husbands and recovering stolen insurance dough, but the Pinkertons who worked in 1920 Spokane were closer to today's Blackwater mercenaries than the slick loners of his detective stories.

Founded when police departments were notoriously corrupt and unprofessional, the Pinkerton Agency had a unique role in American history. Its agents guarded President Lincoln during the Civil War, hunted Jesse James and Butch Cassidy and provided national detective work – for those who could afford it – decades before it occurred to the FBI. At one time the Pinkerton Agency was larger than the standing U.S. Army. But by 1915, when Hammett joined up, Pinkerton's biggest clients were greedy industrialists and mining magnates who wanted security from union toughs and striking workers, protection for their replacement workers, and the occasional skull-cracking of union members who complained too much.

With its wealthy neighborhoods full of mining and timber barons and a downtown bustling with miners' brothels and booze halls, Spokane was a key battlefield in this labor war. Between 1909 and 1920, the IWW (the Industrial Workers of the World, or the Wobblies) was desperately trying to organize Northwest miners. Mine owners were just as desperate to keep them out. In Spokane, IWW organizers gathered on street corners to protest and to solicit members – a thousand people gathered in Manito Park one day alone – at which point police goons would be dispatched to thump on the leaders and arrest them. Three cities – Butte, Fresno and Spokane – became ground zero for what was called "The Free Speech Movement," the demand by union organizers for the constitutionally guaranteed right to hold public meetings.

Brutal violence erupted on both sides. In 1905, the governor of Idaho was killed in a bombing by a former union leader. In 1911, Spokane's acting police chief was gunned down while he sat in his house. The crime was blamed on an IWW member, but never solved.

Pinkerton guards hired by the mines were responsible for much of the violence against union leaders. In Utah, union leader Joe Hill was railroaded and hung in 1916. A year later, in Butte, IWW leader Frank Little was lynched. In 1919, another lynch mob grabbed an IWW member in Centralia and beat him, castrated him, hung him in three different locations and shot him several times. The coroner ruled his death a suicide.

This was all coming to a head in 1920, when Hammett arrived in Spokane. Just weeks earlier, 15 striking miners had been shot, two fatally, by Pinkertons hired to break the strike at the Anaconda Copper Mining Company in Butte. Hammett's first novel *Red Harvest* is loosely based on his work in Butte. He even claimed later that he was offered $5,000 to kill Frank Little, but scholars discount this story since Little was already dead when Hammett came West.

In the 1981 biography *Shadow Man*, Richard Layman writes that Hammett "had pleasant memories of his days as a Pinkerton working out of the Spokane office" and that "his most exciting work ... came during the Anaconda strike." Layman relates Hammett's story of rounding up replacement workers with

*Blackjack Jerome, the strikebreaker Hammett worked with, who would go
into the city early in the morning with a flatbed wagon and round up drunks
... take them across picket lines and dare them to try to go back across alone
before he safely escorted them to the city after a full day's hard work.*

When he wasn't rounding up scabs, Hammett worked other cases in
Spokane, most memorably the midget bandit, who was arrested when
he returned the day after a robbery to beat up a victim who had mocked
his height. Some characters in *The Maltese Falcon* came from Hammett's
Spokane cases, too. According to William Nolan's biography, *Hammett*,
Miles Archer's wife Iva (with whom Sam Spade has an affair) was based
on a Spokane bookseller, and the oily bad guy Joel Cairo, immortalized
in the film by Peter Lorre, was based on a man Hammett "picked up on a
forgery charge in 1920."

But there's no doubt that Dashiell Hammett's lasting legacy to the
Lilac City is the character of Flitcraft, who is shaken loose from his stable
life in Tacoma and ends up living almost the same life in Spokane.

❖ ❖ ❖

If Hammett's goal was to make literature out of the detective novel,
the Flitcraft story is his masterpiece, if for no other reason than the
number of critical studies and literary allusions devoted to it. In his 2002
novel *Book of Illusions*, the brilliant American writer and filmmaker Paul
Auster re-imagined the Flitcraft tale as the story of a silent film star who
disappears and comes to Spokane to start over. Auster followed that
book with another novel, *Oracle Night*, about a writer struggling to rework
Flitcraft. The decidedly less brilliant author of the 2005 novel *Citizen
Vince*... uh, me... used the Flitcraft episode as inspiration for his story
of criminals coming to Spokane to start over in the Witness Protection
program.

In his book, Layman writes that Flitcraft is "the most critically
discussed part of any Hammett work." Writers have called it "the thesis
of noir" and "an existential parable worthy of Kierkegaard or Sartre."
There have been Flitcraft clubs and societies, and at least one website
devoted to the "random philosophy of the falling beam."

Even Flitcraft's alias in Spokane, William Pierce, has a deeper meaning, a reference to William S. Peirce, a logician and philosopher Hammett studied, known for his work with probability, chance and random occurrence (i.e., falling beams).

But in all the pages of criticism about Flitcraft and Hammett, I've never seen a scholar answer this question: Why Spokane?

The cynic, also known as the lifetime Spokane resident, could argue that there's simply no better place to ponder the emptiness of the "appurtenances of successful American living" than Spokane.

But I think there's something else about Spokane that makes it a perfect place for the disappeared to reappear.

It's easy to forget just how remote this city is — and not just because it's 280 miles from Seattle. Surrounded by basalt cliffs and boxed in by mountain ranges on all sides, Spokane is, in the words of the poet Vachel Lindsay, "a walled city" — isolated, foreboding, difficult to get in and out of. Cities Spokane's size are typically suburbs or are strung together. But Spokane just sits here, enigmatic and alone behind its walls.

I have a friend from the Midwest who went to school on the East Coast and now works at the *Seattle Times*. He simply can't figure Spokane out. "Why is it there?" he asked once. "What do people *do* there?" (I told him we do what people do everywhere, except for less money. One striking thing about Flitcraft: Hammett writes that he netted "$20,000 a year" at his car dealership in Spokane, or roughly as much as I made in my second year as a newspaper reporter, *60 years later*.)

Visitors are often shocked to find such a thriving city here, and lifers are surprised when anyone new comes to town. There is inherent mystery in newcomers. Even now, the *Spokesman-Review* does a regular feature on a Spokane transplant, as if we still can't get our arms around why anyone would come here.

And frankly, it just feels like people are hiding here. No wonder legend has Butch Cassidy spending his final years living in Spokane under an assumed name, or that the federal government used to send old mafia guys here. As Hammett knew, Spokane is the perfect place to blend in and start over. In fact, sometimes I think we're all a little like Flitcraft here, going about our business and hiding our real identities, biding our time until the next beam falls. ■

Elizabeth Gurley Flynn first made a name for herself by getting arrested in Spokane.

Wobblies on the Corner:
Elizabeth Gurley Flynn

BY RONALD A. MYERS

First published in the *Inlander* on September 9, 1998

Though it may be hard to imagine today, Spokane was once a hotbed of labor radicalism. And for a month — November of 1909 — all eyes of the nation were trained on the city for outlawing speaking in public. Hundreds of men and women who came to the city to challenge the seemingly un-American policy were thrown in jail.

Well before 1909, the West had ceased being the land of opportunity advertised in railroad circulars; the fertile farmland and hillsides filled with gold had long since been locked up by big business. The thousands of immigrants, then, were left to work for whatever wages were available. Thus the tension between labor and capital — a tension as old as the idea of private ownership — came out West.

In the early-1890s, there were individual unions representing specialized industries. But it became more and more clear to union leaders that the workers willing to work for the lowest wages not only had a natural, common bond but were also in need of a union more than any profession.

The Industrial Workers of the World (IWW) was hatched in Chicago at a 1905 founding convention. Later, the members became universally known as Wobblies. The chairman of that convention was William D. Haywood, known as Big Bill; he was also a key figure in the Western Federation of Miners. Two years after the formation of the Wobblies, Haywood was accused of hiring an assassin to kill former Idaho Gov. Frank Steunenberg, who had been murdered at his Caldwell, Idaho, home in late 1905. Haywood was defended by Clarence Darrow and acquitted in a widely publicized Boise trial. The whole episode – from the labor unrest in the Coeur d'Alene mining district that started it all to socialist radicals on the streets of New York City – was retold in the book *Big Trouble* by Anthony Lukas.

The first sentence of the Wobblies' constitution gives a glimpse into the union's attitude: "The working class and the employing class have nothing in common." And by 1912, the Wobblies had created such an impression that the *New York Times* stated: "Since Camille Desmoulins climbed on that table in Palais Royal in 1789 and unloosed the French Revolution there has been no movement about which it behooved conservative citizens to be more thoughtful." This statement came despite the fact that the Wobblies advocated non-violent means to achieve their goals. They also stood out from other unions for allowing blacks and Asians into their ranks.

It's hard today to transport yourself back, to understand how radical labor advocacy could have such an appeal. But consider: It was still before the bloody Communist revolution in Russia; the United States had just finished a period in which the rich had gotten much richer and the poor had struggled to keep their heads above water. Socialist ideas were accepted by hundreds of thousands of Americans as the antidote to such a state of capitalism run amok.

❖ ❖ ❖

By 1908, Spokane was especially suited to become the site of the Wobblies coming-out party. Its location, central to many labor-intensive operations, made it a gathering place for wage-workers. In Spokane, you could find work in the mines of North Idaho, the orchards of Wenatchee or the pine forests of northeastern Washington. But, as you can imagine with a population of rootless workers, the chance for fraud was high – and workers were taken advantage of by employment "sharks," as they were called.

The Wobblies managed to gain a foothold in Spokane, with its first large membership of nearly 3,000. And their first act was to go after those employment sharks, who they accused of exploiting workers by charging them for finding jobs that either weren't there or didn't pay what was advertised. It's even possible these agencies were working in collusion with the employers.

While the Wobblies went about attracting new members on the streets of Spokane, the employment sharks weren't going to give up the fight for their livelihood – corrupt or not. On December 22, 1908, the owners of the employment agencies pressured the Spokane City Council to make it against the law, "for any person... to do any act which shall tend to draw a crowd." Though clearly unconstitutional under the First Amendment free speech provision, the law was not without local precedence. From back as far as 1891, Spokane's municipal code claimed it was unlawful to "do anything... upon the sidewalks which shall have a tendency to frighten horses, or which shall collect any crowd so as to interfere..."

But with the older ordinance, enforcement was lax; the new law was written to be enforced. This point was driven home in March of 1909, when the city council amended the December ordinance to exempt religious organizations. In short, Wobblies were being singled out to be banned from the street corners they had been speaking from to find recruits and warn workers against the sharks.

❖ ❖ ❖

Two people also came into the orbit of the Wobblies by 1908 – people who would add to the spectacle that was about to be created by the two forces colliding. Elizabeth Gurley Flynn was a black-haired, 19-year-old Irish firebrand of a public speaker from New York City. She began her labor advocacy at age 15, preaching socialism to crowds on the sidewalks of Brooklyn. For her precocious talents, she was tagged by the author/journalist Theodore Dreiser as the "East Side Joan of Arc."

By 1909, she was working full-time for the Wobblies as a speaker and agitator. In the summer of that year, she became the resident speaker at Spokane's IWW hall; in the fall, she and her husband were sent to Missoula to recruit for the IWW. It was in Missoula where free speech tactics were first used in any major way by the Wobblies. The union had recalled Flynn to Spokane in November, where she put those tactics into well-publicized motion.

After her first Spokane conviction, she stated her motivation for being a labor radical: "All my life I have seen my family and my class suffering under the inequalities of the system that makes multi-millionaires at one extreme and toiling slaves at the other. I am in it because I want to see those who produce the world's wealth get better wages and shorter hours." She continued: "This is my first trip to the 'Wild and Wooly' West, but I have failed to see the much-wanted independence and democracy."

Another occasional socialist speaker was Fred H. Moore, a Spokane attorney. He had lived in Spokane since 1901 and was admitted to the bar in 1906 at the age of 23. The IWW retained him in 1908 as their chief legal representative in Spokane.

In the weeks leading up to November, Wobblies were called into Spokane from throughout the West and Midwest to challenge the city's policy. The Spokane Police Department prepared, and the citizens of Spokane were left to follow the unfolding story through their three newspapers: the *Spokane Press*, the *Spokane Daily Chronicle* and the *Spokesman-Review*.

To recreate that month here, we have scoured those three newspapers for first-hand accounts of what happened. Readers should then keep in mind that these are reports of the day. Accounts given from either side may well be tainted by their desire to win the battle for good publicity along with the free speech issue. We have tried to follow events that were reported in all three, using actual headlines to illustrate the news of the day.

MONDAY, NOVEMBER 1, 1909

"7,000 IWW MEN HERE FOR BATTLE," proclaims the *Spokane Press* banner headline. ... Acting Chief of Police John T. Sullivan issues the following order to all officers: "In anticipation of trouble because of threats made by the Industrial Workers of the World to speak on the streets in defiance of the authorities, I will ask all members of the police department to report at this office tomorrow, November 2, 1909, at 12:30 pm, fully equipped and in readiness for duty if the occasion requires it." The chief also promises reporters that the Wobblies will be treated humanely, but "we will not kill them with kindness." ... A special rock pile is reserved for the Wobblies at Monroe and Broadway.

TUESDAY, NOVEMBER 2

"Police keep down riot mobs; station 2 to 6 police on about every corner." ... The IWW fulfills its promise and takes to the streets to violate whatever ordinance might be in effect. ... The presiding judge quickly agrees with Fred H. Moore's argument that Spokane's latest ordinance against free speech on street corners is unconstitutional. But he's just as quick to suggest to the police that speakers could just as easily be charged under the city's broad disorderly conduct ordinance. The street speaking ordinance remains on the books, but Wobblies are now arrested for other crimes. ... Much of the action takes place in the vicinity of Stevens and Front (now Spokane Falls Boulevard). ... Socialist leaders in Everett, Yakima, Seattle, Portland, Los Angeles and Chicago are telegraphed: "Big free speech on in Spokane. Come yourself and if possible bring the boys with you." ... Local Socialists and club women come to the support of the Wobblies in announcing a "Free Speech" mass meeting at the Masonic Temple for the next night. ... IWW leaders and editors of *The Industrial Worker* are arrested at their headquarters. ... A total of 103 street speakers are taken into custody.

WEDNESDAY, NOVEMBER 3

"More than 150 prisoners, mostly enthusiasts, confirmed in jail on charge of disorderly conduct and street speaking." ... Each prisoner; according to plan, demands a separate trial. ... Attorney Moore receives the following wire from IWW headquarters in Chicago: "Use habeus corpus with all arrests. Call governor's attention to state of Colorado's paying $10,000 damages in like actions. We are in this fight to the finish. Instruct any deported persons to return to Spokane at all hazards. Immense defense fund being raised, publicity being given." ... Moore announces that Judge C.E.S. Wood, Portland anarchist and legendary Indian fighter, has been engaged as counsel to assist him in defense of the prisoners. ... Prisoners refuse to go on rock pile and are placed on a diet of bread and water.

THURSDAY, NOVEMBER 4

IWW officials threaten to sue the city over conditions in the city jail, where as many as 24 prisoners are crammed into a six-by-eight-foot cell. Many become sick and faint, but an open window is denied them. ... A bulletin is posted at IWW headquarters stating that last night, Teamsters' local 202 of the AF of L adopted this resolution: "We will stick by the IWW in its fight for free speech until hell freezes over." … Fire hoses are turned on street speakers and some listeners.

FRIDAY, NOVEMBER 5
Wobblies tell the press that, "We do not ask for the privilege of holding meetings on Riverside. We are sure we cannot get recruits to our ranks from the Silver Grill nor Davenport's. We want to work down here among the employment offices where there are wage-earners." … The IWW posts the following bulletin: "The IWW and the police have nothing in common. There can be no peace so long as the police use clubs and hose, and the IWW uses the pen and tongue."

SATURDAY, NOVEMBER 6
"The IWW cases moved along easily and smoothly. 'William Lofholm,' shouted the bailiff. Lofholm took the stand. 'Making a speech?' inquired the magistrate. 'Yes. sir,' came the reply. 'Thirty days,' said the justice." … Prisoners go on hunger strike. … Edith Frenett gives the *Spokane Press* an account of her ordeal in jail: "Arrested on Tuesday at 2 o'clock, in two hours we were covered with vermin, denied the use of soap and towels, prevented from seeing counsel, jeered by the officers as though we were monkeys in a cage. During the first night, the steam heat was first turned up to a suffocating degree and then turned completely off causing the cell to turn ice cold." She had been released on Friday afternoon. … The editor of *The Industrial Worker* gives a statement from his cell to the *Spokane Press*, which sympathized with the Wobblies' cause: "I asked to see the warrant for my arrest, but they refused to show me one. One of the men present said that I would see 'the rope' before I saw a warrant." As for conditions in the jail, Wilson said: "Most of the time there were from 20 to 28 men in the cell. The floor was slippery with vomit. One man who had an ague chill from a malaria attack, and who vomited all afternoon, asked the doctor for medicine. This man was from a malarial district of California, and the doctor simply told him there was no malaria in Spokane, and added, 'If you were not all anarchists, you would not be here, and I will see you in hell before I give you any medicine.'" … More jail scandal: Agnes Thecla Fair is arrested for speaking. She is questioned

by police in a darkened cell. She refuses to answer questions and she alleges that one of the men makes a sexual threat, then another officer begins to unbutton her blouse, sending her into convulsions. She is not able to sleep or eat after this.

SUNDAY, NOVEMBER 7
Socialists hold a free speech fund-raising lecture event in Oliver's Hall at 334 W. Riverside; $100 is raised. The meeting closes with the audience singing, "Keep the Red Flag Flying, Comrades." ... The night is capped off with a packed house at the IWW hall where Louis Catewood, "who admitted with evident pride that he had been a member of the Western Federation of Miners during the trouble in the Coeur d'Alene district, harangued the audience for two hours, uttering fiery, profane tirades against the police, press and pulpit."

MONDAY, NOVEMBER 8
Agnes Thecla Fair is ordered released by the prison doctor. "After being released by the judge on her own recognizance, Agnes Fair is paraded by her comrades through the streets to her rooms on a stretcher. She had appeared rather faint as she left the courtroom." ... "There are three demonstrations, bringing 30 arrestees to court. Police turn over records of those arrested who are not citizens to Federal authorities."

TUESDAY, NOVEMBER 9
"War Department grants police of Spokane use of guardhouse at Fort George Wright for incarceration of IWW members arrested for street speaking." ... Sometime around this time, city officials decide to use the newly constructed Franklin Elementary School, located on 17th Avenue, as a makeshift jail.

WEDNESDAY, NOVEMBER 10
A pregnant Elizabeth Gurley Flynn arrives in Spokane from Missoula to, "take charge of local forces and edit weekly journal." ... City council hears arguments against the speaking ordinance. Moore presents a compromise statute based on the ones in Seattle, New York and Chicago. Flynn gives an impassioned plea for the idea, which is supported by the Central Labor Council. The council rejects the proposal.

THURSDAY, NOVEMBER 11

The *Spokane Press* writes: "The big press associations have taken hold of the agitation, and Spokane is now daily held up to the gaze of the entire country."

FRIDAY, NOVEMBER 12

"STARVATION STRIKE IS OVER; BEG FOR FOOD AND EAT LIKE WILD CREATURES; Prisoners at Fort Wright, Franklin School and Jail Give In." ... A Superior Court judge turns down further writs of habeus corpus on the grounds that they are only wanted to "raise Cain."

SATURDAY, NOVEMBER 13

Streets are quiet ... IWW prisoners bathed by "being put through streams of water as fast as jailers can put them there."

SUNDAY, NOVEMBER 14

Denied the use of a private hall, the Wobblies are given the use of a city courtroom for a public meeting. Flynn speaks: "It is not often that the IWW is permitted to speak in this temple of injustice. If the police and city government refuse the Constitutional right of free speech, the working man should refuse to work, and if the working man refused to work there would not be a single fat capitalist eating turtle soup in Davenport's tonight."

MONDAY, NOVEMBER 15

At a meeting of about 500, held under he auspices of the Socialist Party, a resolution was passed to boycott the National Apple Show, now about to open in Spokane. ... Rumors fly that Clarence Darrow may join Moore in defending the Wobblies. One of Darrow's associates is already bound for Spokane from Chicago.

TUESDAY, NOVEMBER 16

Fred H. Moore proclaims the Goddess of Justice to be dead in Spokane. ... Wobblies announce they will flood the city with lawsuits for false arrest and imprisonment.

WEDNESDAY, NOVEMBER 17

An employment shark at 31 S. Stevens loses his license for illegally selling a job. ... Wobbly John Poss demands that he be allowed to return to jail and suffer with "the boys."

THURSDAY, NOVEMBER 18

Flynn leaves Spokane for a few days to address the Butte Miners Union. ... Wobbly George Smith announces an intention to sue the city over a beating the police gave him at the station. ... Judge Mann declares in passing on one of his street speaking cases: "I may not be right. I may be wrong, but until the higher court decides otherwise, I will continue to rule in these cases as I have been doing."

FRIDAY, NOVEMBER 19

More Wobblies from Montana and California are on the way. ... The editors of *The Industrial Worker*, after spending two weeks in jail, finally get their day in court.

SATURDAY, NOVEMBER 20

"At a conservative estimate, the IWW agitation has cost the city $100 a day," said Chief of Police Sullivan. "In this estimate I include the expense of extra officers, food and fuel. There will be no let up as far as we are concerned," continued the chief. "We have not only plenty of room but plenty of bread and water."

SUNDAY, NOVEMBER 21

Edith Frenette is arrested for the third time, this time for singing "Red Flag" from the porch of a residence near the Franklin School, then on the outskirts of town. After hearing her recite the lyrics in court, the judge sentences Frenette to 30 days. ... Flynn addresses the meeting in Butte, charging that Spokane policemen look and act like "a herd of gorillas," and may even be what, "Darwin could not find." She claims that Spokane judges have no minds to make up and says she fears some prisoners may not get out of jail alive.

MONDAY, NOVEMBER 22

Wobblies point to the death of a union member trying to get to Spokane as the first casualty of the free speech fight. The 23-year-old was killed in Wisconsin, under a train he was hitching a ride to Spokane on.

TUESDAY, NOVEMBER 23

Fred H. Moore puts out the word that the great socialist Eugene Debs has been ordered to abandon his trip to California to come to Spokane. … Wobbly S. Sorenson is arrested. When he gets to jail, a policeman informs him that he is to be thrown in the Spokane River. He is put in a sweatbox, the size of which was six by eight feet. Then, in his words, "They left me and six fellow workers in there for 17 hours with the steam turned on, then they took us out and put us in an ice-cold cell… We were tried in bunches of eight and ten before Judge Mann who was so drunk that he was almost unable to keep his seat." (Sorenson made this report to the U.S. Industrial Relations Commission in 1912, when the commission was collecting reports on free speech fights like Spokane's.)

WEDNESDAY, NOVEMBER 24

Chief Sullivan threatens to arrest Eugene Debs if the famous socialist tries to speak on the street. Sullivan brags, "I am no respecter of persons in this case. I wish the newspapers would call these people by their right name. They are anarchists, pure and simple, and their song of the Red Flag is one of the most inflammatory things I have ever heard."

THURSDAY, NOVEMBER 25

Chief Sullivan announces that IWW prisoners will get only bread and water this Thanksgiving Day. Those Wobblies out of jail vow to also go on a starvation diet of bread and water in sympathy with their comrades.

FRIDAY, NOVEMBER 26

"Refusing to cut or carry in wood for fires to keep themselves warm, members of the Industrial Workers of the World confined at Franklin Schoolhouse last night at eleven o'clock became desperate from the cold and began tearing away the woodwork in the rooms in which they are held prisoner to make a warming blaze."

SATURDAY, NOVEMBER 27

"The chain gang goes out this morning with a membership of 15, all of whom are former street speakers. The chilly weather is bringing the prisoners into submission."

SUNDAY, NOVEMBER 28

"Members of the Industrial Workers of the World confined at the city jail did their best to break up the religious services of the Salvation Army in the jail corridors. All the time the services were going on, the jail rang and echoed with the shouts and noises made by the IWWs in their efforts to drown out the hymns and prayers."

MONDAY, NOVEMBER 29

All remaining criminal conspiracy cases receive a change of venue from Judge Mann at municipal court to Judge Hyde at the courthouse. The grounds are that Judge Mann stated the week before in open court that if he were a practicing attorney he would not defend such cases as those of the IWW. ... More than a score of new Wobblies arrive from Chicago. ... Flynn speaks at the IWW hall, alleging that, "If the gentle carpenter of Nazareth was on earth today he would be fighting for free speech in this city, unless Chief Sullivan had him in jail."

TUESDAY, NOVEMBER 30

Flynn is finally arrested. In her own words: "At about eight o'clock [in the evening] I was walking toward the IWW hall. As I reached the corner of Stevens and Front I was accosted by officer Bill Shannon with the demand, 'Are you Miss Flynn?' I replied yes. When he grunted, 'Well, we want you.' I asked, 'Have you a warrant?' 'Naw, we haven't,' he rejoined, when the other plainclothes man stepped up and remarked, 'There is one in the station.' I accompanied them to the police station where I was booked and the warrant read for criminal conspiracy. I was then taken to the chief's office, where Prosecuting Attorney Pugh put me through the third degree." During the interrogation, Flynn said: "He asked, 'Did you say so and so in your speeches?' To which I replied, 'I talk so much I don't know what I say.' They all gave him the laugh, and he asked if that statement wouldn't probably, if published, ruin my reputation as a speaker. Anxious he was for me to maintain my status as an agitator, indeed!"

❖ ❖ ❖

Despite Chief Sullivan's words to the contrary, with expenses mounting, national publicity casting a shadow over the city and jail space running low, the city lost its nerve. In the weeks after Flynn's arrest, the city quietly slowed, then stopped pursuing the street speakers, as if they had made their point after arresting the Wobblies' leader.

But in the aftermath of the month of November, 1909, all sides could claim victory in some way. Despite perhaps being judged by history as more a fascist regime than an example of democracy, Spokane ultimately regained control of its street corners and had the peace of mind knowing it stood up to an outside threat and survived. And despite having hundreds of its members spend weeks in jail under bogus arrest, the Wobblies not only cemented their national reputation as in-your-face worker advocates, but also saw reforms hit Spokane. In the year following the free speech fight, Spokane wages were raised, matrons were hired to supervise the jails, the city's government structure was scrapped and replaced, the street-speaking policies were moderated and Chief Sullivan and four of his officers were fired. (In 1911, Sullivan was found murdered in his home; no one was ever charged with the crime.) Most importantly, however, the city outlawed the employment "shark" agencies that the Wobblies started their protest over.

The Spokane experience gave great hope to the Wobblies, but by 1920, when the Communist Revolution in Russia had painted radical unions as dangerous, it was smashed by federal prosecutions of its leaders. Federal regulations improving working conditions also marginalized the need for a such a union. But in the meantime, Wobblies continued free speech fighting, descending on towns where a point was to be made – and they continued to be harassed and even murdered, as happened in Everett in 1916. Later, in 1936, a small group of Wobblies that survived was even shot at by hired guns for timber companies in St. Maries, Idaho.

Fred H. Moore moved to Los Angeles in 1910 where he continued to defend labor activists, including those involved in the *Los Angeles Times* bombing of 1911 (with Clarence Darrow as co-counsel) and the Everett Massacre case. He also defended the famed Sacco-Vanzetti case from 1920-24, in which many historians believe the anarchists were wrongfully executed for a bombing. Moore died of cancer in Los Angeles in 1933.

Elizabeth Gurley Flynn was tried and convicted of criminal conspiracy in Spokane on December 6, 1909. Her appeal in February of 1910 was more successful, and she was acquitted, perhaps in no small part due to her advanced pregnancy. Flynn left Spokane, had her baby in New York state and went on to become one of America's most notable Communists. She was arrested, along with 12 others, in 1951, and was convicted under the obscure Smith Alien Registration Act of 1940. As a result, she spent more than two years at the federal women's reformatory in West Virginia. Flynn later became chairperson of the American Communist Party; she died in the Soviet Union in 1964, was given a state funeral and is buried in Red Square. ■

Consfiscated stills on display in front of the Spokane County Courthouse in 1929.
CHARLES LIBBY COLLECTION PHOTO, EASTERN WASHINGTON STATE HISTORICAL SOCIETY

The Prince of Prohibition: Albert Commellini

BY PATRICK HEALD

First published in the *Inlander* on July 6, 1994

Next time you drive along Browne Street in downtown Spokane, take a turn into the alley between Spokane Falls Boulevard and Main, and you'll find yourself in the middle of what was once the Inland Northwest's most notorious nightspot. You'll be standing in what was called "Trent Alley," where 70 years before, you could have had a drink sold to you through a small hole in a door; or you could have gone underground into one of the alley's speakeasies for a more social whistle-whetting. Between 1916 and 1933, Trent Alley was the place in town to go if you wanted to drink. Never mind that those were the Prohibition years, when the sale, possession and consumption of alcohol were all illegal.

Downtown Spokane crawls with the ghosts of those days, when gambling, drinking and prostitution roared into the early-morning hours, seven nights a week. In a time when the nation mandated a curb on partying, the record shows that Spokane seemed to party even harder than before.

"My own personal opinion is that people drank during Prohibition who would have never drank if it was legal," says Clyde Phelps, a 91-year-old Spokane resident who was the chief of police in the 1940s and '50s and a beat officer during Prohibition.

City officials, including police, knew about these various houses of ill repute but did little to curb the activity, perhaps because, in some cases, they were among the patrons.

The "Noble Experiment" that started in Washington state in 1916 and lasted until 1933 spawned a whole slew of entrepreneurs who profited from the public's thirst. Many of the places they built are gone now, and most forgotten, but fortunately some of those who lived in those days are still around. Their memories and the historical record tell the tale of a uniquely wild chapter in the history of the Inland Northwest.

❖ ❖ ❖

In the early 1900s, as more and more men moved their families into cities and became reliant on a weekly paycheck rather than the fruits of their land to put food on their tables, the alcohol problem began to rear its muddled head.

The sentiment that led to Prohibition was based on a legitimate concern over the problem of abusive drinking and its effect on the family unit. Men, the reasoning went, would work all week, get paid in cash and then squander the week's grocery money and rent in one night of carousing. In some cases, the man would come home drunk and proceed to take out his frustrations on his wife. Law enforcement tended to overlook domestic violence in those days, and since most married women depended on their husbands to support them, fleeing from the situation was not an option. Welfare was still nearly two decades away.

In Spokane, the population swelled as the city became a major distribution point to and from the great natural resource lands that surrounded it. But the city's recent Wild West past coupled with the independent nature of the people who were willing to make the trek out West perhaps combined to make up a less compliant population.

Washington voters enacted a prohibition in 1916, a full three years before the Volstead Act made Prohibition the law of the land in January of 1920. Spokane County voted to go dry by a total of 948 votes, in a time when the city had approximately 80,000 residents.

Although it was still legal to import liquor from a non-dry state, that practice ended in 1917 with the enactment of federal legislation prohibiting the importing of liquor from a wet state to a dry one.

December 31, 1915, was the last day liquor would be legal in Spokane County for 18 years, and by all accounts it was some party. Taxis made out well that night, as many people hauled away free booze from bars that could not keep the stuff on site after midnight.

"CROWDS STORM SALOONS, SUPPLY FAILS AS DRY ERA DAWNS." Thus read the front page of the *Spokesman-Review* on January 1, 1916. The article stated: "There was much drunkenness, but it was not sufficiently disorderly to be reflected on the blotter at police headquarters, where a quiet evening was spent."

Hotels, bars and restaurants all had huge stocks of soon-to-be-illegal liquor that needed to be consumed or sold. In his book *A History of Spokane*, Carl H. Trunk details the panic that swept Spokane after the state vote on its version of prohibition: "There was a great rush for this liquor as businessmen knew it would be worth five times its value within a few short months."

Prohibition came to pass, but that didn't mean people had to like it – or, apparently, obey it.

Longtime Spokane resident Pearl Keogh remembers what it was like. She says Spokanites of the '20s were in no mood to "just say no" when it came to taking a drink. "It was everywhere," says Keogh. "I know we had some neighbors that had it all the time."

Keogh says people flaunted the law because alcohol had been legal for so long.

"I think it was because people were used to it," says Keogh. "[Prohibition] was just one of those things that happened, and they just ignored it, of course. But there were a lot of arrests made, too. A lot of people were being caught and put in jail and fined for it."

But she adds that the money that came into Spokane through bootlegged liquor was an overall plus.

"They did a lot of things after the money came in. I think the liquor helped, because whoever was selling it was making money, and they were spending it. It was just a going thing for everybody."

❖ ❖ ❖

A going thing, indeed. An entire industry grew up in response to the passage of the law. Bootleggers traveled between Canada and the United States, or from other states like Montana, where a variety of backwoods distilling operations were underway. There were even stills in and around Spokane.

The Canadian government, far from discouraging American bootleggers, heavily taxed the sale of alcohol to them. Because of the proximity to Canada, and the relative ease with which the border could be crossed, Spokane enjoyed one of the finest supplies of Canadian liquor in the nation.

In his book *Rum Road to Spokane*, Edmund Fahey details the exorbitant profit margins enjoyed by bootleggers who made the run from Fernie, British Columbia, back to Spokane. A case of Canadian whiskey cost a bootlegger $36, but in Spokane it could be sold for closer to $190 – about a 400 percent profit.

But by producing the booze yourself, many secretive entrepreneurs realized, you could make even more of a profit. In a *Spokesman-Review* article from 1972, Jay Kalez detailed the production of "Mica Peak Moonshine" or "Mica Moon." Rugged terrain and the relative isolation of the Mica Peak area, Kalez wrote, coupled with the close proximity to Spokane created an ideal setting for a moonshining operation.

After making the trek down the twisting backwoods trails from the Mica Peak area, "Bottlemen" would travel into Spokane and check into hotels with one or two suitcases filled with the goods. Most Spokane residents who wanted to drink usually had one or two reliable bottlemen they depended on to bring their pick-me-up.

And, on a smaller scale, there were other stills operated all over town. One bootlegger leased what was then Old Bart's Cigar Factory across from Lewis and Clark High School. The place was soon churning out a hundred barrels of "shine" a day. One woman, Trunk wrote, who lived near Downriver Golf Course, turned her home into a beer parlor. As thirsty golfers finished up their rounds, she would supply them with beer served in tomato cans.

But perhaps the most brazen moonshining going on in the city was the still in the basement of City Hall. Historian Trunk relates the story of Mate Hammond, a city engineer during the Prohibition years. Hammond had an office in the basement of the Old City Hall Building. When stills were confiscated, or liquor casks seized as contraband, they were stored in a room next to Hammond's office. Hammond cleverly drilled a hole through the wall and tapped into the booze that was being held as evidence.

But apparently the quality of the confiscated booze wasn't good enough for Hammond. He dismantled the stills that had been confiscated and rebuilt one of his own right there in the basement of City Hall. The good times did not last long, however. The still was discovered, and Hammond was asked to seek employment elsewhere.

Hammond's censure seems unique among the stories of Spokane during Prohibition. How were so many distillery operations, bootleggers and social drinkers allowed to flourish? Historians and those who lived then agree it was due to a lack of enforcement. It was an unpopular law, and many police officers conveniently looked the other way.

Former Chief of Police Phelps has very clear recollections of a time when people had to duck down in a basement to take a drink.

"People who drank before still drank," says Phelps. "The general public did not want the Prohibition laws enforced. There was no doubt that getting whiskey by the drink was no problem in Spokane."

Probably the strongest proof in support of Phelps assertion was the fact that the people charged with upholding and enforcing the law – like judges, prosecutors and cops – were also providing bootleggers with a substantial portion of their business. "Some of the people who made the most noise about liquor in the police department were the ones who drank the most," Phelps remembers.

Dorsey Griffin, in his memoir *Memories of Moonshine Days*, recalls how his father used to supply whiskey to Frank V. Girand, a Spokane County judge in the 1920s. Hubert Hoover, who joined the Spokane Police near the end of Prohibition, remembers how people would get upset if the cops arrested the "wrong" bootlegger. "If you pinched a bootlegger, everybody screamed," says Hoover. "If you pinched the other guy's bootlegger, that was fine."

Not that it mattered much, as you could get it "anywheres," Hoover recalls. "It was a mockery."

Hoover claims that the power structure of the police, far from going after bootleggers, instructed beat cops to lay off certain well-known rum-runners in town. "They were told by the city commissioner which ones to leave alone," says Hoover.

The indifference of the police, the thirst of the public and the entrepreneurial spirit of the bootleggers all came together in Trent Alley, the natural place for speakeasies to spring up. Speakeasies, the underground bars that served alcohol at night, dotted downtown Spokane, but Trent Alley was like Grand Central Station.

"My parents used to tell me, 'Don't get off the streetcar between Division and Washington, no matter what!'" says Louise Engle, a longtime Spokane resident. "That was the bad part of town."

It was an area that catered to whatever whims men with cash might care to indulge in – usually flowing drinks and "sporting ladies."

Trent Alley had always been a rowdy neighborhood, situated as it was right near the Great Northern Railway Station, a major transfer point for men going to work in the mines and timber stands of North Idaho and northeastern Washington. Or, more important, coming back when work was slow – or, even better, just after payday. But residents of the city were also attracted to the alley.

Sam Huppin, owner of Huppins' Hi-fi and Video, remembers his days as a paperboy in the district. "There used to be a place along the alley where you could walk along and drop your money down a hole," recalls Huppin. "A hand would reach up and give you a drink."

❖ ❖ ❖

But not all exchanges were so impersonal. One of the reasons the Prohibition years make up such a colorful chapter in the history of the Inland Northwest and Spokane is the people. The characters who operated the speakeasies were well-known, and their stories shed as much light on the times as anything.

Ninety-year-old Keogh, who was a nurse at Sacred Heart in those days, says there were a lot of speakeasies in Spokane. One of them belonged to Jim Young. "He was a big, colored man," Keogh recalls. 'We knew Jim real well."

She says she was only in his speakeasy once, however, and it was not a glamorous experience. "It was on the alley. My brother and his wife said, 'Let's go down and see old Jim Young.' We went up these steps and went in a great big open attic. He had beer barrels for tables, then he had boards on top of them. It was the most crude thing. I said, 'You'll never catch me up here again.'"

Hoover remembers it, too. "Jim Young's was one of the hot spots," says Hoover. "It was just off Browne between Trent and Main. He was upstairs. The socialites all patronized him, too."

Another well-known provider of good times was Jimmy Durkin, who ran the speakeasy in the basement of the Durkin and Ulrich Dining Room, now the site of Jake's Pawn Shop on Main Avenue. Durkin, apparently sympathetic to the original intention of Prohibition, had a sign behind the bar that read, "If your kids need shoes, don't buy booze."

But no discussion of Prohibition in Spokane would be complete without mentioning Albert Commellini, who was in the restaurant and "import-export" business in Spokane; Commellini's Corner, near Wandermere Golf Course, is named after him.

Commellini bought land on Moran Prairie and built a house there called "Glenrose" – the name the South Hill neighborhood is still known by. According to local historian Jean Oton, the home became one of the first speakeasies in Spokane. Glenrose burned to the ground in 1936, a fate suffered by many of the properties Commellini owned.

Commellini also owned Commellini's Import House at Browne and Pacific. A substantial portion of the bootlegging in Spokane ran through Commellini's Import House. "He had everything you wanted," says Keogh. "He even got it from Canada. He was kind of the boss."

Keogh knew Commellini, describing him as a "likable man. I remember he had these two great big dogs, as big as a Shetland Pony, that lived in the back. They were gorgeous."

"Albert Commellini was the kingpin here," adds Hoover. "He had a big Cadillac, and he would drive the streets all night long. He used to tell the commissioner [Leroy Lambert] which cops he wanted on the beat."

But Commellini was civic-minded as well. He was instrumental in starting up the Hotel De Gink in the Schade Brewery building, a place for the many unemployed men of the area to sleep and get a free meal during the Depression. He even went so far as to run for city commissioner in 1933.

In 1936, Commellini had Al Capone's brother Frankie look over the Ambassador Club on East Trent with an eye toward buying it. Capone declined; the next year, the club burned to the ground.

When the Volstead Act was repealed in 1934, Commellini focused on other enterprises, including an Italian restaurant on Dartford Drive near Wandermere, run by his sister, Elide.

❖ ❖ ❖

But Trent Alley was not the only place to get a drink, only the most notorious. Traces of old gin-joints still exist throughout downtown Spokane if you know where to look.

Since many of the speakeasies were in converted basements, they required a considerable amount of "dressing up" to make them acceptable places in which to take a drink. Murals were painted on the walls of Durkin's place at 417 W. Main. Similar murals could be found on the walls of the basement of the Four Seasons Coffee Shop at 222 N. Howard. The murals depict rugged scenes of Northwest life, including grizzly bears in combat and ranchers in action.

There was also a network of tunnels that linked several downtown buildings, and those tunnels played a bit part in Spokane's Prohibition scenario. Originally built as convenient ways to provide cleaner and safer passage from one building to another (remember, this was a time when streetcars made life a challenge for pedestrians), the tunnels were perfect for moving booze back and forth between hotels and speakeasies. A former employee of the Spokane Club recalls how tunnels originated at the club, spider-webbing out to the *Spokesman-Review* building, the Davenport Hotel and who knows where else.

In the end, Prohibition was simply not popular enough to last. To quote Edmund Fahey's *Rum Road to Spokane*: "The chief aid to rum-running along the border was the resentment of honest citizens against the tyranny of Prohibition. Many people who scarcely ever touched a drink themselves — and would not have touched a dollar of rum-running profits — still refused to tip off the authorities, or to testify against rum-runners. It was the pure resentment of people being denied their rights and freedoms.

"Adding fuel to the citizens' disregard of the law were the enforcement officers, who, for mercenary reasons, allowed an unending stream of spirits to flow to a defiant public."

So, as in all of America during Prohibition, the saying in Spokane was: "If you want a drink, go see the three wise men — the cabdriver, the policeman and the bootblack." ∎

Kirtland Cutter's original watercolor for the Idaho State Building
for the World's Columbian Exposition in Chicago in 1892.

GLEN CLONINGER COLLECTION

In 1897, Cutter built an eclectic palace in Spokane for mining magnate Patsy Clark.

EYMANN ALLISON HUNTER JONES, PS, PHOTO

Frontier Dreambuilder: Kirtland Cutter

BY TED S. McGREGOR JR.

First published in the *Inlander* on November 18, 1998

There are lost civilizations in Central America that had no written language. Archaeologists puzzle over the buildings they left behind to discern whatever they can about the people who built them. Architect Kirtland Kelsey Cutter is similarly mysterious; his buildings say a lot about the city they give character to, but until now little has been known about the man behind the plans. All that changed with the publication of the first book on Cutter's life, *Kirtland Cutter: Architect in the Land of Promise* by architectural historian Henry Matthews. But even after 14 years studying his life, Matthews says Cutter remains something of an enigma.

"One of the things about Cutter," says Matthews, a professor at Washington State University, "is that he never wrote anything down."

Still, Matthews' exhaustive research sheds more light than ever on Cutter's life, especially the influences that made him design buildings the way he did. Matthews also documents the chapter that is little known in these parts: What happened to the architect after he left Spokane.

What we do know about Cutter is enough to make him one of the most recognizable and important figures in Spokane history. He grew up outside Cleveland, Ohio, in an upper-crust family, was well educated, spent time traveling in Europe and, as a young man pursued painting – an aspiration that slowly transformed into architecture. At the suggestion of his uncle, an official at an upstart bank in the 10-year-old settlement of Spokane Falls, Cutter came west by rail in October of 1886, with no formal training in architecture.

On August 4, 1889, much of Spokane burned to the ground. It was a tragic event that paradoxically offered Cutter his first big break, since city fathers resolved to build back the city better than before. Commissions began to pour in to the firm of Cutter and John Poetz (the first of his many business partners).

Over the next 34 years, operating out of Spokane, Cutter designed homes and buildings in the Adirondacks, Montana, Colorado, Tacoma, Seattle, Spokane and even England. Some of his best work can be seen in Browne's Addition, where the Finch and Campbell homes still stand. He also designed the Spokane Club, the Washington Water Power Substation and elements of the Monroe Street Bridge. He was comfortable working in all styles, and he blended them at will. Cutter built the state's first true Arts and Crafts home in Browne's Addition in 1893; he built rustic lodges at Lake McDonald and Hayden Lake; and he created fantasies on Venetian (the Davenport Hotel) and Moorish (the Patsy Clark mansion) themes.

Matthews' continental sensibilities (he's English) allow him to see through the popular myth that the West was wild by choice; rather, he points out that the breed of entrepreneurs heading west was interested in bringing the niceties of the East, or even the traditions of Europe, to the frontier as soon as they could afford to do so. Cutter's extensive travels, studies of contemporary design and innately elevated sense of style made him perfect to help his clients realize those desires in any combination they wanted. It's also important to note that Cutter benefited from historical chance, as his early career coincided with an unprecedented flow of money from the mining fields of North Idaho into Spokane.

"He is expressing the dreams of these people," says Matthews, "to be more elegant and civilized. All that money could have produced horrible buildings, but Cutter made it work. He thought about how people could enjoy living, and he knew how wealthy people lived, and that's why he was successful. Cutter could give them something they wanted in a way even they couldn't have imagined."

In a time when Western cities competed for acclaim, Cutter's work was singled out by architectural critics who passed through Spokane, including the influential Albert Hubbard, who compared 1905 Spokane to Pericles' Athens.

"When Cutter first came to Spokane, he described its architecture as savage," says Matthews. "I think he was on a long mission to civilize Spokane, and he really succeeded. One lesson is that a single individual can have a tremendous influence on a place. He really put Spokane on the map."

❖ ❖ ❖

Anyone who has walked through a Cutter building, or merely scanned the outside of a Cutter home, knows it's something special. He imparted a lasting legacy of pride on a community that never again hit such a high economic point since those heady days known as Spokane's "Age of Elegance." That's why the rest of the Cutter story is especially poignant, and it parallels the shifting fortunes of Spokane as well as any person's life could.

By 1923, mining money was dwindling, competing architects were nibbling away at prospective jobs and many of Cutter's patrons were aging or even passing away. Ruined by debt, his home – the stately Chalet that sat on West Seventh until it was torn down in the early-1970s – was repossessed, and his personal belongings were auctioned off. Cutter and his wife Katharine left Spokane penniless the same year he was elected to the American Institute of Architects. And for decades, that was the end of the story.

The epilogue would only be learned years later through a serendipitous bit of preservationist sleuthing, which also sucked Henry Matthews into its vortex and brought his new book into being, a century after the peak of Cutter's practice.

For maybe three or four decades after the devastation of the Depression, most people didn't appreciate the architectural legacy of Cutter – or anyone else. Legend has it that one of Cutter's best designs – the F. Rockwood Moore home – was torn down in the 1940s to save $200 a year in taxes. Even as late as the 1970s, when Spokane was preparing for Expo '74, important buildings like Union Station were torn down. As in Seattle, where a small group fought to save the Pike Place Market, a last-minute appeal in Spokane saved the Great Northern

Clock Tower, now a beloved link to Spokane's past. Around the time people started looking at Spokane's old mansions with renewed appreciation, the cult of Cutter was revived. His sumptuous interiors, as in the Davenport Hotel and the Patsy Clark mansion, created a whole new generation of admirers.

The Cheney Cowles Museum, which took ownership of the Cutter-designed Campbell House in 1924, has always tried to keep the architect's flame alive. And when the preservationist revival began, museum officials tried to gather as much on the man as they could. Were there any remaining drawings or plans? They asked the family of Cutter's last Spokane partner, Henry Bertelsen. No, they were told. So why did Cutter plans continue to pop up at local antique auctions? Over a two-year period, Larry Schoonover, then curator of history at the museum, started sniffing around. Through chance and some dogged detective work, he found out there was indeed a cache of Cutter's work.

"It was pretty exciting when we walked into a basement of a home on the South Hill, and there were ink-on-linen drawings rolled up in cardboard boxes," recalls Schoonover. "There were 10 to 20 drawings per residence, including floorplans."

The museum purchased the collection, 290 drawings in all, and planned an exhibition, which ran in 1986. Ivan Munk, then a producer for KHQ-TV, convinced his station to do an hour-long show on Cutter.

"We did the show because Larry found the plans," says Munk, now a full-time artist who has recreated many Cutter homes on his canvases. "Suddenly there was a Cutter mania again, and all those plans gave us a better idea of what he had done."

But Munk knew to do the job right, he'd need an architectural historian to lend the program the proper authority. The late Spokane architect Ken Brooks recommended Henry Matthews, a newly transplanted Brit, whose sagacious accent could only help in Munk's mission.

"I remember when Ivan asked what I knew about Cutter," says Matthews. "I said, 'Well, a little.' Looking back on it, maybe I shouldn't have said anything," he adds with a chuckle at how consuming the resulting book became for him.

Just after the museum acquired the Cutter collection, one of the librarians received a momentous letter from one Phyllis Poper of Long Beach, California, who wondered if the museum knew anything about a Kirtland Cutter who had built a number of homes in her area. This was yet another major break, since Poper knew Cutter's post-1923 story. Poper's husband Richard had acquired Cutter's practice, including all his personal letters, his library and his architectural sketches.

Matthews, Munk and Schoonover decided to tackle the subject that had been so elusive for so long: What happened to Cutter after he left Spokane? So the production team went to Long Beach, and with the Popers' help found a treasure trove of Cutter homes and buildings. In the Poper collection, Matthews found a flurry of communication from 1923 between Cutter and Frederick Dawson, a former business associate who happened to be married to the niece of the Campbell House's Helen Campbell. Dawson was involved in developing a prime piece of real estate in California – Palos Verdes Estates, a high peninsula that overlooks Long Beach on one side and Santa Monica Bay on the other. At the time, Palos Verdes was being developed as a colony for millionaires, and it remains today one of the ritziest addresses in all of Southern California – a perfect match for Cutter, who "always went where the big money was," as Munk puts it.

"The whole Southern California thing was completely new and surprising to everyone involved in the project," says Schoonover. "We had no idea what Cutter did after he left Spokane."

Cutter had his first commission built at Palos Verdes within a year of leaving Spokane, and his final years were spent in an upstairs office in Long Beach, designing homes and working on plans for more grandiose projects that weren't realized due to the onset of the Depression. However, the homes he designed there – most in the Mission Revival style so popular in California then – remain as prized as the ones he left in Spokane. In 1933, he designed a beach house on Balboa Island for legendary film director Victor Fleming, who liked the cottage so much he had Cutter build him a permanent residence in Bel Air in 1937. Fleming had a pretty good year in 1939 with the release of two of his films, *Gone With the Wind* and *The Wizard of Oz*.

Cutter died in 1939 at the age of 79; his ashes were spread over the Pacific Ocean by a young associate.

❖ ❖ ❖

Such a man, such a story and such a tangible legacy are what captivated

Matthews, who hopes his book will bring Cutter the kind of professional recognition he deserves. But Matthews is not just writing for academics – his book also succeeds as a popular history with a hefty dose of photos, some of which are being reproduced for the first time.

Matthews says Cutter deserves a place on the short list of important architects working in the turn-of-the-century Western United States. Ironically, it has probably been Cutter's strength – his hard-to-pigeonhole, eclectic style – that has kept him from such status, outside of Spokane and Los Angeles, that is.

"Yes, he built in such a variety of styles, but that's what makes him the quintessential architect of his time," says Matthews. "My point is he goes to the extremes; he does the very ostentatious mansions for millionaires that express the American fascination with escapism, and then he does the rustic buildings that have to do with nature. And there are the two poles of American obsessions."

Or, as Matthews puts it at the end of his book: "The celebration of the primeval forest in Lake McDonald Lodge and the enthusiasm for the exotic in the Hall of the Doges [in the Davenport Hotel] speak eloquently of opposing forces of nature and artifice tugging at the American psyche."

Cutter in the White City

BY TED S. McGREGOR JR.

First published in the *Inlander* on March 13, 2003

The Chicago World's Columbian Exhibition of 1893 was like a beacon to the architects of the United States, attracting the best and brightest; sculptor Augustus Saint-Gaudens called it "the greatest meeting of artists since the 15th century." And Spokane's own Kirtland Cutter was no exception. In his new book, *The Devil and the White City*, Erik Larson points out that more than 200 buildings erected by states, corporations and foreign governments covered the Chicago fairgrounds; the collection was commonly called the White City.

In his biography, *Kirtland Cutter: Architect in the Land of Promise,* Henry

Matthews devotes a long passage to Cutter's contribution to the fair – the Idaho State Building. Cutter won the commission for his eye for detail, which was apparent throughout as he used exclusively Idaho materials in its construction: Timber from Shoshone County, a giant shield of magnesia stone from Nez Perce County, lava rock from Logan County and huge sheets of mica from Latah County.

"Among the pretentious classical architecture of other state pavilions," writes Matthews, "the Idaho Building symbolized, in a romantic way, the virtues of nature against the competing forces of civilization."

Cutter and his partner John Poetz won the prize "for a type of architecture and construction which expresses the character of the state erecting it." Fair officials estimated that 10,000 people a day visited the chalet-inspired, three-story building, which featured an enormous stag's head above the entrance.

Larson says as he has crossed the country on his current book tour, he has heard many stories of what happened to the buildings and smaller artifacts from the fair – one Chicagoan who came to a reading said he saw an ornate old ticket booth in the back yard of a home he considered buying. Some buildings were torched by arsonists; the Palace of Fine Arts was rebuilt as a permanent structure and remains the city's Museum of Science and Industry. What happened to the Idaho State Building is typical for its serendipitous fate.

Designed for easy transport, despite its 475 tons of timber, Cutter's structure was put up for auction after the fair ended. Captain Pabst, whose own brew won the coveted blue ribbon at the fair, wanted to move it to Milwaukee; another buyer wanted to drop it among the attractions at Coney Island. But a Chicago socialite bought it for $4,000 and had it moved to Lake Geneva, Wisconsin, as a summer lodge. It fell into disrepair and was finally milled in 1911 for planking used to build a new pier on the lake.

An Englishman recently enriched who lost out in the bidding couldn't forget the building, however, and hired Cutter to build him an exact replica among the trees of his estate all the way across the pond in Hampshire. Cutter sent one of his key employees to England to oversee the construction. Failing to secure logs of the necessary size in Norway, the project required the shipment of Washington state logs to England – around the horn, no less. Having a taste of the Wild West, the owner apparently wanted to experience the real thing and soon moved to British Columbia. His estate was sold, and Cutter's work appears to have been demolished sometime in 1903.

The Patsy Clark Mansion

BY HENRY MATTHEWS

Excerpted in the *Inlander* on November 18, 1998; reprinted by permission from *Kirtland Cutter: Architect in the Land of Promise*, University of Washington Press

In eighteenth-century New England, the social elite were content to live in houses of very similar design, conforming to classic rules of composition and proportion. In Spokane in the late 1890s, entrepreneurs rejoiced in the opportunity to build exactly as they pleased. Kirtland Cutter's new clients were from a new generation of capitalists who had understood how the potential of the region could be realized, and had profited enormously. Some, from wealthy East Coast families, were educated, shrewd and ready to seize opportunities. Others were self-made men, who by hard work, experience and sound judgment had flourished in a field of heavy competition. Unfettered by convention, they could invoke memories of whatever they had admired in the places they had left to go west; or they could indulge in fantasy about places they had never seen. The parvenu who had traveled the path from rags to riches could display symbols associated with old wealth; he could imply through a time-honored design that his newly built mansion was an ancestral home. And the educated investor backed by old money could bring customary signs of civilization to the frontier. The key to Cutter's success was that he possessed both the familiarity with old traditions and the imagination to give substance to new desires. His years of travel and the many hours he had spent poring over illustrated books had given him roots in the language of architecture; his association with John Poetz and Karl Malmgren (his partners) had made up for his lack of professional experience.

The wives of the high-powered men who commissioned houses from Cutter undoubtedly were influential in decisions reached between client and architect. They had far more time to devote to artistic matters than their husbands, and many of them were active in promoting the arts in Spokane. Cutter was comfortable in the society of women, and they most likely acted as his allies in negotiations for costly or unusual design features.

Between 1897 and 1900, Cutter and Malmgren designed eight mansions in Spokane that represent a peak in the success of the practice. All but one client chose to build in the two most fashionable residential districts: Browne's Addition, on a spur of land west of the downtown overlooking the gorge of the Spokane River, and the South Hill, near the sites under the cliffs where Cutter had erected his first architectural works. In both places the architects juxtaposed houses in radically different styles, which a century later still set the character of the neighborhood. At the head of First Avenue stands the Neoclassical house, complete with columned portico, built for mining magnate John A Finch. Next to it, similar in color but very different in form, is the Mission Revival house of lawyer and capitalist. W.J.C. Wakefield; beside it, the red brick and half-timbered home of Finch's partner, Amasa B. Campbell, which followed an "Old English" theme. Only two blocks away they created a unique mansion for the most colorful of Spokane's mining millionaires, Patrick Clark. ...

❖ ❖ ❖

Known to his friends and associates as "Patsy," Clark came from a poor family in Ireland. He had crossed the Atlantic in 1870 when he was 20 years old, and had gone almost at once to the gold mines in California. Brighter prospects lured him to Virginia City, Nevada, and then to Ophir, Utah, where he was employed by the copper magnate and fellow Irishman Marcus Daly. They had both labored in the Californian mines and worked their way to success; more important, both men had an instinctive understanding of the art of making successful mines. Clark was not a trained geologist or a technician, but Daly recognized his extraordinary ability to manage the complex operation of a mine. At Ophir, Daly took him on as foreman and mine superintendent, but he soon moved with his employer to Montana, where at the age of 30 he became superintendent of the Moulton Mine. It was not long before he was managing Butte's famous Anaconda Mine.

In the late 1880s, at about the time Cutter began his architectural practice, Clark moved his family to Spokane and made the city his center for mining operations. With Marcus Daly he developed the Poorman Gold Mine in the Coeur d'Alenes and as co-owner reaped enormous profits. Then he joined with a Spokane syndicate, including Cutter's clients, Finch, Campbell, Wakefield and Austin Corbin, to exploit the riches of Slocan and Rossland in British Columbia.

He was now ready to commission Cutter to design him a house without any budget restrictions. According to legend, he asked the architect to create the most impressive house west of the Mississippi. In 1897, as the walls began to rise on Second Avenue in Browne's Addition, he made his best investment ever. He grubstaked two prospectors at a claim in the Eureka Basin of north central Washington and thus started operation of the Republic Mine, the richest in the Washington and British Columbia region. The crux of Clark's wealth was his uncanny genius for buying mines of great potential when the price was low and selling them at the zenith of their value.

The design of a mansion for such a man was a challenging opportunity for the architect. We do not know what specific demands Clark made on him, but Cutter decided to work in an opulent, eclectic style, drawing inspiration from Islamic architecture. ...

❖ ❖ ❖

It appears that Clark wanted to build a residence that stood out from all the others in Browne's Addition. But he can hardly have envisioned the striking originality of Cutter's design. It was bold in form and extremely rich in color. Built of a warm, honey-colored brick with sandstone dressing, it was covered with a hipped roof of brilliant red metal tiles. The colors of the materials were heightened by the use of white paint on the columns and arches around the upper windows and deep red on the balustrades. The front, facing south onto Coeur d'Alene Park with its central entrance arch and round corner towers, has an appearance of powerful symmetry. Yet Cutter deliberately broke the symmetry by allowing one tower to rise higher than the other, and projecting out a veranda on the west side only. ...

The experience of entering this house and moving through it fulfills the promise of the façade: The exotic interior confirms the suspicion of a Mughal influence on the design. The entrance hall, finished in dark oak, appears gloomy at first. But out of the darkness, rich colors glow, and mysterious, complex forms create an unforgettable atmosphere. Several cusped arches of Mughal or Mudejar origin enliven the space. Three of these arches separate the hall from the stair; three others, near the front wall, lead to the vestibule and to recessed bays on either side. At right angles to them, springing from the same eight columns, elaborately carved brackets in the form of identical half arches rise to support the ceiling beams. The two freestanding columns opposite the front door dominate the space. Their branching, multifoliate structure, reminiscent of the audience chamber of the Red Fort at Delhi, suggests that Cutter aimed to give his client nothing less than the palace of an oriental potentate. He may, however, have gained inspiration from a source he had actually seen, the East Indian Building at the World's Columbian Exposition in Chicago in 1893.

Beyond the arches that spring from these columns, stairways lead up and down. To the left, steps descend to a smoking room; in the center, an arch opens like a proscenium to the grand staircase. Its first flight ascends to a landing, spacious enough to accommodate a sofa and armchair on either side of a fireplace. The climax of the framed vista is a pair of superb Tiffany stained glass windows, whose warm, subtle colors and flamboyant peacock motif proclaim the joys of the Gilded Age. ...

As in the other mansions of the period, the principal rooms open through broad doorways to the hall. Each has its individual character and none but the smoking room follows the Islamic theme of the hall. To the right, Patrick Clark's library conveys a feeling of masculinity. Its beamed ceiling and millwork in fine walnut and mahogany combine with the dark green velvet tapestry on the walls to suggest the quiet luxury of a gentlemen's club. The onyx fireplace and gilt mirror above provide a touch of opulence. From the library, a glass door opens out onto the spacious veranda whose brick-built arches were ornamented with sandstone. To the left is the reception room, where Mrs. Clark presided as grand society hostess. This domain of high society ladies, finished elegantly in rose, white and gold, appears strikingly light compared with the hall. Cutter adapted the Louis XV Style to design this room in an original manner. At the far end of the room toward the back of the house, an elliptical barrel vault supported on Corinthian columns forms a canopy over the fireplace. On either side, under a lowered ceiling, a deep couch fills the space between four columns. Cutter had taken the concept of the humble inglenook and reinterpreted it in the elegant manner of 18th-century France. Above the fireplace, a broad mirror gives the illusion of continuing space; in each corner, beside the couch, a stained glass window lights the cozy seating area...

More in tune with the realities of life for a mining millionaire, a huge safe was concealed behind the paneling of the dining room wall, beside the entry to the butler's pantry. Behind the north wall of the dining room, Cutter planned the kitchen and servants' quarters to allow for all the needs of the Clark family and their guests. He placed the service wing, as in the Campbell and Finch houses, to one side at the back, so as not to interrupt the light of the window over the staircase. Detached from the house on the west side, but matching it in design, stands the carriage house, where, in addition to horses, carriages and a sleigh, a cow was kept to provide milk for the table. ...

Cutter followed the architectural trends of his day, but continued to excel in the creation of homes to suit the lives of his clients in the Gilded Age. ... His excursion into an exotic world of fantasy for Patrick Clark shows both originality and a successful fusion of disparate elements. ■

Natatorium Park in 1924. Louis Vogel ran Nat Park for more than 40 years; his wife Emma's dad, Charles Looff, gave the couple a hand-carved carousel that's still in use.

EASTERN WASHINGTON STATE HISTORICAL SOCIETY PHOTOS

The Ringmasters of Nat Park: Louis and Emma Vogel

BY ROBERT M. WITTER

First published in the *Inlander* on March 23, 1994

Not too long ago, tucked away atop a bank along a bend in the Spokane River was a magical place… Sounds a bit like the beginning of a fairy tale, doesn't it? But in the memories of many Spokane natives, it's a place that has taken on the aura of a fairy tale – a place that recalls a simpler, idyllic time. That place was Natatorium Park.

It could be found at the far western end of Boone Avenue, hidden below Summit Boulevard – Spokane's own version of Coney Island. Nat Park, as it was called, was a picnic ground, nature conservatory, performance venue and amusement park all rolled into one.

At the end of Boone, the road sloped down a gradual curve to deposit auto traffic and, in the earlier days, streetcar passengers at the front entrance. The 40-acre park was nestled on the hillside leading down to the Spokane River. Although visitors felt as if they had escaped to a place far away from the hustle of the city, the park was actually within city limits.

In its heyday, which spanned more than half a century, you, along with thousands of your neighbors, could listen to a John Philip Sousa concert, swim in the indoor heated pool, ride the Jackrabbit roller coaster or spend the evening in the always-hopping dance hall at Nat Park. So it was with great sadness that the eyes of Spokane watched, after a decade of declining attendance, as the remnants of the park were burned on site in the summer of 1968. Only the Looff Carrousel, which continues to delight thousands each year as the centerpiece of Riverfront Park, was saved.

But despite the sad ending to the tale, most of the lingering memories of the Nat are pleasant.

❖ ❖ ❖

Prior to the great fire of 1889 that destroyed much of Spokane, the park was simply a picnic ground for the fledgling town. Under the original name of Twickenham Park, this rustic site was poised for development due to its proximity to the center of town. Originally owned by local businessmen, the land was purchased around 1891 by the Spokane Street Railroad Company – a subsidiary of the Washington Water Power Company. A gentleman by the name of Audley Ingersoll was one of the original park directors, and there is some evidence that suggests the park may have been called Ingersoll Park at one time.

As Spokane's growth continued into the new century, efficient urban transportation soon became a necessity. And in answer came the era of the streetcar. The history of streetcars is a fascinating story in itself, but most important to Nat Park is that the streetcar went out to the park, opening it up for use by residents from all over the city.

Park developments around this time – from the turn of the century until the late 1920s – included the addition of a baseball field, a band shell, a dance pavilion and a huge indoor pool, or natatorium. The Natatorium Plunge, as the pool was called, was the major attraction at the park.

So for the pool – the only public pool in the city for many years – the name of the park was officially changed to Natatorium Park. Not long after the name change from Twickenham to Natatorium Park, Spokanites nicknamed it Nat Park – a name that stuck throughout the years.

The designers of the park left heavily wooded areas to surround the amusements. The forested areas offered a natural setting to those in search of escape from the bustling, rapidly growing young city. You could walk a pathway to a grand set of steps leading down to a huge water fountain surrounded by beautiful gardens and ponds. As a complete package, the park accommodated any mood or recreational need.

The stands of the baseball park, which was built in the early 1890s, were full each summer as the Nat hosted games between Spokane and the other teams of the early Pacific Coast League. Babe Ruth played an exhibition game in the ball field, heroically smacking a ball through a nearby window. There are also historical reports of a Thanksgiving Day football game played there in 1894.

And the park was even alive at night, as the enormous dance hall hosted many of Spokane's largest social events. At one time, dances were a daily feature at Nat Park, and all the big name bands played there. In addition to townspeople, soldiers stationed in Spokane at Fort Wright and as far away as Farragut Naval Station in Idaho flocked to Nat Park. In the 1940s and '50s, bandleaders such as Benny Goodman, Harry James, Kay Kyser and Phil Harris played to packed houses. At one point, the hall was so jammed that some floor supports gave way.

❖ ❖ ❖

During the early period of development, Nat Park owners, looking for ways to expand the attractions, sought the advice of Charles I.D. Looff of Rhode Island. Looff was a craftsman who got his start, and gained national recognition, by hand-carving Coney Island's first carousel.

Now operating an amusement factory specializing in custom-built carousels, he visited Spokane in 1907 to consult with Nat Park's owners – the Washington Water Power Company. Looff made a strong pitch for the purchase of one of his hand-carved carousels. Although WWP executives agreed in principle, they balked at his $20,000 asking price.

As fate would have it, one of Charles Looff's daughters, Emma, was married to a man by the name of Louis Vogel who had doctor's orders to move out West. So Looff gave the carousel to Emma and Louis; some reports say it was their wedding present. WWP agreed to let the Vogels operate the carousel and take charge of all amusement operations at Nat Park, living on a percentage of the income.

Louis Vogel, who had no prior experience operating an amusement park, moved to Spokane, and on July 18, 1909, opened the Looff Carousel. The carousel was, and remains, a work of art, with 54 hand-carved horses, one giraffe, one tiger and two dragon chariots. As well as authentic horse-hair tails, the teeth on each horse were carved to be anatomically correct; eyes were fashioned out of fine, cut glass. The carousel spins to music created by its own organ. The elaborate musical device, which was manufactured in Germany, has over 300 pipes and creates the musical equivalent of a 60-piece band.

This beautiful amusement ride is believed to be the last carousel that Looff himself actually carved. Because of a marked increase in his amusement business, later carousels were carved by hired craftsman at the Looff Company. Today, it is considered to be one of the finest hand-carved carousels in existence.

Another feature of this special carousel was the building designed to shelter it and highlight its beauty through a three-tiered roof. Underneath the eaves of the first two tiers were panels of stained glass completely circling the building. The stained glass was aligned with reflective mirrors and light bulbs on the carousel that created a beautiful spectacle of light for riders and those waiting to ride. Looff knew the importance of the building and had it designed to be constructed in sections, so it could be moved if the carousel ever was to change location.

Other popular Nat Park attractions included the Dragon Slide, Chute the Chutes, the Whip, Dodgem Cars, Joy Wheel, Custer Speedway and the famous Jackrabbit roller coaster.

The Chute the Chutes took its riders down a steep chute in a boat, splashing down at the bottom in a pond. As the boats hit the pond, hundreds of gallons of displaced water flew everywhere, often soaking the riders. Another big draw was the Dodgem Cars, later called Bumper Cars. The Custer Speedway offered young drivers an even more realistic driving experience. Kids would line up at this popular attraction for the chance to get behind the wheels of authentic miniature 1930s and '40s vintage automobiles.

But the biggest attraction among the young was the wood-framed roller coaster. A sign posted at the start of the ride read, "Hold your hat; don't stand up!" As the train of cars started out, they wound through a dark tunnel and suddenly broke into the bright sunlight to immediately start a steep ascent up the first and largest grade. No sooner would you reach the precarious summit, with its wide, breathtaking view of the Spokane River, and… Whooaaaa! After riding the Jackrabbit, you could take on the world.

❖ ❖ ❖

Louis Vogel became a success, and his background in banking proved to be very valuable when matched with his budding flair for showmanship. Always adding new attractions and refining existing park venues, Vogel turned the Nat into a profitable venture.

Louis Vogel worked hard to keep the park a safe and clean place that catered to the entertainment desires of all ages. Outside concerts became a summer mainstay, and like the dance bands, many big names played Nat Park. With the band shell placed at the bottom of a large, pine-shaded grassy slope, it was an ideal place to finish the day.

Throughout the first week of August, 1915, John Philip Sousa's band played a series of 15 concerts at Nat Park and attracted nearly 60,000 people. At times that week, Spokane's trolleys were running down the line just 30 seconds apart shuttling crowds into the park.

But more than any other time, the Fourth of July was Nat Park's most special day. Louis Vogel produced a fireworks show that would be hard to match today – rockets exploding high over the park and reflecting in the swift current of the river below. On days like the Fourth, the park was literally a sea of people.

Success continued for Vogel, as an employee of the Washington Water Power Company, and later on his own. In 1929, he purchased the entire park from WWP. As owner, Vogel became even more aggressive with park upgrades. Soon Vogel's son, Lloyd, joined in his father's efforts, specializing in booking the big bands to play Nat Park.

Louis Vogel died in 1952, which left his son to take over park operations. While the operation was financially healthy, it was clear that the recreational activities of Spokanites had begun to expand beyond city limits. With automobile travel now at everyone's disposal (trolleys were removed from the streets in 1936), lakes and other far-off destinations became stiff competition. Lloyd Vogel also needed to update several attractions. One was the Aeroplane ride, which in the early days featured a fast, circular spin in a miniature biplane tethered to a central tower. After a few years into the Buck Rogers era, the Aeroplane was transformed into the Rocket Jets, made up of classic 1950s rocket ships. One of the surviving rockets can be seen in the playground of a daycare center on north Maple Street in Spokane.

After many years of hard use, the Natatorium Plunge building fell into such a state of disrepair that Lloyd tore most of the structure down, leaving just the pool, which was no longer in use. Instead of demolishing the pool, Vogel purchased seals and created a live seal pond attraction. Another change was a miniature train ride that wound around the park, even through the heavily forested section of Nat Park. The train's route also took riders through the old baseball field, which was by then closed down.

Lloyd Vogel stayed the course with Natatorium Park traditions like the Fourth of July, and, until the late-1950s, regular dances in the Nat Park Dance Hall. But for whatever reason, attendance began to dwindle.

Finally, after nearly 10 years of declining park attendance – and profits – Lloyd Vogel sold Nat Park to the El Katif Shrine Temple in late 1962. Vogel retained ownership of the Looff Carousel, however. Newspaper accounts of the day predicted that this was the end of Natatorium Park. The Shriners were not certain how to use the park and kept it closed down throughout the 1963 season.

There was plenty of speculation over its future use – even discussion of devoting it solely to Shriner-related functions. Finally, just in time for the 1964 season, Nat Park got a reprieve. After some renovation work, Bill Oliver (an assistant to Lloyd Vogel) was hired by the new owners to oversee park operations. Oliver's relationship with Natatorium Park started as a young child when he would retrieve carousel rings in order to earn free rides, so he was a natural for the job.

Lloyd Vogel moved to New York to take charge of the fireworks display for the 1964 New York World's Fair. Less than one week after the close of that World's Fair, Vogel was found dead from a fall off a roof in New York City. In his will, Vogel left the Looff Carousel to Oliver.

❖ ❖ ❖

Nat Park continued operations each year through the 1967 season. The final curtain fell in March of 1968, when the Shriners announced that Nat Park would not reopen and would be sold. The Shriners cannot be faulted for the demise of the park as greater societal forces conspired against such parks across the nation. And they should be credited for keeping it open during those last few years.

The 1960s and '70s were a cruel time for treasures like Nat Park because the movement toward preservation of historic buildings hadn't yet begun. Not only was Spokane losing another historic treasure, but also a beautiful public gathering place.

Bill Oliver just couldn't bear the thought of the carousel leaving Spokane. He offered it for sale to the City of Spokane for a very reasonable price, and soon enough private and city funds were raised to buy it. City officials never mobilized to purchase the available land for a park, which would no doubt have enhanced the West Central neighborhood, as well as the rest of the city.

While the purchase of the carousel was a major save for the community with lasting benefit, it could not erase the sadness of that summer of 1968 as the buildings that made up the Nat were demolished. The scraps from the many historic structures were burned right on site, closing a chapter of Spokane's history that now only lives in the memories of those who visited the park.

A further travesty was the failure to save the beautiful carousel building, which was also demolished after the removal of the merry-go-round. Although the building was built in a way to be movable, the wrecker's scheduling requirements apparently took precedence. After leveling all structures and removing almost all recognizable features of the park, the new ownership eventually turned the site into a high-density mobile home complex.

❖ ❖ ❖

Taking in the view from way above the Spokane River before taking the plunge on the Jackrabbit, dancing to the sounds of Phil Harris and his band or just kicking around the back woods with brothers and sisters on a family outing are common Nat Park memories that seem just a bit tarnished by the knowledge that future generations here will never know such a special place.

The Looff Carrousel now graces Riverfront Park, and continues to thrill thousands of new riders each year. Although most children today are too focused on grabbing the gold ring to wonder where the carousel came from, to many of us it will always rekindle fond memories of the Nat. ∎

The 150-foot *Georgie Oakes* (pictured here in about 1905) was Norwegian boatbuilder Peter Sorensen's masterpiece. The wood-fired steamer could haul 100 tons of ore out of the Silver Valley mines.

Captain Coeur d'Alene: Peter Sorensen

BY E. J. IANNELLI

Published for the first time in *Inlander Histories, Volume 2*

It's Independence Day, 1927 – six weeks after aviation pioneer Charles Lindbergh has completed the world's first transatlantic solo flight, and three months before the premiere of *The Jazz Singer*, Hollywood's first feature-length "talking" film. Revelers have gathered along the beaches and docks in the town of Coeur d'Alene, having made the pilgrimage to its Fourth of July celebration, an annual highlight throughout the Inland Northwest. At some point during the festivities, a huge stern-wheel steamboat is towed out onto the water and set alight. She is the *Georgie Oakes*, erstwhile queen of Lake Coeur d'Alene.

The flames rise up, burning brighter and than any fireworks display. They quickly consume the wooden decks that once held freight, soldiers, miners, loggers, homesteaders and sightseers at various stages throughout her 35-year career spent plying this nexus of lakes and rivers. But it isn't the glorious Viking funeral that guides will recount through nostalgia's haze some 90 years hence. The blazing vessel soon drifts too close to valuable storage docks, and the fire is extinguished before it's able to complete this act of nautical cremation. For weeks afterward, the charred wreck of the *Georgie Oakes* will struggle to remain afloat until at last she yields to her injuries and slips beneath the lake's surface.

❖ ❖ ❖

Nearly 50 years of steamboating history on Lake Coeur d'Alene were
brought to a close as the remnants of *Georgie Oakes* sank. Although
it would be more than a decade before the prestigious *Flyer*, a sleek
excursion steamer, met the same pyrotechnic end, by the early 1920s the
steamboat's primacy in regional transportation was already in irreversible
decline. The automobile would deal the finishing blow to any rugged
vestige that survived the Great Depression.

During that tumultuous half-century, however, steamboating shaped
expansion in the region. Steamboats were present almost from the
moment Coeur d'Alene mustered enough bravado to declare itself a
town. Traversing the second-largest lake in Idaho and its network of
navigable waterways along three rivers – the St. Joe, Coeur d'Alene
and Spokane – steamers opened transportation routes that were all but
unreachable by rail or without considerable difficulty by foot. They
determined areas of settlement, making now-forgotten Idaho villages
like Stinson, Black Rock, Omega Landing, St. Joe City and Ferrell into
colorful centers of recreation and commerce, albeit fleetingly. And they
allowed fortune hunters to relieve the region of its natural resources –
chief among them timber, lead and silver – while delivering ever more
farmers and homesteaders further into its forested interior.

Although steamboats were powered by the area's vast supply of
cordwood, their existence was always at the mercy of the prevailing
socioeconomic winds. On Lake Coeur d'Alene, they morphed from
supply transports when the town was little more than a glorified garrison,
into ore haulers during the mining boom, into shuttles for laborers and
goods during the timber harvests, and finally into pleasure boats for
throngs of day-trippers. At the height of all this activity, Lake Coeur
d'Alene was home to more than 50 steamboats and the site of more
steamboat traffic than any lake west of the Great Lakes.

❖ ❖ ❖

Steamboating on Lake Coeur d'Alene had its origins in the construction
of the Mullan Road. Starting in the spring of 1859, Lt. John Mullan
and his team of more than 200 U.S. Army troops, engineers, workmen

and surveyors began work on the 611-mile overland route designed to connect Fort Benton, Montana (Dakota Territory at the time), which lay at the head of the Missouri River and linked to important ports eastward, to Fort Walla Walla, located in Washington Territory not far from the confluence of the Snake and Columbia rivers. Nearly two decades earlier, Jesuit missionary Father Pierre Jean DeSmet followed a similar path and described the difficulties it presented to would-be travelers:

> *Imagine thick, untrodden forests, strewn with thousands of trees thrown down by age and storms in every direction; where the path is scarcely visible, and is obstructed by barricades, which the horses are constantly compelled to leap, and which always endanger the riders.*

Completed in 1862, the Mullan Road primarily conveyed wagons and pioneers, but its occasional military traffic would have a lasting impact. In 1877, General William Tecumseh Sherman – he of controversial Civil War scorched-earth tactics – camped with a detail near Lake Coeur d'Alene and was inspired by the site's natural splendor to suggest it for a fort. Within a year, the Army had established Camp Coeur d'Alene at the point of land where the Spokane River flows from the lake. The military presence was intended not only to quiet growing unrest among Native Americans whose tribal land was gradually being usurped, but also to protect crews who were busy laying communication and transportation infrastructure so essential to Manifest Destiny. The camp officially became a fort (renamed Fort Sherman several years later) in April of 1879.

It was in that same year that post commander Lt. Colonel Henry Clay Merriam commissioned the construction of the very first steamboat on Lake Coeur d'Alene in case the Mullan Road's unreliable supply lines were ever disrupted. The stern-wheeler was to be 85 feet long with a 14-foot beam, capable not only of regularly transporting supplies but also, in emergencies, soldiers. Its cost was $5,000. Captain Peter C. Sorensen, a 46-year-old Norwegian immigrant then based in Portland, Oregon, was summoned to oversee construction, which, according to contemporary accounts, went as smoothly as one might expect of any untried major project undertaken in frontier wilderness.

"Sorensen actually disassembled an engine and brought it by boat and by wagon to be used in the first steamboat," says Robert Singletary, an authority on Coeur d'Alene history who frequently gives talks and walking tours in Sorensen-inspired costume and character. "He had problems getting that engine to fit the structure, so that was a bit of a struggle."

When the vessel was finally given its delayed launch late in 1880, Sorensen christened her the *Amelia Wheaton* after the daughter of the new post commander, Colonel Frank Wheaton. Sorensen never went back to Portland, instead putting down roots not far from what was little more than a tent city at the time, and becoming the ship's captain. Over the next three years he steamed across the lake in the *Amelia Wheaton*, mostly ferrying hay and grain for the fort's cavalry mules.

As a civic leader and master shipbuilder, Sorensen's presence would loom large over Idaho steamboating until his death on January 16, 1918. On those sleepy trips piloting the *Amelia Wheaton* or his own *Lottie* back and forth on the lake, he found ample time to bestow names, still in use today, upon natural features, among them Cougar Bay, Black Rock Bay, Echo Bay, Beauty Bay and Powderhorn Bay. Sorensen built his home on the bluff above Kidd Island (he named the spot North Cape) and acquired a reputation as a tinkerer and inventor. He built an automated contraption to tend his chickens while he was underway and maintained a large telegraph apparatus of his own. Sorensen's great grandson said that he was the one responsible for building an eight-foot musical cube out of glass bottles on Kidd Island along with other "scientific displays," as well as a not-so-scientific painted wooden monster that floated on the lake. Singletary cautions against accepting tales of Sorensen's wilder experiments too readily: "You have to take that with a grain of salt. I haven't been able to verify any of that outside of his expertise in shipbuilding."

That expertise is well documented. Sorensen, along with his gifted shipbuilding partner Peter Johnson, was behind more than half of the boats on the lake, including the *General Sherman, Volunteer, Schley* and *Torpedo*. He constructed his last boat, *North Star*, in 1907, by which time he was well into his 70s.

❖ ❖ ❖

A.J. Prichard's discovery of gold in the Coeur d'Alene district in 1881 and the mercenary scramble that followed in 1883 had an effect that would be repeated as long as steamboats plied the lake. The *Amelia Wheaton*, which had hauled fodder until that point, soon became a shuttle for starry-eyed prospectors who dreamt of striking the next motherlode. Steaming roughly 20 miles across Lake Coeur d'Alene and then 30 miles up the Coeur d'Alene River, the *Amelia Wheaton* deposited passengers at the Old Mission, where, depending on their wherewithal, they could travel by foot or by horse to Prichard Creek Valley, now known as Murray, Idaho. This water route had the advantage of bypassing a good portion of the overland journey via the Mullan Road. Tens of thousands of miners, settlers, speculators, claim-jumpers and other assorted fortune hunters flooded into the area. More frenzy ensued when abundant silver veins were discovered in 1884, giving the valley the name that stands today.

Regional historian Ruby El Hult, who grew up near Harrison watching steamers chug by, explains in her book *Steamboats in the Timber* (1952) how railroads and steamboats indirectly began to work in tandem at the start of the gold rush:

> *The Northern Pacific Railroad Company was partly responsible for the magnitude this first wild stampede attained. The railroad had been built through this undeveloped country in 1881-1883 at colossal expense, and the railroad officials eagerly seized upon the news of the mining strike as a means of stimulating travel over the line. They put out glowing, exaggerated pamphlets which lured people from all over the country to come to Idaho.*

The Northern Pacific's consecutive rail stops of Rathdrum and Spokane benefitted from this massive and spontaneous influx, and so did the steamboat landing at Coeur d'Alene. To accommodate the crowds arriving by stagecoach in the settlement, hotels, restaurants, saloons, warehouses, wharves and, yes, more steamboats were quickly built. One was the stern-wheeler *Coeur d'Alene*, with a length of 120 feet and a 14-foot beam, constructed under the supervision of Captain Irwin B. Sanborn. The other was Sorensen's smaller, propeller-driven *General Sherman*, built for businessmen James Monaghan and C.B. King. Launched in 1884, the two vessels established another defining trait of the steamboat era, namely, fierce competition in which monopolistic control was seen as the only desirable outcome. They engaged in fare wars so cutthroat as to be comical until the *General Sherman*'s owners struck a deal that allowed their ship – and *only* their ship – to be resupplied from the piles of cordwood chopped, stacked and sold by Native Americans along the waterways. Without fuel to stoke its boilers, the *Coeur d'Alene* had to concede defeat.

Daniel Chase (D.C.) Corbin, the shrewd and aloof younger brother of Long Island Railroad president Austin Corbin, Jr., arrived in Rathdrum around this time. No sooner had he alighted from the train than he began to envision an interlinked regional feeder network that would help the mining interests part more easily with their precious metals. He proposed a standard-gauge spur that would branch off the Northern Pacific at Hauser Junction and lead to Lake Coeur d'Alene, where steamboats would bridge the watery expanse between that line and a narrow-gauge railroad into the mountains starting at the Old Mission.

Similar ideas had already occurred to other entrepreneurs like J. J. Browne, but Corbin, who compensated for a legendary lack of magnanimity with an excess of opportunism, was the first to put the necessary pieces in place. His lines operated by the Spokane Falls & Idaho and the Coeur d'Alene Railway & Navigation Company were completed in 1886.

For the nautical leg, Corbin purchased the *General Sherman* as well as the *Coeur d'Alene*, making allies of the two former competitors. In 1887, he added the broad-shouldered *Kootenai*. According to *Steamboats in the Timber*, this was "a big, powerful boat" that "could break ten inches of ice and still make good time, and could plow through ice as thick as twenty-two inches." That made her perfectly suited for the harsh winter runs. Though the lake might be frozen, ore and goods could still flow freely.

Yet Corbin's calculating gaze soon drifted northward, and with customary prescience he sold the Coeur d'Alene Railway just two years later. Assisted by construction engineering whiz Edward J. Roberts, he then concentrated on a series of lines to connect the mines of southeastern British Columbia to Spokane.

Between 1887-1891, technological advances (and the installation of industrial mining machinery) led to exponentially more ore being extracted from the area's lead and silver mines. Combined yields rose from $800,000 in 1887, to $1.2 million in 1888, to $4 million in 1890 and up to $9 million in 1891. The ever-growing output taxed the small fleet of steamboats that hadn't been designed for hauling ore. The *Coeur d'Alene*, for example, was only able to haul 50 tons of ore (compared with the *Kootenai*'s 300-ton capacity), so its cabins and superstructure were removed and installed onto an impressive new hull built in 1891 by Sorensen and Johnson. This new ship measured 150 feet in length and 28 feet in beam. She could haul double the *Coeur d'Alene*'s capacity and would immediately be put to work on the mining run. She was the famed *Georgie Oakes*, named for the daughter of the president of the Northern Pacific, which had purchased the line from Corbin in 1888.

The *Georgie Oakes* had a cameo in the July 1892 labor unrest at the Bunker Hill and Sullivan mines, another byproduct of the introduction of machinery. New hydraulic excavators had enabled mine operators to transfer many of their skilled workers to menial jobs. The mass demotion was accompanied by a longer workday plus a seven-day work week. All of this came without a corresponding increase in wages when most of the workers' paychecks were already going toward the high cost of company lodging and overpriced goods at the company-owned commissaries. For the laborers, who toiled under the additional threats of flooding and cave-ins even as their bosses were off being fêted as estimable captains of industry by Spokane society, this was one grievance too many. Unionized miners struck in protest. Mining companies retaliated with scabs and strong-arm private security, including the infamous Pinkertons.

During the early hours of July 11, a gang of union men surrounded the Frisco mine in Burke, Idaho, loaded an ore car with 750 pounds of gunpowder, and sent it down the narrow-gauge rail. The explosion "shatter[ed] the mill to splinters, making it a complete wreck," the *New York Times* reported the next day. Meanwhile, violence spilled over from the Gem mine to the Bunker Hill mine, where another group of armed union men chased roughly 130 non-union workers from the area. As these fleeing miners waited to board the *Georgie Oakes*, they were assaulted and chased, presumably by union men, although subterfuge on the part of the mining companies wasn't unheard of. After martial law was declared throughout the neighboring county, four companies of soldiers departed from Fort Sherman to restore order. They chugged out to the mining district on the *Georgie Oakes*.

❖ ❖ ❖

Miners at least had the power to protest their forced obsolescence.

Steamboats could only silently accept their fate. Once the Oregon-Washington Railroad & Navigation Company had finished constructing a direct route to the Coeur d'Alene mining region in 1890, it was no longer necessary or cost-effective to transport the ore downstream, and the role of steamboats was diminished – for that purpose, at least. In the waning years of the 19th century, the water routes once essential to the mining industry became the new thoroughfare for timber.

The expansive forests along the banks of the St. Joe, the St. Maries and the Coeur d'Alene rivers were rich with white and yellow pine, tamarack and fir. The St. Maries Valley alone boasted the largest stand of white pine in the world. This made the area especially attractive to timber barons, who had been clear-cutting the forests around the Great Lakes region and were now beginning to eye the virgin bounty that lay westward. El Hult notes that the fawning pleas of the local paper might have helped to draw their attention:

> In 1893 the Coeur d'Alene Press said wistfully, "Mill men, why don't you come and take a look over this country? You are letting a good opportunity slip through your fingers. There are millions and millions of feet of timber in close proximity to this place, and this is a most advantageous location for a good mill."

The logging companies obliged, giddy over the prospect of 15 billion feet of densely packed timber that could be used to sustain the explosive growth occurring all over the country, particularly in the Inland Northwest and along the West Coast. Two years before the turn of the century, Idaho mills cut 65 million feet of lumber. A decade later, that number had increased almost eightfold. By 1910, Idaho was producing and distributing 745 million board feet each year, and new residents had swarmed into Coeur d'Alene, which saw its population climb to more than 7,000 that year.

William "Bill" Dollar was one of the first timbermen to arrive. He and his improbable name swaggered into town in 1899 on behalf of the F.S. Robbins Company. In 1901 he was joined by Frederick A. Blackwell of the William Howard Land and Lumber Company. Their respective corporations would go on to log 200 million and 1.25 billion of the nearly seven billion feet of timber cut from the region's precipitously steep hills by 1905. To achieve such staggering output, they relied on the backbreaking labor of loggers and millhands, who in turn relied on the steamboats to ferry them and their kit from Coeur d'Alene to points along the timber route – isolated outposts like Ramsdell, Silvertip Landing and Cosmo's Landing, or remote towns like Harrison, St. Maries, Ferrell and St. Joe City. Steamboats were these towns' only connection to the wider world. A Wild West atmosphere developed along the riverbanks, replete with gambling, drinking, prostitution, scam artists and shootouts. As the timber boom was largely responsible for conjuring these waterfront whistle-stops into existence, its eventual bust would cause many of them to shrink or disappear completely.

Freight and passenger haulers like the *Queen*, *Schley*, *Shoshone* and the regal, propeller-driven *Spokane* (another Sorensen and Johnson build) weren't the only steamers on the lake. In 1902, the aptly named Boom Company began sorting the thousands of logs that were chuted down the steep hillsides into the St. Joe. Each was identified by a log mark, similar to a ranch's cattle brand, that identified which company had felled and claimed it. Steam-powered tugs, such as Johnson's 85-foot-long *St. Joe*, would then tow the vast rafts of bound logs, or brails, to the appropriate mills near Coeur d'Alene. The painstaking journey could take two days or more. When the logs were destined for mills farther west in Post Falls, they would be released into Cougar Bay, where they would eddy like pools of giant matchsticks before being carefully fed into the mouth of the Spokane River. If the logs filled the waterways too snugly, lumberjacks had to walk out over the floating terrain, plant dynamite into the logjam and blast the passage back open again. The job carried the constant risk of death.

Logging would continue at a brisk pace until the Great Fire of 1910, when the flint of an unusually hot, dry summer struck the steel of human carelessness and natural mishaps. Over two days in late August, the firestorm destroyed three million acres of timberland – equal to 7.5 billion board feet of timber – across Eastern Washington, North Idaho and Western Montana. A contemporary observer reported flames several hundred feet high, "fanned by a tornadic wind so violent that the flames flattened out ahead, swooping to earth in great darting curves, truly a veritable red demon from hell." Cities more than 800 miles away reported skies thick with smoke. Inexperienced firefighting teams from the fledgling United States Forest Service pressed into the heart of the inferno; some perished. Mining and logging camps were abandoned in haste. The populations of the tiny timber towns along the rivers, unreachable by rescue trains, were prepared for evacuation. The *Idaho* was dispatched to St. Maries; the *Colfax*, big sister to the *Spokane*, went to St. Joe. For three days and nights the *Colfax* docked there with a full passenger load, its steam up and ready to go if given the word. Fortunately, St. Joe and St. Maries were spared the worst.

Lumber production in the 10 counties of North Idaho would slowly resume after the Big Blowup, reaching a zenith of 950 million board feet in 1926, the year before the *Georgie Oakes* was consigned to the lakebed. By 1932, output had fallen to 200 million board feet.

❖ ❖ ❖

A civil engineer and bon vivant named Joseph Clarence (J.C.) White had been summoned to Coeur d'Alene by D.C. Corbin back during the mining boom to help construct his narrow-gauge railroad. Once that was completed, for several years White lived and worked out of Spokane before returning to Idaho in 1892. There, much like every other businessman in the area, he became connected with the timber and transportation industries. And, much like every other businessman in the area, he watched with keen interest and no want of envy as boats like the plush *Colfax* and the *Spokane* steamed virtually unchallenged over the lake and rivers, making money hand over fist for co-owners George Reynolds' and E.D. McDonald. Before long White was approached by the father-and-son timber baron team of James H. and Harry Spaulding, who suggested establishing a rival company to outperform and undercut Reynolds and McDonald's modest fleet of steamboats.

The 38-year-old White secured $30,000 in backing from Bill Dollar — who, as it happens, would soon be granted a federal license to print money as the Exchange National Bank of Coeur d'Alene — and co-founded the Coeur d'Alene and St. Joe Transportation Company with the Spauldings on October 8, 1903. They contracted an outsider to build a 147-foot side-wheeler with a 23-foot beam at a cost of $45,000. The new *Idaho*'s size and 1,000-passenger capacity would give the noble *Georgie*

Oakes a run for her money; her grandeur would make the *Spokane* and *Colfax* look like third-class economy fare.

For the benefit of turn-of-the-century commuters and weekend excursionists, the *Idaho*'s dockside arrivals and departures were scheduled to coincide with the new electric railroad running from Spokane to Coeur d'Alene operated by Frederick Blackwell. The Transportation Company's machine was so well-oiled that Reynolds and McDonald couldn't keep pace. The pair sold out to White and his partners in 1905, and the *Spokane* and *Colfax* changed hands. To humiliate their former owners even further, red bands proclaiming Transportation Company ownership were placed around the boats' smokestacks. The victor became known as the Red Collar Line and would officially change its name accordingly some years later.

In his *History of Idaho*, published little more than a decade after the Transportation Company launched the *Idaho*, Hiram T. French maintains that this monopoly was a benefit to convenience and efficiency:

> *Citizens had long felt the need of a properly managed steamship line between Coeur d'Alene and St. Joe. Boats were manipulated by single owners, without definite method, without satisfactory regularity and without the needed equipment and conveniences. It was with a realization of the much-desired improvements that Mr. White organized the Red Collar Steamship Line, which has brought about a new era in transportation in this locality. All the former shipowners were induced to merge their interests into that of an organized company; new and modern boats have been added; a double daily schedule service was established; arrangements were methodically differentiated for passenger, mail, express and freight service. All this service is first-class, and for its initiation Mr. White is almost wholly responsible.*

One effect of this "first-class" service was that the public developed a passion for excursions. Every Sunday, crowds of people – families, couples, bachelors, travelers, sightseers – would ride in to Coeur d'Alene on the electric line and catch a round-trip steamboat to idyllic St. Joe or rustic St. Maries. They would eat, sing, converse, carouse, court and dance as the boats glided close to 30 miles across Lake Coeur d'Alene and then up the St. Joe River, famed for its shadowy waters lined by pine and cottonwood. On the return journey, passengers could enjoy hearty suppers in the dining room, and the merrymakers who weren't already in their cups from a day spent picnicking or saloon-hopping could visit the onboard bar (that is, until the Volstead Act took effect in 1920) and hope to avoid staggering overboard before reaching the depot that evening.

Coupled with the weekday mail and shipping runs, this regular activity kept the Red Collar Line comfortably in the black. Crowds numbering in the thousands turned out year after year for the Fourth of July events. El Hult writes, "On some Sundays... there would be such a mob around the Electric Line depot that the sidewalks were jammed for two blocks." Business was so good, in fact, that Reynolds and McDonald wanted back in despite their previous assurances of non-competition to White. They used the money from their first sale to the Transportation Company to hire Johnson to build another boat – the *Boneta*, a 96-foot long stern-wheeler with an 18-foot beam – and reincorporate as the White Star Navigation Company. The *Boneta* made an excellent freight hauler, which did nothing to assuage the mounting ire of the Red Collar owners. This would lead to a widely recounted incident in which the *Idaho*, captained by Jim Spaulding, rammed the more petite *Boneta*, captained by Reynolds. Spaulding called it an accident; Reynolds called it malice. The *Boneta* sank within minutes, and it was no small feat to raise and resurrect her.

White Star added the graceful two-deck *Flyer* to its fleet in 1906. With the low-slung sweep of her hull and almond-shaped top profile, she looked every inch her name as she glided across Lake Coeur d'Alene. Two years later, Reynolds and McDonald saved the *Georgie Oakes* from scuttling and rebuilt her at a cost of $10,000. She featured the grand interior staterooms and elegant dining that excursion passengers now sought. But it still wasn't enough. The petty, underhanded tactics that White Star and Red Collar were using against one another – cutting mooring lines, deliberately obstructing cargo or vessels, and complicating ticket redemption, to name just a few – were part of a slow war of attrition that only the Red Collar had sufficient resources to withstand.

On February 1, 1910, White and Spaulding's operation subsumed Reynolds and McDonald's for a second time. As part of the buyout, they took possession of the stalwart *Boneta*, stately *Georgie Oakes*, the nimble *Flyer*, brawny *Telephone* and others. With such a massive fleet and complete dominance of Lake Coeur d'Alene transport, the Red Collar Line enjoyed a heyday until the mid-1910s, when it came up against outside forces that were beyond even a monopoly's control. The rail lines had slowly expanded their reach, offering passengers more direct overland alternatives: In 1909, the Milwaukee Road, later known as the Route of the Hiawatha, opened along the south end of the lake, with trains running from the Great Lakes to Puget Sound through St. Maries and Plummer. And the gasoline-powered automobile, the pinnacle of individual convenience, was becoming more widespread. Not even the Spokane-to-Coeur d'Alene electric line had been able to hold out against it. In 1922, the Red Collar Line went into receivership after a few desperate and costly attempts to retain its former glory. A handful of steamboats would linger on the lake for a few more years.

❖ ❖ ❖

Peppered with anecdotes about desperate rescue missions to save stranded passengers and full-throttle races between rival captains, the history of steamboating on Lake Coeur d'Alene and its tributaries is as deep as the lake itself. Some time should be taken in closing to recount the fates of several steamers, each of which took on a character all her own and became the centerpiece for stories that were passed along over the decades by passengers, captains and crew.

In 1888, the *Amelia Wheaton* was sold by the government to a private party. She steamed up and down the St. Joe until 1893, when part of her was transferred to a new hull and she was renamed the *St. Joseph*. Her old hull became a freight barge. The *General Sherman* was abandoned around 1891 and sank in shallow water before being raised and repaired in 1894. It too steamed the St. Joe for several years until its mechanicals were salvaged and installed into the new *Schley* in 1899. Its hull was towed out onto the lake and sunk. The *Coeur d'Alene*, having been partially refashioned into the *Georgie Oakes*, became a barge on which floating dances were held. In 1914, the pillaged hull of the *Spokane* was burned as part of the town's Fourth of July celebrations. After just 10 years of service, the palatial *Idaho* was retired and used as a massive floating shed for storing apples before it caught fire and sank in 1915.

The *Kootenai*, that burly ice-breaker, was docked for several years and then purchased by someone who neglected her for several more. She was ultimately towed to Three-Mile Point – a slight bulge in the shoreline now guarded by colossal summer "cabins" – and sunk. She would later be joined by the *Colfax* and the steam-powered tugs *Samson*, *St. Maries* and *Bonanza* at a site still known as the Steamboat Graveyard.

The prominent figures of Coeur d'Alene's steamboat era would also end up congregating after their time had passed. Captain Sorensen's grave lies within a few dozen paces of the resting places of Frederick Blackwell (d. 1922) and J.C. White (d. 1953). All three are buried in Forest Cemetery, not far from the lakeshore and just a short distance from where Fort Sherman stood before it was abandoned in 1900.

There are a few steamboating relics scattered around the Lake City, too. Just off the Kidd Island shore, below Captain Sorensen's old perch, is the rusting boiler of the *St. Maries*, salvaged by divers as scrap metal. A singed and weatherbeaten fragment of the *Idaho*'s paddlewheel remains in front of the Museum of North Idaho, where you can see many more artifacts of the era. Next to it sits a huge propeller, which divers recovered from the *Flyer* years after the swift steamer was set alight – just like the old *Georgie Oakes*.

The *Flyer*'s retirement was the last major event in the Coeur d'Alene steamboating era that Sorensen had helped to launch. On February 4, 1938, in front of a crowd that had gathered on City Beach to bid her a final farewell, she was burned down to the waterline and slowly foundered, joining her illustrious predecessors in steamboating history. ■

The final voyage of the *Flyer* on February 4, 1938.

Geogology iconoclast J Harlen Bretz

Expo '74 organizer King Cole

Native American writer Mourning Dove

Parks pioneer Aubrey L. White

People of the Century: 1900 - 2000

LEADERS
ARTISTS AND ENTERTAINERS
EMPIRE BUILDERS
NORTHWEST ORIGINALS

First published in the *Inlander* on October 6, 1999

Just before the turn of the millennium, the *Inlander* tapped local historians to come up with a list of the most important, interesting and/or influential Inland Northwesterners of the 20th century. Developing such a list is, by nature, a subjective process. In an attempt to be as complete as possible, a variety of local historians were consulted to compile their own lists and ultimately agree on a final 80 men and women named as People of the Century. (Here in *Inlander Histories Vol. 2*, 16 of those profiles are included, with the remaining 64 people listed in brief.)

Our selection committee included: ROBERT CARRIKER, Gonzaga University history professor and editor of *Great River of the West: Essays on the Columbia River*; NANCY GALE COMPAU, director of the Northwest Room at the Spokane Public Library and co-author of *Our City... Spokane*; JOHN FAHEY, author of *The Inland Empire: Unfolding Years, 1879-1919*; HENRY MATTHEWS, architecture professor at Washington State University and author of *Kirtland Cutter: Architect in the Land of Promise*; TED S. McGREGOR JR., editor and publisher of the *Inlander*; IVAN MUNK, artist and author of *Spokane Country: The Way It Was*; JACK

NISBET, natural historian and author of *Singing Grass, Burning Sage*; WILLIAM STIMSON, author of *A View of the Falls: An Illustrated History of Spokane* and a journalism professor at Eastern Washington University; and J. WILLIAM T. YOUNGS, Eastern Washington University history professor and author of *The Fair and the Falls*. Profiles written by Ted S. McGregor Jr. unless otherwise noted.

❖ ❖ ❖

LEADERS

KING COLE

BY J. WILLIAM T. YOUNGS

He is known as the "father" of Expo '74, one of the most important events in Spokane's history. Offering a more modest appraisal of himself on the 20th anniversary of the fair, King Cole said he was the one who would have been "blamed" if the exposition had failed.

Cole would be the first to admit that he did not originate the idea of a world's fair in Spokane; he liked the concept and went to work promoting it, but he was not the first to propose it. Nor did he manage the exposition – that task fell to an out-of-towner, Petr Spurney. Moreover, other Spokanites played key roles in raising funds for the exposition and building the site, most notably perhaps Jim Cowles, Tom Adkinson and Rod Lindsay. And yet Cole was arguably the essential person in leading Spokane to become the smallest city ever to host a world's fair.

Cole was born in Grand Junction, Colorado, in 1922. Two years later, his family moved to California. During the 1950s, he became interested in urban renewal. At the time, "every city in the United States looked pretty dreary," Cole recalled. He wanted to take part in the movement to change that. Cole became head of redevelopment for San Leandro, California, and helped renovate the city core and waterfront. In 1963, word of Cole's success spread to Spokane, where a private organization known as Spokane Unlimited hired him to help revitalize the city.

At the time, dark trestles separated the downtown from Spokane Falls. An industrial laundry sat on present-day Canada Island and belched soap suds into the river. Warehouses occupied Havermale Island. Most Spokanites had forgotten the falls. There was even talk of paving over the south channel of the river to provide more parking.

Arriving in 1963, Cole hit the ground running. During his first full year in town, he delivered 52 speeches. Again and again he plugged away at a single, central theme: the importance of a strong urban core. "The center of the city is its heart," he said. "And with any organism, no matter how healthy the extremities and other members are, if the heart is sick, the total community is going to get sick."

Cole brought to these meetings, as well as to his many speeches, a personal enthusiasm that inspired others. During his first year in town, a Rotarian concluded a report on his recent talk with the remark: "I hope that he returns with another message, and more of that sparkle, with which he is filled."

Cole's "sparkle" was infectious, and references to Cole as "a merry old soul" were inevitable. When Spokanites rallied around the idea of a world's fair in the early-1970s, many supported the idea because they were moved by Cole's vision of a better Spokane. When the Bureau of International Expositions in Paris endorsed the fair, they associated Spokane with the ebullient Cole. And when the Soviet Union agreed to exhibit at the fair — assuring Spokane's success — their exposition members had already met and liked the promoter from Spokane.

Spokane's success came from imaginative leadership among local businessmen and astute political maneuvering in Washington, D.C., by Tom Foley and Warren Magnuson. It also depended on the work of thousands of volunteers and overworked staffers.

On his return from Paris, after Spokane won approval for the fair, Cole claimed that no previous event in the city's history "can compare with what is going to happen here in the next few years because of Expo '74. I am not basing my remark just on dollars or new construction. I'm talking about the whole community attitude, the competitive 'can do' spirit that will make and keep this a tremendous community."

From other promoters, such words could be dismissed as clichéd. In

Cole, such words were part of a faith, deeply held, in the transforming power of a common vision. Many Spokanites believed in Expo because they believed in Cole. Urban renewal in the city had a face and a personality. Anyone who knows Spokane history recognizes that, like the city itself, Spokane's great exposition had a heart. The heart of Expo '74 was King Cole.

JULIA STUART DAVIS

In 1960, Julia Stuart became the first woman from west of the Mississippi to serve as president of the National League of Women Voters, serving two terms. It wasn't a huge surprise, since her actions as president of the Washington state chapter had captured the attention of the national organization. In 1956, the voters of the state threw out a legislative districting system that was grossly unfair as it failed to reflect population growth. Few thought the reform had a chance, as the status quo had its fervent supporters, but the proposal brought forward by the state's League of Women Voters, led by Stuart, proved everyone wrong. Stuart, who came to Spokane in 1945, was also active in pollution abatement and outdoor recreation issues, and received the Izaak Walton League's Honor Roll Award. In 1964, she was one of a dozen American women singled out for special honors at the New York World's Fair.

C.C. DILL

While many played key roles in the construction of the Grand Coulee Dam, perhaps none had the impact of Clarence Cleveland Dill. In 1931, the Democratic U.S. Senator from Spokane visited then-candidate Franklin D. Roosevelt and secured a simple promise in return for his support: If elected, Roosevelt would build the dam. Dill also intersected with history in 1933 when two kids from Wenatchee got in trouble for playing music over the radio without permission. Dill's conviction that the airwaves should be public space was carried through the Federal Commerce Committee he chaired, and he drafted the landmark Federal Communications Act. Dill, who started his career as a high school teacher and served in the Senate from 1922-35, returned to Spokane after his political career concluded to practice law.

INA AND ERIC JOHNSTON

BY IVAN MUNK

Eric Alan Johnston is one of Spokane's true golden boys. Born in 1896, his pharmacist father moved the family to Spokane at the turn of the century. Johnston graduated with a law degree from the University of Washington just in time to join the Marines for service in World War I. With a partner in 1923, Johnston established a local electrical supply company known today as Columbia Electric. Within a year, he was elected president of the Spokane Chamber of Commerce.

After Johnston's unsuccessful bid for Congress in 1940, President Franklin Roosevelt called upon him for the touchy task of serving as his personal representative to Joseph Stalin in Moscow. In 1942, he was the youngest man ever elected president of the United States Chamber of Commerce. In 1950, he became president of the Motion Picture Academy. As Congressional committees searched Hollywood for communists, his style of diplomacy satisfied neither the red-baiters nor the leftists. After such a storied career, he and his wife Ina were chosen by journalist Edward R. Murrow to be the subject of a half-hour interview program that was broadcast nationwide.

Johnston died in Washington, D.C., in 1963, and Ina returned to Spokane, becoming a strong force in her own right. She was instrumental in getting the Spokane Civic Theatre off the ground and helping fund the Dishman Hills Natural Area, along with other causes, through their Johnston Foundation.

ELEANOR AND JIM CHASE, a professional singer and social worker, and Spokane's first African American mayor, respectively

ROD CLEFTON, KHQ-TV broadcaster, producer of *High School Bowl*, televised historic reenactments and public service programming on the Spokane Aquifer

FR. BERNARD COUGHLIN, Gonzaga University's 23rd President (1974-97), Fulbright Lecturer, Spokane Chamber of Commerce President

TOM FOLEY, Spokane native, Congressman (1965-95), Speaker of the U.S House of Representatives (1989-95)

NEAL FOSSEEN, Spokane Mayor (1960-67), advocate for bringing the World's Fair to Spokane in 1974

LEONARD FUNK, Spokane public servant for 29 years, including Spokane Mayor (1929-35)

JOSEPH GARRY, great-grandson of Spokane Garry, Coeur d'Alene tribal member, six-term President of the National Congress of American Indians

BENJAMIN H. KIZER, Spokane attorney, Director of the United Nations Relief and Rehabilitation Administration in China (1944-46)

MARGARET LEONARD, Spokane City Councilwoman (1962-77), community activist

CLARENCE MARTIN, Cheney native, Washington State Governor (1933-41)

JOHN OSBORN, Spokane physician, Founder of the Lands Council, clean water activist

MARY LOU AND SCOTT REED, Coeur d'Alene residents since 1953, an Idaho State Senator for 12 years, and a noted pro bono environmental attorney, respectively

JOHN ROSKELLEY, mountaineer, author, Spokane County Commissioner (1995-2004)

LEWIS B. SCHWELLENBACH, Spokane native, U.S. Senator (1935-40), U.S. Secretary of Labor (1945-48)

LUKE WILLIAMS JR., Spokane Valley native, owner of American Sign and Indicator, inventor of alternating time and temperature display

VIVIAN WINSTON, Founder of Spokane's Planned Parenthood, Women Helping Women and the Crisis Residential Center

❖ ❖ ❖

ARTISTS AND ENTERTAINERS

MOURNING DOVE

BY JACK NISBET

Mourning Dove was the pen name of Christine Quintasket, an Interior Salish woman who wrote a novel and collected tribal stories in the early decades of the 20th century. Her mother was of Lakes and Colvile ancestry, and her father belonged to the Nicola band that lived among the Okanagan people. In an account of her life, Mourning Dove wrote that her mother gave birth to her while crossing the Kootenai River in a canoe, then wrapped her in the steersman's shirt. It would be an appropriate beginning for a woman who traveled restlessly through the Intermountain West and battled against prevailing currents for the rest of her life.

She spent her formative years near her mother's traditional home at Kettle Falls, joining in the great salmon fishery there each summer. She spoke Salish as her first language, but attended Catholic mission schools intermittently at Kettle Falls, Colville, Fort Spokane and Fort Shaw near Great Falls, Montana. While at the Fort Shaw school, a teenaged Quintasket spent time with her grandmother Maria and witnessed the 1908 roundup of the last free-ranging bison herd. In 1909, she married a Flathead tribal member she had met at the school, but it was a stormy partnership, and by 1912 Quintasket was living by herself in Portland. There she took the name Mourning Dove and began to write.

Unsatisfied with her skills, she migrated to Calgary and studied typing and composition at a business school. By 1915, she had a draft of a novel dealing with the life of an Indian girl. In that same year, she met Yakima businessman and Indian advocate L.C. McWhorter at the annual

Frontier Day festivities in Walla Walla, and he encouraged her to tell her people's stories. They began a correspondence that continued for more than two decades.

In a 1916 interview in the *Spokesman-Review*, Mourning Dove stated her ambition to shatter white stereotypes of the American Indian. "We do feel, and by and by some of us are going to be able to make our feelings appreciated, and then will the true Indian character be revealed." In the same interview, she spoke of the imminent appearance of her novel, perhaps the first one ever published by a Native American in a traditional setting. It did not come easily. McWhorter became involved in the editing of the book, initiating a series of frustrating delays.

Mourning Dove taught school for a time in Oliver, B.C., then in 1919 married Fred Galler, an enrolled Colvile of Wenatchi and pioneer white ancestry. They lived in East Omak on the Colvile Reservation, and worked together as migrant laborers in hop fields and apple orchards along the east front of the Cascades. When *Cogewea: The Half-Blood* was finally published in 1927, it was an awkward blend of Mourning Dove's fictional story and McWhorter's ethnographic footnotes and angry political statements. Mourning Dove continued to work in the fields during the day and write at night, and the novel was followed in 1933 by a collection called *Coyote Stories*. This book was influenced by both McWhorter and Yakima newspaperman Heister Dean Guie, who envisioned the collection as bedtime stories that would be appropriate for children. Many of the stories, as published, were unrecognizable to the Colvile-Okanagan elders who originally told them to Mourning Dove.

Although criticized by members of both the white and tribal communities, Mourning Dove never stopped working to realize her ambitions as an Indian and as an artist. It was not an easy path, and since her teens she had suffered from various physical ailments. In the summer of 1936, she became disoriented and was taken to the state hospital at Medical Lake, where she died within nine days. She left behind 20 folders of written papers in the care of Guie; in 1981, his wife turned them over to the University of Washington Press. Reorganized and edited by researcher Jay Miller, they appeared as *Mourning Dove: A Salishan Autobiography* in 1990.

Even if the words are not exactly her own, Mourning Dove's autobiography contains images that do not surface in the European perception of the Inland Northwest. Her description of the fishery at Kettle Falls, for example, separates itself from accounts of early male fur traders, missionaries and painters by going inside the encampment itself. Mourning Dove visits each family in their traditional established campsite. She details the exact materials used to fashion the basket traps and spears, and recalls the specific jobs of women and girls in preparing the catch. She remembers the buzz of yellowjackets around the drying fish, and the joy of dancing and playing around the tents. She took a centuries-old tradition that she had lived and captured it not by telling a story, but by writing it down. In this way she provided a springboard for a host of contemporary native artists — male and female, from tribes all over the continent — whose creative work weaves an individual vision into the rich history of their people.

VACHEL LINDSAY

Although he only stayed in Spokane for five years, starting in 1924, the Illinois-born Vachel Lindsay brought a great deal of celebrity with him. Based on volumes he published in the 1910s, Lindsay was one of the world's preeminent poets when he moved to Spokane. But the move was aimed at creating some stability in his life, which had consisted of traveling the country — often paying his way with poems he would write on the spot. Lindsay, who lived in a suite in the Davenport Hotel, married a local woman, and fathered three children, but the stability he sought was not to be. During his stay, however, he did expose the city to a larger cultural context, and he used the city as fodder for his poetry, writing about its affairs and environs. By the end of his stay, his writing came in the form of columns in the newspaper. But he began to sense that his patrons' attentions went no deeper than his celebrity, and his finances soured. While his stay created local pride at the time, and Spokane played a role in an important literary career, Lindsay never found happiness and took his own life in 1931 in his hometown of Springfield, Illinois.

PATRICE MUNSEL

One of the great opera singing careers of the 1940s and '50s was launched in the Spokane conservatory of music teacher Charlotte Granis Lange in 1935. That's when Patrice Munsel, then 12, started taking voice lessons.

Five years later, she became the youngest member of the Metropolitan Opera Company in New York City. While Munsel's career, which spanned three decades, kept her away from Spokane, she always voiced her pride over her hometown and returned to sing frequently.

KEN BROOKS

While most Inland Northwesterners link the name Kirtland Cutter with architecture, another name gained more stature in the middle part of the century. Ken Brooks was ahead of his time in many ways, not the least of which is in his designs – especially the Washington Water Power building at Mission and Upriver Drive, which won the First Honor Award from the American Institute of Architects in 1959 for its innovative style. But Brooks also led the charge to reclaim the downtown from decay, leading a series of initiatives he called "Spokane: A Place in the Sun." Brooks' legacy is hard to categorize because of his varied interests, from the environment to engineering to planning, but perhaps that's the way he liked it, as he once remarked, "All our endeavors finally distill to the art of living."

SHERMAN ALEXIE, Spokane and Coeur d'Alene tribal member, author

HAROLD BALAZS, Spokane visual artist

JANE BALDWIN, founder of the Works Progress Administration's Spokane Art Center, woodblock printer, painter

FIRTH CHEW, Spokane Civic Theatre board member, accountant

BING CROSBY, Spokane native, Gonzaga University alumnus, recording and movie star

KIRTLAND CUTTER, Spokane architect, designer of the Davenport Hotel

JOHN FAHEY, Spokane historian

BRUCE FERDEN, Spokane Symphony Director (1985-91) credited with saving the orchestra

THOMAS HAMPSON, Spokane native, professional baritone singer

STODDARD KING, *Spokesman-Review* columnist, poet

MIKE KOBLUK, Founding member of the Gonzaga University-based Chad Mitchell Trio, program director for Expo '74 and the Spokane Opera House

CHARLES LIBBY SR., Spokane photographer whose 200,000-plus negatives now reside at the Northwest Museum of Arts and Culture

PATRICK McMANUS, Sandpoint native, author, humorist

LENO PRESTINI, Terra cotta artist with the Washington Brick and Lime Company of Clayton, painter, muralist

BOB AND JOAN WELCH, Spokane arts advocates, founders of Interplayers professional theater

HAROLD C. WHITEHOUSE, Spokane architect, designer of St. John's Cathedral

❖ ❖ ❖

EMPIRE BUILDERS

AUBREY L. WHITE

As a young man in Spokane, Aubrey White worked in a bookstore, spending his off hours wandering the city's natural areas, imagining what might be there in the future. But he didn't imagine an empire of homes, businesses or factories − instead he imagined a system of parks that would make the city a better place to live. After traveling back East as a representative for mining companies, he returned to find the city growing rapidly. He immediately posed his ideas about parks to local leaders and founded a City Beautiful Club. As a result, he was appointed chairman of the Park Board and oversaw the passage of a $900,000 park bond. But he didn't stop there; White pressured Spokane's leading citizens to donate land to the cause, too. Manito, Comstock and Corbin parks, to name a few, all date to his leadership. Later in life, he became editor of the *Spokesman-Review*'s Garden and Betterment section, continuing to beat the drum of setting aside land for the common good. At the time of his death in 1948, Spokane had more parkland per capita than any similar sized city in the country.

W.H. COWLES

Although his career straddles the 19th and 20th centuries, W. H. Cowles laid the foundation for an Inland Northwest empire that endures to this day. Within six years of getting off the train from Chicago in 1891, Cowles, the second son of the *Chicago Tribune*'s business manager, had established a newspaper enterprise that has more or less defined Spokane's media landscape ever since. Cowles was a civic leader in matters of cleaning up the residue of the wilder side of westward expansion, too – from gambling to prostitution to corrupt government. He was also instrumental in creating the system of parks we enjoy to this day. He freely used his newspaper's clout to accomplish these ends. Cowles ran the operation, continuing to expand into other areas like real estate and paper production, until his death in 1946.

DUANE HAGADONE

There's a local myth that, some years ago, *National Geographic* named Lake Coeur d'Alene one of the world's five most beautiful lakes. Even though it never happened, it's great grist for the public relations mill that has helped put the Coeur d'Alene Resort at the top of many a traveler's list of favorite places. From the floating green at the Coeur d'Alene Resort

Golf Course to the lake view from Beverly's restaurant, the resort has taken the idea of transitioning a resource-based economy to a tourism-based one and run with it. Behind it all is the singular vision of Duane Hagadone, primarily a newspaperman but more recently a kind of concierge for the region he grew up in.

Hagadone took the reins of the *Coeur d'Alene Press* and other newspapers owned by his family when he was only 26, as his father passed away unexpectedly at age 49. Hagadone managed to buy more newspapers, from Iowa to Hawaii, and then he went after another dream. In 1986, his resort opened to hackles in the national and local press. It was a significant risk for his company, but just a year later his rooms were sold out, and Japanese tourists could be spotted in downtown Coeur d'Alene.

E.H. STANTON

Today the Stanton name is linked to Washington Trust Bank, but there was a time when the name Stanton meant one thing: meat. E.H. Stanton came West and settled in Sprague, Washington, where he started a meat packing plant. He later moved to Spokane and started the Spokane Meat Company. Eventually he sold his meat packing concerns to Armour, using the proceeds to get into a new line of work. In 1918, he purchased the Washington Trust company. Soon he pursued other interests, including real estate, apple orchards and timber, leaving Washington Trust in the hands of his son Fred Stanton. E.H. Stanton died after a full day of work at the bank in 1931.

JOE ALBI, co-founder of the Athletic Round Table, driving force behind the construction of Albi Stadium

DON BARBIERI, urban planner, principal with Spokane's Goodale and Barbieri, which also spun out Cavanaugh's Hotels, TicketsWest and the Best of Broadway series

RALPH BERG, heart surgeon, co-founder of the Heart Institute of Spokane

SISTER PETER CLAVER, Sacred Heart Hospital chief administrator (1962-88), nurse, Sister of Providence

D.C. CORBIN, Spokane banker, land surveyor and railroad builder

W.H. COWLES 3rd, *Spokesman-Review* publisher, civic advocate, member of Momentum and Spokane Unlimited

GEORGE WASHINGTON FULLER, director of the Spokane Public Library for 25 years, donor of the Fuller Collection to the downtown library's Northwest Room

RAYMOND A. HANSON, inventor, founder of the international engineering firm R.A. Hanson Company

HENRY J. KAISER, industrialist who started his career in Spokane, builder of the Grand Coulee Dam, founder of Kaiser Aluminum

ROBERT B. PATERSON, founder of Spokane's Crescent Department Store

DENNIS AND ANN PENCE, founders of Sandpoint-based Coldwater Creek

MERTON ROSAUER, founder of the Rosauers supermarket chain

PAUL SANDIFUR SR., founder of Spokane's Metropolitan Mortgage

FR. WILFRED P. SCHOENBERG, official archivist for the Oregon Province of the Society of Jesus, author, founder of the Museum of Native American Cultures (MONAC)

D.W. TWOHY, founder of Old National Bank in Spokane

LOUIS WASMER, founder of KHQ, Spokane's first radio station

❖ ❖ ❖

NORTHWEST ORIGINALS

J HARLEN BRETZ

BY JACK NISBET

Born in rural Michigan in 1882, J Harlen Bretz always refused to put a period after the initial in his name. His first love was astronomy, and as a kid he set up an observatory in the cupola of his father's big red barn. From there he learned both that he loved field work and that he did not have a clear head for numbers: "My first real discovery was that I never could master the mathematics in astronomy."

Bretz switched to biology, took a degree from Albion College and married his college sweetheart in 1906. He landed in Western Washington as a high school biology teacher, where for four years he spent his weekends and summer days tracing out the evidence of glacial action around Puget Sound. By 1913, he had earned a doctorate from the University of Chicago and a new job at the University of Washington.

A library encounter with a topographical map of Dry Falls and studies in the Columbia Gorge lured Bretz inland to the wonders of the Columbia Basin, and soon he was driving his new colleagues at UW to distraction with pleas for them to join him in the field. When they responded by dismissing him from his post, Bretz resumed his schedule of outdoor observation, this time on the faculty of the University of Chicago. At first unable even to afford a car, he spent years tramping through the Columbia Basin with family and students, typically clad in khakis and a steel hardhat. There he sifted through massive gravel bars, measured huge ripple marks, mapped erratic boulders and scrambled up dry cataracts.

At the beginning of the 20th century, geologists clung to ironclad rules about the gradual formation of landscapes and river drainages. The textbooks said that wind and water ate away at rocks over eons of time, grinding the earth down in smooth and predictable ways. When Bretz published the first of a long stream of strident papers in 1919, all based on the cockeyed notion that a flood of apocalyptic proportions had roared across the Columbia Plateau, the community of academics was aghast. Bretz coined terms like "Channeled Scablands" to describe the effects of the deluge, and focused all his energy on answering a single question: "After a receding cataract has destroyed itself, what features of the gorge it made will record its former existence?" While an entire discipline believed what their textbooks told them, Bretz believed his eyes and his intuition.

The maverick ignored a 30-year storm of withering criticism, continued his work and inspired a host of talented students not only to refine his ideas, but also to become vocal disciples for the cause of catastrophic Ice Age floods. It was gradually accepted that between about 12,000 and 15,000 years ago, a series of several dozen major floods swept from glacial Lake Missoula across Pend Oreille Lake, Spokane and the Columbia Basin, sculpting the landscape that we live in today. Bretz, who remained active in the field right up until his death at age 98, lived to see his carefully formulated concepts radiate outwards from the Columbia Basin to modify theories of landscape formation all over the world.

Although Harlen Bretz was a remarkable original, he was also a man of his time, who saw the control of nature as the logical next step after understanding it. In 1932, in his landmark paper on the Grand Coulee, he recommended the exact site for the great dam and explained how the captured water could be steadily diverted for agricultural use. "Man's ingenuity now promises the Columbia Plateau an optimum of water, delivered through the long cloudless summers. Wheat farming will give place to alfalfa growing and fruit raising. In the unclaimed or abandoned dry gravel soils, sagebrush and bunch grass will vanish and orchards will spread a summer greenery over the gray landscape."

Bretz visualized the Columbia Basin as a green utopia without any of the problems of erosion, soil depletion, water contamination or habitat destruction that must enter into the equation today. In reading his work, it's easy to get the feeling that if he was out there now, sweating through his khakis, he would have some clear and controversial ideas about the future of his favorite flood-torn landscape.

SONORA SMART DODD

Father's Day seems such a part of the American calendar that you'd think Hallmark invented it. In fact, it took Spokane's Sonora Smart Dodd several years to turn her idea into the annual observance it has become.

Dodd traced her idea to a cold night in the late-1890s, when her own father, William Jackson Smart, had to tell his six young children, including her, that their mother had died. Her father raised all six kids on his own, and the enormity of that task came back to Dodd one Sunday morning at Spokane's Central Methodist Church, just after her pastor delivered a Mother's Day sermon. She told the minister that there should be a day for fathers, too, and he took up the idea with other religious leaders in Spokane, then the city council. Eventually, the governor declared the third Sunday in June to be Father's Day in Washington state. The first Father's Day was celebrated in 1910, and newspapers picked up the story, ensuring that the holiday was embraced around the country.

FRANCES AND CLARENCE FREEMAN

Through perseverance and hard work, Frances and Clarence Freeman overcame racial barriers to build a successful life in Spokane – and helped erode the racial divide in the process. The couple, married when Clarence was 29 and Frances 24, had the kind of prospects you'd imagine for an African American couple in the 1930s. Despite some time in school and after putting in applications all over town, Clarence stayed on with the Ridpath Hotel, where he had worked since he was 14. Clarence later joined the Army and excelled in uniform, being promoted to company commander while in Europe.

But when he returned to Spokane, the same old lack of opportunity stared the couple in the face. Clarence remembered how one of his pastors used to tell him to buy up real estate, even empty lots: "They're going to be worth a lot someday," Clarence recalled the pastor as predicting. So the couple used every spare dime to buy apartments, lots, whatever. One of those apartments was such a squalid mess that Clarence got a couple people together to take it down, and the next thing he knew, he was in the construction business. He went on to build projects on his own property and eventually began working with white people, too – something he had been conditioned not to expect. "Thank goodness the good people outnumber the bad people," Clarence said of the handful of bankers and others who supported him. "That's how Frances and I made it – the good people showed up."

Frances was an accomplished citizen in her own right, and she became the first African American to serve on the Spokane Park Board, a post she held for 10 years. Frances went to business school and helped the war effort while Clarence was overseas. An active gardener, she also raised money to beautify the Finch Arboretum and Liberty Park.

WILLIE WILLEY

A hippie before anyone knew where Haight-Ashbury was, Willis "Willie" Willey arrived in Spokane in 1905, appearing to embark on a normal Spokane career path. But after a failed romance and a falling out with his congregation, Willey decided to go back to nature. From about that time forward, the only clothing he wore – rain, snow or shine – was a pair of shorts. While the novelty was fresh, he was known around town as "Nature Boy," but soon he ran into trouble with the law. His ranch was auctioned off after a legal squabble, but he refused to leave the property, and during a repeating cycle of going to jail and then squatting back on the ranch, his story was syndicated in newspapers across the country. Someone coined the phrase "Williecana" to describe the fascination. Celebrity fit Willey well, as he showed up in the newspaper almost weekly with some new stunt. Soon, Willey took his show on the road, and in Portland (where he was arrested for recommending fewer clothes to a woman he met), Chicago, Boston and New York, the "Spokane Nudist" caused a sensation. But he eventually returned to Spokane, again fighting for his land – a battle he waged unsuccessfully into his sixties. In 1956, Willey died in his car, which had served as his home for many years.

BOBBY BRETT, principal with Brett Sports, owners of the Spokane Chiefs and Spokane Indians

ALBERT COMMELLINI, restaurateur, bootlegger, founder of the Hotel de Gink, a soup kitchen for the poor during the Depression

LOUIS DAVENPORT, Spokane's arbiter of style, owner of the Davenport Hotel

MARY GAISER, community volunteer and benefactor who funded the Spokane Symphony, the YWCA and the Spokane Arts Commission

DAVID GUILBERT, president of the Inland Automobile Association, road-building advocate

HENRY HART, principal of Lewis and Clark High School (1907-37)

MAY ARKWRIGHT HUTTON, Silver Valley mining magnate, feminist, suffragette

JAY J. KALEZ, Spokane Works Progress Administration manager, engineer, historian

DON KARDONG, Olympic runner, founder of the Lilac Bloomsday Run

CARL MAXEY, Spokane attorney, civil rights activist

FRED MURPHY, Coeur d'Alene Lake tugboat captain, dockbuilder

PAULINE FLETT AND LAWRENCE NICODEMUS, local Native Americans who worked to preserve the Salish language

JOHN STOCKTON, Gonzaga University graduate, NBA Hall of Fame member, Olympic gold medalist

BILLY TIPTON, female jazz musician who lived life in Spokane as a man, marrying five times

ED TSUTAKAWA, artist, founder of the Mukogawa Institute, Spokane Sister Cities supporter

LOUIS VOGEL, manager of Natatorium Park, son-in-law to Charles Looff, who carved the famous Nat Park carousel that still resides in Riverfront Park ■

Sisters of Providence on a "begging tour" through the Silver Valley, where miners helped fund their mission at Sacred Heart Hospital.

Healing Pioneers: The Sisters of Providence

BY WILLIAM STIMSON

First published in *InHealth* in January of 2005

With calamity and moral failings on full display every day in the news, it is hard to avoid becoming jaded. We learn to look away, to reign in our emotions, become "realistic" about what we can do. But for the founder of the Sisters of Providence, Mother Emilie Gamelin, looking away was never an option.

Born in 1800, little Emilie was already filled with empathy by the age of 3, when she saw a beggar and sobbed until her mother allowed her to give the man her little-girl possessions. Her own family was beset by Job-like tragedy: Her mother died when she was 4, nine of her siblings died at an early age, and when she was 14, her father died. At age 23, Gamelin seemed at last to have found happiness when she married one of the leading men of Montreal.

Even then, her world slowly collapsed. Two of her children died within months of their births, and then her husband took sick and perished. A few months later, her 21-month-old son died. Just five years after her marriage, Emilie Gamelin found herself all alone.

She took comfort in caring for others. Her husband had expressed a last wish as he was dying: Would Emilie care for a mentally disabled friend after he was gone? She did, and the care of the mentally afflicted became a lifelong concern.

But she didn't stop there. She discovered dozens of elderly women who had outlived their families and had no place to go. So Gamelin collected donations from her society friends and established homes for them. The epidemics that swept through Montreal had left whole families of orphans. Eventually, she was caring for more than 600 of them.

In fact, Gamelin had uncovered so many needs that, in order to cope, the bishop of Montreal established a new order of nuns. Gamelin became the guiding spirit of the Sisters of Providence. She was nursing cholera victims in 1851 when she contracted the disease and died.

❖ ❖ ❖

Word of the zealous Sisters of Providence spread, though, and bishops around the world sent pleas for assistance. In 1856, the bishop of Montreal responded to one of these requests by dispatching a delegation of four nuns to the rugged Pacific Northwest.

Leading this group was a close friend and confidante of Mother Gamelin, Sister Joseph of the Sacred Heart. A city girl who did not even speak English, Sister Joseph wrote back to Montreal to admit that, "with my inexperience, my unpleasant nature, my ignorance," she felt inadequate to the task. But she also wrote a letter saying, "More and more, I feel that to be happy, I must reach out and relieve the destitute."

She reached out, all right. Over the next 30 years, the little platoons of nuns she dispatched from the headquarters on the Columbia River traveled east as far as the Indian reservation at St. Ignatius in western Montana, and north to New Westminster, British Columbia. They created 17 hospitals (and 15 schools), including Seattle's Providence and Spokane's Sacred Heart hospitals.

Sacred Heart Medical Center is a good example of Mother Joseph's technique. In 1886, Father Joseph Cataldo, who that year was overseeing the creation of Gonzaga University, asked the sisters to build a hospital in Spokane Falls, a place being swamped by miners and settlers but sorely lacking in facilities to care for them. It was the kind of frontier outpost where the sick might die on the streets.

Mother Joseph, now 63 years old, boarded a train with one other nun and went to Spokane. After looking over the town, she selected and purchased a site on the river between Browne and Bernard (where her statue can now be seen). Drawing on 30 years experience, she sketched a brick hospital on a tablecloth, and within three weeks workmen were digging the foundation.

❖ ❖ ❖

Mother Joseph, who had grown up helping her father in his wagon-building shop, supervised every step and even helped carry the wood and lay the bricks.

The imposing three-story brick building was almost complete just six months after her initial sketch; their first patient was a desperately ill man found alone in a shack in downtown Spokane. In its first year of operation, the six nuns cared for 122 patients in the hospital and made 1,040 home visits.

The hospital's advertisement read: "Admission and Attendance Free to those Unable to Pay." Their policy, as expressed to the staff by the nun Mother Joseph left in charge, was "to receive everyone that knocks on our door, even if we have to give up our own apartments."

They paid for it by conducting "begging tours" to nearby towns and through the rough mining camps of the Coeur d'Alenes. It turns out their reputations had preceded them, and miners gave generously to an institution they knew was made for the likes of them.

Mother Joseph died in 1902, 46 years after arriving to take on her Pacific Northwest mission. Her last words were an echo of Mother Gamelin. "Do not say: This does not concern me, let others see to them. My sisters, whatever concerns the poor is always our affair."

❖ ❖ ❖

Mother Joseph's spirit of service carried through to another era and another Sister of Providence who was paid $40 a month and sewed her own clothes on the way to building the modern Sacred Heart Hospital we all know today.

Sister Peter Claver, who died in 1991, was a nurse with a Master's degree in hospital management when she was appointed administrator of Sacred Heart Hospital in 1964, six decades after Mother Joseph's death. She took over a Victorian building that was hopelessly outmoded for modern medicine.

By the time she retired in 1988, most of what is now Sacred Heart Medical Center had been built under her direction. Sacred Heart employment had grown from 900 to more than 3,000, making the hospital the second largest employer in Spokane after Kaiser Aluminum. The hospital had gained a national reputation for innovation and excellence in medical care.

Sister Peter Claver herself collected boxes full of awards and honorary degrees, which, those who knew her agree, only surprised her.

Since joining the Sisters of Providence at the age of 22, she had one interest in hospitals, which was to help people who were sick. She did this instinctively and emotionally, as one might rush to the aid of a person who collapsed on the street.

But a large institution offers lots of potential diversions from this simple purpose: careers, egos, schedules and so on. (And lately, profit. In 1985, when she was selected one of the nation's top women executives, Claver told a reporter: "I'm sure that for-profit hospitals have dedicated people working for them, but I find the practice of making money from sick people repugnant.")

She referred to the hospital budget as "the patients' money" and was notoriously frugal with it, always asking whether something could be repaired rather than replaced.

She would grill a room full of physicians along the same lines about a million-dollar piece of medical equipment. She wasn't easy to bluff, either, because she read the same technical data they did. Those who worked with her estimated she must have had a very high IQ, because she immersed herself in the details of everything connected with one of the most complex institutions. Frank Bouten of Bouten Construction, builders of the medical center, said he had never had client who understood construction better or paid more attention to technical detail than Claver.

Yet her secretary, Jay Staebell, believes Sister Peter Claver's most outstanding talent was negotiation. Time after time, doctors or other experts came to her office with grim faces and big requests, and left satisfied, whether they got what they wanted or not. "She could negotiate so they would feel they won."

❖ ❖ ❖

When she got away from blueprints and out of the meetings, Claver roamed the halls of the hospital, chatting with nurses and patients, looking for glitches. One employee remembers being with Claver when she pulled on a door and found it stuck. Claver reached into the deep pockets of her nun's habit, pulled out a screwdriver and adjusted the lock.

From the time she awoke at 5 am and asked for guidance at morning mass, she devoted every moment of the day looking for ways to make the hospital run better. C.F. Legel, her finance officer, remembers she would personally attend tests of the emergency transformers that took over when hospital power went out. When the test worked, she would smile with satisfaction.

The hospital was her life "pretty much 24/7," says her lifelong friend and colleague, Sister Michelle Holland. Claver was at the hospital 12 hours a day. On evenings and weekends, she read medical literature she needed to master. Even when asleep she wasn't off duty, says Holland. "In the middle of the night, she'd hear if the transformer went off. The other sisters would sleep through it."

This devotion gave Peter Claver a great moral authority and self-assurance. In his homily at her funeral mass, Gonzaga University President Bernard Coughlin, S.J., told a typical story about the seemingly quiet nun. Claver and her chief hospital assistants went to Olympia to have dinner with Spokane area legislators to discuss the hospital's legislative problems. After dinner, one of the legislators rose and said he must hurry off.

Sister said, "Well, you know we've traveled a long way to talk with you, and I'd like to share a few more comments with you. Please sit down." And he did.

Coughlin was careful to caution this could only be part of the myth by adding, "as the story goes."

Was that likely? Did that sound like Claver? Her colleagues say it did. "She would have said it very nicely," says Sister Dorothy Byrne, who knew Claver since they were both young nurses. But, yes, the authority and conviction in the story were typical of Peter Claver.

"I was there," recalls C.F. Legel, Claver's chief financial officer. "I won't say who it was," he adds, "but I can confirm it." ∎

Tom Foley's official portrait as Chairman of the House Agriculture Committee.

The Speaker from Spokane: Tom Foley

BY TED S. McGREGOR JR.

First published in the *Inlander* on July 7, 1999

Perhaps all you need to know about how Tom Foley ticks is that unlike nearly all upper-echelon politicians these days, he's the rare exception who didn't parlay his prominence into a tell-all book that hit the shelves while his Speaker of the House seat was still warm. Nearly five years have passed since he became the most prized trophy in the 1994 Republican takeover of Congress, and that passing of time has allowed *Honor in the House* (WSU Press) to tell his amazing story without the bitterness or blame you might expect from someone who became a human lightning rod. It also leaves a more fitting final impression of Foley; rather than remembering his defeat, readers will be left with a more complete and hopeful picture of the man whom newsman Jim Lehrer and others predict will be treated very well when this chapter of the history of the United States is written.

Foley's longtime press secretary Jeffrey Biggs tells the tale with the kind of authority that could only come from having been in the thick of things during much of Foley's career. And Foley himself co-authors the book through an innovative structure that pairs Biggs' narrative with extended first-person ruminations by the former Speaker of the U.S. House of Representatives; having Foley's voice loom so large is the book's strongest point.

The linear narrative works just fine as pure biography, tracing the arc of Foley's career from his Spokane youth to Congress to one of the highest offices in the land. But it may be of more significance as a window on one of the nation's most important but (the book argues) least understood institutions.

❖ ❖ ❖

The fact that Tom Foley's father was a prominent Spokane attorney (and later a judge) helped pave the way to a career in politics, but his background as a Roman Catholic of Irish immigrant stock made his political aspirations seem somewhat dreamy. And if that wasn't enough disincentive, he was an active Democrat in a district that had been served by Republican Walt Horan since the 1940s.

Just a few years after earning his law degree from the University of Washington, Foley somewhat impulsively decided to run for Congress in 1964 – with the blessing of his mentor, Sen. Henry Jackson, whom he had worked for as a staffer. The fateful story of his filing for office is one of the book's funnier anecdotes; he had to borrow money for the filing fee, and after running out of gas on the way to Olympia, he made it in to the filing office just 15 minutes before the deadline.

Foley beat the odds and defeated the entrenched Horan, and was swept into office in the landslide that accompanied Lyndon Johnson's presidential victory. Foley's recollections of those days are instructive for how much things have changed in Congress since then. Committees were all-powerful in those days – he even remembers being shocked at an orientation session when he was advised by a senior member that the biggest mistake he could ever make would be to think for himself.

Biggs gives ample attention to all Foley's reelection campaigns, and Foley's popularity in the rural counties became the secret of his success. Once at the Omak Stampede, he was embarrassed when he fell off his horse in front of the crowd. His assistant that day, Dale Larsen, said it was the perfect thing to have happen: "You proved that you were from Spokane, that you couldn't ride worth a damn," Larsen told him. "But you got out there and made them feel good about the fact that they could. You'll win this county, I predict it."

Foley cemented his relationship with the rural parts of the district by serving on the Agriculture Committee, which he ultimately chaired.

Foley's early career was also highlighted by his involvement with a reform movement within the party. His work helped spread the power more evenly through Congress, slowly loosening the grip of committee chairmen.

But it's Foley's rise to power — and fall from it — that's the real story here.

❖ ❖ ❖

Coming to power after the embarrassing departure of Speaker Jim Wright, Foley was the first Speaker from west of the Rocky Mountains. But he inherited a Congress that was chafing under the slash-and-burn politics of the minority, which was increasingly managed by Whip Newt Gingrich. Wright made a plea for a return to political sanity as he left in 1989: "When vilification becomes an accepted form of political debate, when negative campaigning becomes a full-time occupation, when members of each party become self-appointed vigilantes carrying out personal vendettas against members of the other party, in God's name that is not what this institution is supposed to be all about… All of us in both parties must resolve to bring this period of mindless cannibalism to an end."

History, however, shows that things only got worse from that point.

Biggs airs all the criticisms that surrounded Foley's tenure, chief among those being that he was too nice a guy to get things done. As Foley puts it, his party was often hoping for more confrontation to match the emerging style of the Republicans — why give George H.W. Bush any free rides? "In their eyes," Foley writes, "I was failing in my partisan duty if I didn't get up every morning with a fresh attack on the administration."

Foley even prevented the Savings and Loan crisis from being used as a partisan issue by House members eager to pin the blame on the Republicans — a gesture that seems almost quaint by current standards. But Foley had a reason for his conciliatory approach: His years in Congress taught him that a single party cannot govern.

When Bill Clinton was elected in 1992, everything changed. Now a Democratic Congress had a Democrat in the White House. Conventional wisdom said that now was the time to really get things done. And initially, at least, there were successes, especially the deficit reduction plan. It was one of Foley's finest hours, as the *National Review* wrote: "Without [Foley's] help, Congress might not have shifted gears to reverse 12 years of Republican fiscal policy."

But trouble was not far behind, as Republicans began to literally oppose everything as a matter of strategy. Perhaps Foley's harshest words in the book are reserved for this turn of events: "That they would be so obvious about their obstruction and about their desire to see any bill… defeated is a remarkable confession of their putting politics above the interests of the people."

The Republicans in the Senate did their part, too, with a record 28 filibusters in the 103rd Congress, including one on campaign finance reform – an issue that still remains unresolved by the Congress. And the Clinton administration began to overreach, especially on its health care reform proposal. So by the time the 1994 elections rolled around, Clinton's approval rating in the Fifth District of Washington was around 27 percent, and Foley was easily portrayed as a Clinton loyalist. In the book, Foley uses hindsight to discuss how he could have done things differently, wishing he had made his personal feelings better known at the time, especially on the health care reform package, which he felt was too large a pill to be swallowed all at once.

After years of poorly financed and politically naive opposition, Foley also faced perhaps his toughest challenger in 1994. George Nethercutt was a party official who jumped in because the only other Republicans interested had already lost to Foley in previous elections. Nethercutt benefited from huge independent expenditures by the National Rifle Association (which had formerly given Foley its highest award but turned on him when he supported keeping military style machine guns out of the American weaponry mix), term limits backers and even people opposed to Washington, D.C., statehood. Nethercutt also had the services of Ed Rollins, one of the nation's most prominent campaign strategists.

Foley sounds almost admiring when he describes how his opponents defeated him, calling one strategy a "rather clever approach," which he paraphrased as "the wonderful argument that you here in the Fifth District are empowered more than any other people in the country. If you're sick and tired of what's going on in the federal government and

Washington, D.C., you have a voice amplified beyond imagination in other parts of the county. They can only fire a member of Congress. You can fire the Speaker."

Perhaps the almost Zen-like acceptance of his fate comes from his recollections of when he unseated Walt Horan. Nethercutt beat Foley by about 4,000 votes, ironically by winning in the nine timber- and agricultural-based counties that Foley had always worked so hard to appease.

But the strength of Biggs' narrative is that it describes Foley's loss as years in the making and probably beyond his control. Much of the blame is pinned on the Republicans' successful strategy to vilify Congress, and Biggs questions whether those means were justified by the end result.

"Newt Gingrich," Biggs writes, "spent the 1980s and early-1990s undermining the legitimacy of Congress in an effort to so repulse the public that it would throw the longtime Democratic majority out and allow the Republicans to govern."

And Biggs lets the record speak for itself, too, as he quotes a *Roll Call* editorial charging that, "often, the attitude seems to be that [Republican leaders] feel they have to destroy Congress in order to save it."

Even Republican Minority Leader Bob Michel, who was retiring, was saddened about the direction his party was taking, decrying members for "trashing the institution" as well as "those who choose confrontation before compromise."

Biggs shows a little bias when he sums up the situation by quoting former Speaker of the House Sam Rayburn, who used to say: "It takes a skilled carpenter to build a barn. Any jackass can kick it down."

In a departure from the book's linear narrative that follows Foley's life, Biggs gives a significant amount of space to what Congress became after the Republican takeover. Biggs looks at how rules changes made by Gingrich defied House precedents and created strong, centralized control. Foley himself criticizes another innovation introduced by Republicans: letting lobbyists write legislation. Biggs also describes Gingrich's flameout, which began when he shut the government down, boasted about doing it and then was offended when the country got mad. Since that "Contract With America" Congress, the Republicans seem to have learned what Foley always knew: One-party rule does not work.

In fact, Foley himself blames one-party rule as the chief reason behind his own demise. When Clinton won in 1992, he says Democratic hegemony created a predictable reaction from voters – a return to divided government.

❖ ❖ ❖

As a lesson for current students of the institution, perhaps the concept that divided government works best is this book's most important message. The accomplishments of LBJ's "Great Society" have largely been undone, and 1992's Democratic control wasn't accepted by the majority of the nation's voters. Meanwhile, it can be argued that divided governments, as under George H.W. Bush or Ronald Reagan and their Democratic Congresses, have been more effective.

Foley is an important figure because of what he learned in all his years in Congress, and an agenda toward a better Congress can be gleaned from these pages. Among other things, he sees the unpopular public financing of campaigns as a necessity. He sees centralized power and discipline in the Congress as a hindrance to creating good policy. And he sees the media as overly negative, and all too willing to "stroke public dissatisfaction and encourage doubt" rather than help people understand Congress better.

Foley and his wife Heather, who served as his chief of staff for years, landed on their feet. After a few years with a D.C. law firm, Foley was appointed by President Bill Clinton as Ambassador to Japan, a post he held until April of 2001.

Perhaps Foley's style as Speaker – fair to members of both parties and focused on solving problems rather than gaining partisan advantage – will come back in style and become his imprint on the institution. Many readers, who'll see the accomplishments of three decades carrying his fingerprints, will probably come to hope so.

As former Senate Majority Leader and Ambassador to Japan Mike Mansfield of Montana writes in the book's preface: "On Tom's last day as Speaker of the House, Republican Leader Bob Michel of Illinois rose to bid him farewell. He spoke of the virtues the departing Speaker had for so long typified: integrity, decency and a commitment to crafting reasoned solutions to difficult problems. What struck me in the highly partisan world of today was that these qualities were being highlighted by the leader of the opposition." ■

After this story was published, Tom Foley passed away, in October of 2013 at the age of 84.

Ed Tsutakawa at the Mukogawa Tea House in 2001.

Blending In, Standing Out: Ed Tsutakawa

BY DAN RICHARDSON

First published in the *Inlander* on December 20, 2001

Spokane must be one of the most Western of cities with its history of Indians, mining and railroads – its landscape poised between the mountains and the rolling prairie of the Palouse. There are cosmopolitan flourishes, though. Across the river from downtown is the campus of the Mukogawa Fort Wright Institute, where 180 Japanese students arrive each semester to study English. In the heart of the city is Riverfront Park, its Pavilion a reminder of the 1974 World's Fair, when the global community gathered on the river's banks. And up the South Hill rests the reflective Oriental quietness of the Spokane-Nishinomiya Japanese Garden.

One thing these three flourishes have in common, along with many other Spokane institutions, is Ed Tsutakawa, (pronounced "Soot-a-kawa") who labored inside the small circle of volunteers, financiers and planners that brought these landmarks to fruition.

The paradoxes of Spokane – a Western city with flourishes of the East – mirror those of Tsutakawa himself. Born in the United States, he spent many formative years in Japan. Though raised in a family business, he pursued art as a calling. Despite native citizenship, he was hauled behind barbed wire with other Japanese Americans during World War II; interned, he turned patriot, using his art for the war effort.

"I didn't want to let the grass grow under my feet," recalls the 80-year-old Tsutakawa.

In person, Tsutakawa possesses a gentle, friendly demeanor. It's like a current of warm water atop the depths of his personality, where he is energetic and driven. He gets passionate, for example, during a conversation about the 24-foot wooden bridge in the midst of the Japanese Garden. It's too clunky for the garden, he says.

Tsutakawa stands in the foremost ranks of Spokane's citizens. He's devoted time – in several cases, decades –to groups like the Boy Scouts, United Way and the YMCA, plus numerous local government boards and committees. Tsutakawa's "voice of sweet reason cuts silkily and softly through to the heart of the issue. Not much noise, but things happen immediately," wrote a *Spokesman-Review* columnist in 1987.

Rob Higgins, the president of Spokane's City Council, has seen Tsutakawa in public service for 20 years, as has every city mayor in recent times.

"They all knew Ed Tsutakawa and loved him," says Higgins, who describes him as a "very humble man. A very gracious individual. Very well connected."

Edward Masao Tsutakawa was born on May 15, 1921, in Seattle, as was his wife, Hide ("He-day"). He is closer to five feet tall than six, and stooped with age. His swept silver hair retains a hint of its youthful black. Back pain has hobbled his beloved golf game – he once drove overnight from Seattle to attend a morning golf tournament in Spokane – and he laughs off minor surgeries as "timely adjustments." But his voice is firm. His hands are steady. He readily picks up an ink pen and sketches illustrations to accompany his conversation.

His is a cheerful demeanor, and his face often wrinkles up with smiles. Tsutakawa still works, half-time, at the Mukogawa Fort Wright Institute, where he is vice president.

His ambition and energy brought Tsutakawa to the halls of power on two continents. He counts as good friends the mayor of Nishinomiya and the chief of the prestigious Mukogawa Institute in Japan, and former Speaker of the House Tom Foley here at home. Everyone at the Spokane Club knows him. "Hey, Ed," they call, and several stop for a handshake and a quick word. Scholars, business owners, politicians – Tsutakawa is one of them, one of the movers and shakers. It was not always so.

❖ ❖ ❖

The Tsutakawa family operated an import-export business with a branch office in Seattle. They maintained close ties with the home country, though, and the family is rife with the cross-cultural currents of American immigrants. The second-generation boys were given Anglo first names – George (the well-known painter and fountain-builder), Henry (now an attorney in Japan), Ed – and Japanese middle names. The family moved to Japan when Tsutakawa was five, and he grew up there, in the village of Nauro, on the banks of the Mukogawa River. Their house was an American-style timber frame structure, with cedar shingles. The village was then a suburb of Nishinomiya. Ten years later, in 1936, the family moved back to the States. Ed and his cousin George were both interested in painting and sketching. Ed Tsutakawa entered the University of Washington in 1939; he took a few pre-med classes but quickly switched to art.

His parents "didn't like the idea at all," recalls Tsutakawa of his artistic pursuits. "I kind of believed in being independent, more of my own thing, to see how far I could go with it."

Tsutakawa thrived at school and was a college junior well into his art studies in December of 1941. The Japanese attack changed everything. "Pearl Harbor," Tsutakawa says, "was the worst thing that happened to me and to the world."

He says he and other Japanese in the U.S. felt betrayed by their home country and hated its military government; simultaneously, they were alienated from other Americans. "We didn't like the kind of things that were being said. Things like, 'Once a Jap, always a Jap.'"

Fearing disloyalty, President Franklin Roosevelt issued Executive Order 9066 two months after Pearl Harbor. It was the order that forced 110,000 people of Japanese descent from their homes into internment camps in the Western U.S. Tsutakawa was yanked from school and sent, along with his family, to a holding camp at the Puyallup Fairgrounds ("Camp Harmony") outside Tacoma. Then in August 1942, authorities shipped them to Camp Minidoka, near Pocatello, Idaho.

Many behind the barbed wire fences grew angry, says Tsutakawa. Others, including him, joined the war effort. Tsutakawa joined the Japanese American Citizen's League and, inside the camps, helped to organize art classes and other projects for internees. He and several other artists – including Keith Oka, a "darn good artist" who later moved to Spokane – turned their talents to the war effort, painting giant canvas signs urging Americans to buy war bonds.

There were hard feelings and hard times, but the camps are far from the final chapter of Tsutakawa's story. Indeed, internment spurred many Japanese Americans like Tsutakawa to leap into civic affairs after the war. Contemplating the police concentration today on some Arab Americans in the wake of the Sept. 11 attacks, Tsutakawa says the internees hung on to their belief in the American way of life. Arab Americans, he says, "have to learn to do that." Tsutakawa also believes the United States learned a lesson when it locked up Japanese Americans, and he believes widespread roundups of all Arab Americans will never happen as a result. "I don't think it will get that bad."

Times were difficult in the internment camp. Tsutakawa's father Jin died in camp at just 52. "He didn't have a chance," lacking adequate medical supplies, says Tsutakawa. Meanwhile, his brother Henry, who had been in Japan when the war broke out, was drafted by the military there and sent to Manchuria.

While interned, Tsutakawa came and went often, having volunteered to work on Idaho farms and to drive the coal truck for camp. He was also painting watercolor scenes, a kind of muted visual record from an internee's eyes. Those paintings are still displayed in museums along the West Coast. In camp, Tsutakawa also met his future bride, Hide.

It was the military authorities who imprisoned Tsutakawa's family in the camps, and the military that got him out. Two Army captains asked him if he wanted out to help the war effort. He did.

In April of 1943, Tsutakawa left the camp. His first stop: Spokane. His friend Oka was getting married in Spokane, so Tsutakawa attended the wedding. He had been through town once before, prior to the war, as an art student sketching the old mines around Coeur d'Alene. This time, he was in town only briefly, but the taste of freedom lingered – it would be a fine place to start his own life, and other artists were gathering there, like Oka, Paul Horiuchi and Herman Keys, with whom Tsutakawa would later share a studio.

The Army assigned him to an intelligence unit in Chicago to teach Japanese language to military officers. His service time was a sort of limbo, though. Perhaps because he was just 23 years old, the Army gave him small assignments like carrying papers between schools. He didn't have enough to do. The grass was growing under his feet.

"I had all kinds of time, so I went to school," he recalls. Living in relative luxury at the YMCA – he'd later serve on its board for more than 20 years – Tsutakawa for a while attended design school and took classes at the Chicago Art Institute. Meanwhile, his Japanese buddies were in Europe fighting the Nazis. "That's where I wanted to go," he says. He volunteered, but the war ended.

Tsutakawa landed back in Spokane and immediately immersed himself in art. Eminently practical, he turned his talents to graphic design: "not real serious art," he says, but commercial work for logos, letterheads and catalogs. Working first as a freelancer, then for a letter shop and later at his own business, Tsutakawa flourished when his creative and pragmatic sides merged.

"It was the right time, the right business. And it was busy. I worked 16 to 17 hours a day… whatever had to be done," he says.

It was a time of paradox and adjustment, too. Though he'd gained his freedom, Tsutakawa's portion of sorrow was not over. He met a young woman, Tama, and they married in January 1946. They had a daughter, Nancy. Mother and daughter "were in the hospital together, but never saw each other," says Tsutakawa. Tama died that December.

Influenced by Tama's Christianity, Tsutakawa was baptized on Jan. 1, 1947, the day after he buried her.

"I was still young," he says. "I think about that time. I started to find out life was very fragile."

Fragile, but resilient, too. Tsutakawa reconnected with Hide, whom he'd met in camp, and they married in 1949.

With the addition of two children, Margaret and Mark, the family's roots in Spokane grew deeper, and the city became their home.

"Sometimes you put your priorities, but they're not fitting," says Tsutakawa. "For instance, the artist's life. Then, you want a family. It changes your way of thinking, your way of living. I wanted to stay at the best place for raising children."

In 1954, Tsutakawa and Morris "Ed" Jeffers founded LithoArt Printers. With help from friends and even a previous employer, the partners' company grew rapidly. Meanwhile, the young Tsutakawa could be found at all kinds of groups about town. He was, according to one report, a member of at least five professional Spokane art associations. Jeffers' wife Elaine lent a hand at the shop and knew Tsutakawa for years.

"He was always the outstanding one who had the membership at the City Club," she recalls. Tsutakawa was often gone on civic affairs, but the shop was a good fit for the partners, she says. "He was a fabulous artist, and my husband was a very good printer, so it worked out."

By 1960, Tsutakawa and his family were well established in Spokane. He was, however, just getting started in public life.

❖ ❖ ❖

For many Americans, the 1960s were a period of rebellion, of casting off Middle American values. Not for a core of civic-minded Spokanites, though, among them Ed Tsutakawa. With his civic action and artistic vision, this was to be the decade he began making his mark on Spokane.

In the 1950s and '60s, the sister city movement was taking root. Old-timers and news reports generally credit resident Ken Maddocks and the Rev. Shigeo Shimada, of the Highland Park Methodist Church, with raising the idea of a Spokane sister city in 1961. Then-Mayor Neal Fosseen supported the idea. Tsutakawa, who attended Shimada's church, got involved early on. So what city should Spokane look to? Why, Nishinomiya, of course.

"I didn't think we could find anything in common with Spokane and Nishinomiya," says Tsutakawa. But he became one of the principal leaders of the sister-city committee and later bore a letter to the Japanese city from the mayor. The idea caught fire. The two cities exchanged gifts, students and delegations. This October, a group of Spokane politicians and community activists visited Nishinomiya to celebrate 40 years as sister cities. That's one trip of more than 120 Tsutakawa says he's taken to Japan in his 57 years in Spokane. He's gone there for business, to visit family and for pleasure; many Japanese visitors have stayed with the Tsutakawa family in Spokane over the years.

Growing out of the sister city relationship was another idea that would make a lasting change in the Spokane landscape: a friendship garden. The 12-year tale of the Spokane-Nishinomiya Japanese Garden is an epic in itself. Suffice it to say that when the 1.5-acre corner of Manito Park opened in 1974, Tsutakawa was one of the central figures in its creation. Others included gardening guru Polly Mitchell Judd and garden designer Nagao Sakurai.

Sakurai had designed more than 100 gardens in Japan, including one at the imperial palace. Tsutakawa says, "Traditionally, a Japanese garden is a reminder of life. It uses sadness or tragedy or those kinds of things and finds the beauty in it."

The garden's creation was not entirely placid. Sakurai was commissioned in 1967, but part way through construction he was stricken by a stroke. Reports from the time credit both Judd and Tsutakawa with visiting the convalescing Sakurai, showing him outlines of the emerging garden and in turn taking his sketches to the construction site. Judd and Tsutakawa had, reports say, somewhat competing visions of the garden. Tsutakawa acknowledges tensions with Judd and others caused at least in part by his passion for the project. "I was too hard on the people working on it," he says. Judd wanted a park reflecting more sadness, a purer Japanese garden with Eastern religious touches, Tsutakawa says, while he wanted to celebrate the sister city bond.

Visiting with Sakurai, he asked the designer, "Is there any way you can build or emphasize friendship in it?"

Sakurai looked at him, eyes wide with surprise. He thought for a moment, then answered: Yes, he could do that. And, Tsutakawa says, "He did."

Three decades later, Tsutakawa is still passionate about the garden. He recalls donations that people made to build the garden, like the money – around $10,000 – that Davenport Hotel dishwasher Wasaburo Kiri gave to jump-start the construction. (The garden's reflection pond is named in his honor.) He names with pride the stone lanterns that grace the garden and describes the sound of the waterfall, a signature piece in any garden, as "chatting, a light sort of conversation." (Beside the waterfall is the small Tsutakawa Pagoda.) He bristles a little when talking about the bridge, which has high safety rails that defy Japanese garden bridge convention.

The Japanese speak of *shibui*, meaning a natural beauty or understated elegance. A garden gains *shibui* with time as trees grow and moss embraces stone. "Does the Japanese Garden have *shibui*?" a visitor asks Tsutakawa. He nods. "It's getting there."

The garden was dedicated in 1974, but capturing the city's more immediate attention was a construction project in the heart of downtown: Expo '74.

The World's Fair opened in May of 1974, just weeks after the garden. Although it featured a disappointingly small number of exhibitor nations, observers praised the size and magnificence of their pavilions. The Soviet Union boasted the largest, but nearly as big was the Japanese pavilion, which drew 30,000 Japanese visitors. In charge of the pavilion was Tsutakawa.

When organizers King Cole, Neal Fosseen and others began discussing the idea of hosting a World's Fair in the late-1960s, Tsutakawa was still, he says, a somewhat struggling businessman. But he had vision and strong ties to Japan, an integral place in the sister city program (one observer calls him the "glue" of that relationship). The organizers placed Tsutakawa on the coordinating board. By the time the Expo landed in Spokane, Tsutakawa had journeyed to the East on a six-month sabbatical from work to negotiate for Japanese involvement. It paid off handsomely in their participation, further strengthening Tsutakawa's contacts there.

In 1980 or shortly after, Tsutakawa sold his share of LithoArt to the Jeffers and retired from printing. He started a freelance company to broker negotiations between Japanese and American firms and also dabbled in a number of businesses. One of these was a Seattle-based, Japanese-language newspaper (now shuttered), which, he says, he was hired to overhaul. Perhaps Tsutakawa brought a too-aggressive vision of growth to the paper; it was the only job from which he was ever fired.

The Mukogawa Institute in Japan is a school with five divisions from junior high school through doctorate programs. It was sending students on U.S. field trips in the early-1980s, and officials there began thinking about opening an American branch campus for its students. The Institute needed a trusted scout, someone with knowledge of its needs and of the United States. In 1988, school officials approached Tsutakawa.

In scouting for Mukogawa, Tsutakawa visited potential campus sites in San Francisco and Portland before settling on Spokane. Mukogawa officials loved the historic brick buildings of Fort Wright, some of which were vacant. Mukogawa closed on the property in July 1990, and students began arriving two months later. The school poured millions into renovating the campus, says Tsutakawa. Higgins, the city council president, calls

Mukogawa the "crowning achievement" of Tsutakawa's civic career.

"I knew Spokane had a lot of potential," Tsutakawa says. He points to things like universities, a comfortable size and natural resources; available land, open buildings and excellent medical facilities.

"It's a great place to incubate businesses. But I think we need to look at the world outside and study their needs," Tsutakawa says. Because of its airport, Spokane can be a vital player in the Pacific Rim, he says. Forget "Spokane, Washington; think, Spokane, U.S.A. We need to get away from the Inland bit," he says.

❖ ❖ ❖

"I told my wife, this is where I want to be buried," Tsutakawa says of Spokane. (He ought to know, having served on the city's cemetery committee for 28 years and having personally designed the memorial at the Japanese American cemetery.)

Tsutakawa's legacy is born of competing tensions, his yin and yang of Japanese and American influences, striving yet balanced.

"We are born to actually work on, unconsciously, legacies to pass on — better work, better world to future generations. I believe that," says Tsutakawa. "I'm very lucky I got to do these things, and people let me do it." ∎

After this story was published, Ed Tsutakawa passed away, in October of 2006 at the age of 85.

Bill (standing) and Bevan Maxey have followed their father into the practice of law, but they've grown up in a different place from where Carl Maxey was raised.

Father's Footsteps: Carl Maxey

BY LUKE BAUMGARTEN

First published in the *Inlander* on January 12, 2012

You can see Carl Maxey in his two sons, and you can't. He's there in Bevan Maxey's national-caliber athleticism, in his son's locker-room swagger and easy demeanor. And he's also there in the casual way Bill Maxey's left lip curls slightly to meet a joke he has heard.

Maxey is there in the men's career choice (law) and in their pursuit of excellence, which keeps Bill working deep into the evening and causes Bevan's internal alarm — spring-loaded with worry — to shake him awake at night. The brothers also have their father's sense of duty and his disdain for failure. This sense of duty causes Bevan to wonder — as his father did — if he has done enough to make things better.

There are the ways the two try to improve upon the man's good deeds — Bevan tries to spend more time with his children than his father was able to spend with him — and there are the ways in which they could not improve upon Carl Maxey if they tried.

No matter what, Bill and Bevan Maxey will never be:

✓ The first black lawyer in Eastern Washington to pass the state bar.

✓ A collegiate national champion light-heavyweight boxer.

✓ An anti-Vietnam War candidate for U.S. Senate.

✓ The man the *New York Times* credited with "with virtually singlehandedly desegregating much of the inland Northwest."

They will never have the fire of an orphan. They will never know the shame or rage that comes with being denied service at lunch counters.

Like their father, they are people of color, but they are not, strictly speaking, black. Their mother, Ninon, is a white woman originally from Ashland, Oregon, whom Carl met at the University of Oregon. Whether the brother's mixed heritage has made their life easier or more difficult is "tough to tell," Bill says.

If the brothers had their way, there would be no comparison. "No one is ever going to be like Carl," Bill says. But people always compare fathers to sons.

Paul Mack, a former prosecutor now in private practice in downtown Spokane, tried his first case against Carl Maxey 26 years ago and has worked both collaboratively with Bill on personal injury cases and against Bevan in divorce court. Mack lauds Bill's diligence and Bevan's sharp-mindedness, and says they treat the law as a calling rather than a business. "They are both very good at what they do," Mack says, adding in the same breath, "They have big shoes to fill."

"They are such wonderful men," says former Spokane Mayor Shari Barnard, who considered Carl Maxey a personal mentor. "They haven't been in the public eye the way their father has."

The Maxey brothers have taken up many of the same causes — economic equality and social justice — but they've done so more often from the boardroom than the bully pulpit. Carl Maxey worked his will on the world at a time of tremendous social change. His sons have lived in the aftermath.

As a result, the Maxey brothers occupy a unique place in the world that is partially given and partially earned. It has something to do with their race, something to do with their family name and something to do with pure human ambition.

The place they occupy has to do with a lot of things, not the least of which is the fact that their father had, in his own words, started from "black scratch."

❖ ❖ ❖

Carl Maxey had his troubles in school. He had gotten a late start. He loved to read and was a diligent student but struggled throughout college. Speaking was never an issue, though. A born fighter — he'd win the national light-heavyweight boxing championship for Gonzaga in 1950 – Maxey loved to spar verbally. He became a student of rhetoric, and he understood, Bevan says, the knockout force of a potent idea.

Bevan says he learned from his father how to pull quotes from classic literature and use them to good effect in the courtroom. (A plaque with Robert Frost's words about diverging roads sits atop a shelf at Maxey Law.) The concept of "black scratch," however, was a Carl Maxey original.

The idea is that if you are born to absolutely nothing in the world, that is difficult enough. But if you are born to absolutely nothing in America, and you are black, that is a whole other kind of hard-up.

Author Jim Kershner, in his biography *Carl Maxey: A Fighting Life*, likens "black scratch" to starting from Square Zero. Maxey may have argued, in his darker moments, that it was starting at Square Minus-One. He didn't just grow up at a disadvantage to whites; he grew up as the sometimes-sole target of their distaste of black people.

Born in Tacoma in 1924, Maxey never knew his parents and was put into the Spokane Children's Home at age 5 by his adoptive mother, Carolyn, after his adoptive father, Carl Sr., ran off. Carolyn died of heart failure when Carl was 8, and he remained a ward of the county.

The Children's Home was Dickensian and, at times, verged on sadist. Milton Burns was the only other person of color in the place (he was mostly Native American, but everyone considered him black). Burns recounted to Kershner stories of nighttime beatings by the facility's assistant superintendent. Eventually, it came to light that the superintendent and later the assistant had sodomized a number of boys in the home. Maxey said he was never touched. Burns said he hadn't been either, but later thought he might have repressed the memory. It was at the orphanage, his first wife would say, that Maxey lost his fear of the establishment. Maxey believed it was one of the places where he got his fire.

That fire took him places, eventually, but first he was sent to jail. Within a year of the sodomy scandal, the Ladies Benevolent Society, which ran the Children's Home, voted to kick Maxey and Burns out. (Maxey suspected the ladies were trying to sweep the pedophilia mess under the rug.) The minutes from the society's meeting, as quoted by Kershner, read matter-of-factly: "It was moved... that the two colored boys, Carl Maxey and Milton Burns, be returned to the County, having been in the home for years. Motion carried. It was moved… that the Board go on record as voting to have no more colored children in the Home from this time forward."

With his mother dead and his dad nowhere to be found – and Milton Burns in similar straights – the county decided to house the boys at the Juvenile Detention Center. They spent a year in an annex of the Spokane County Courthouse, schooled at Audubon Elementary by day and locked up with the delinquents at night.

It says something about Maxey's lot that the first place he considered home was a Catholic mission school for Indian children on the poverty-stricken Coeur d'Alene Indian Reservation. He was sent there after Father Cornelius Burns saw him in juvie and offered to take him and Milton off the county's hands. Maxey would thrive at the reservation – learning to box, picking up other sports, developing a love for reading and a Jesuit sense of social justice – and come to view the priest as a surrogate father figure.

In *A Fighting Life*, Lou Maxey, Maxey's second wife, says the school had had sports teams before, but never won anything until Maxey came along. Despite this prowess, he wasn't afforded star treatment in the racially tense North Idaho Panhandle. Prior to his first football game in Wallace, someone in town hung a sign that read, "N---er, see this sign and run." He spent the night at the sheriff's house and then won the game the next day.

After graduating from Gonzaga High School, Maxey entered the Army as a private in the medical battalion. He credited the racism and segregation he encountered in the service with adding fuel to his burgeoning social awareness. He decided to become a lawyer after coming home to Spokane and promptly being denied service at a local cafeteria – despite standing in his full Army dress.

Maxey went to college at the University of Oregon and law school at Gonzaga. During his career, Maxey would integrate clubs by threatening to take away the liquor, and barber shops by threatening to rescind their licenses. He would strong-arm Spokane's school board into hiring the district's first black teacher. He became famous for being able to achieve results by simply threatening to sue and made a good deal of money by helping make the world just a little more fair to rich, white women divorcing their rich, white husbands.

The husband in such cases would retain a country-club lawyer. The wives increasingly turned to Maxey, who developed a reputation for squeezing every cent out of a divorce settlement. "I can't tell you, as I grew up, how many people have come up and said, 'Your dad represented my mom,'" Bevan says.

Bevan says his own divorce practice, which takes up about half his time, is more equitably split between the sexes. The one exception to that continues to be with rich, white women. "The men still have their country-club guys," he says.

For Carl Maxey, even divorce was a matter of equality. Bevan says his father would paraphrase the iconic lawyer Clarence Darrow: *Even the rich have rights.*

Before any of that, though, Maxey had to graduate law school, which proved difficult for him. He was a devoted student but was hampered by his spotty early education and the distractions of the boxing ring. And of course, there was the fact that, in the middle of law school, his first son, Bill, came along.

❖ ❖ ❖

Bill and Bevan Maxey's lives have not been their father's. Carl and Ninon made sure of that. When Bill was in grade school and Bevan was an infant, the young family moved from southeast Spokane, off Perry near Grant Elementary — about as diverse a neighborhood as Spokane has — and into a split-level on F Street near Finch Arboretum. To Bill's recollection, they were the first non-white family in the neighborhood.

Neither son remembers specifically speaking with their father about why they moved, but Bevan says he thinks it was part of a desire in his father "to establish some precedent that there can be successful black men and women, [and that they] can be incorporated in other parts of society." Not just the black parts of town.

While Carl Maxey may have wanted to make a larger point when deciding things like where to live, his sons have not.

When Bevan bought his house on Spokane's South Hill, "I just needed a house." And though it has been a home for his family, he has come to regret the decision in one sense. The house sits within the boundary of Ferris High School, not Lewis and Clark, the school where he and Bill were star athletes. "I guess I should have paid more attention," he says, laughing, while taking care not to cast aspersions on Ferris. "I still have two kids there."

And while their father kept a mental ledger of specific incidents of hate and bias to his dying day, his sons have a hard time pinning single, discrete memories down. They speak in vague terms — "there were certain situations like…" and "maybe somebody says something to the effect of…"

Growing up in the hills of southwest Spokane, the brothers remember neighborhood altercations. "I got into a couple of physical fights with people," Bill says. It might have been racism, or "[I] might have been just a new kid on the block, too." Once they got to know him, these kids became his friends.

Bill recalls grumblings from neighbors and a certain iciness at times, but mostly it was a quiet, tight-knit little neighborhood. Bevan says the same: "I grew up in a very small neighborhood, and we're all friends from as far as back as we could remember."

There were exceptions, though. Bevan's biggest memory from childhood is a phone call he received when his parents and Bill were away.

"Is your mom there?" Bevan recalls,

"No," he answered

"Is your dad there?"

"No."

"Are you alone?"

"Yes."

"Then I'm coming to get you."

Their recollections of a mostly idyllic childhood have shaped the brothers' outlook on how progress might be achieved. It will not necessarily be in courtrooms (though there will certainly be more of that) or even in the Legislature, but neighborhood by neighborhood, industry to industry, as more people of diverse color and background enter communities historically closed to them. It is much easier to hate a stranger than it is to hate your neighbor.

By middle school at Sacajawea, "people started coming up with these little pet phrases that are kinda racial," Bill recalls. He became something of a target. "There weren't a whole lot of mixed-race kids like me at Sacagawea," he says. "And I had curly, bushy hair, so there was teasing about that."

Like their father, both men fell into sports. In athletics they found recognition and pride. Both were standouts at Lewis and Clark High School. Bill ended up playing basketball at Oregon. Eight years behind him, Bevan went on to play wide receiver for the Washington State Cougars and had a brief courtship with the Seattle Seahawks.

Still, Bill found clear racial divides at LC in the '60s — even among athletes, who, after practice, would break up along color lines and go their separate ways. Bill adds, though, that by the time Bevan came up eight years later, things were much more inclusive. "I saw things changing even in the class behind me," Bill says.

Bevan found the strata at the school more social than racial ("we had the jocks and the soshes") and agrees that he had a pretty good time in high school. He credits the '70s — "those were funky, funky times" — and his massive red afro, which became something of a status symbol. It also helped him come to terms with the negative self-image that had sprouted in middle school. "There's a point where, you know, you realize, 'This is who I am and I'm proud to be who I am,'" Bevan says. "I'm not, you know, ugly because of who I am."

Race seemed to always be on their father's mind. With his sons, it is present, without being overwhelming. "It is something that's always in the back of our minds and frequently in the forefront of our minds," Bill says. Bevan sees this, in a strange way, as progress, a step toward people being judged by their character and not their color.

There is a sense that the elder Maxey, for all his bombast, met his biggest trials with quiet, grit-teethed perseverance. Milton Burns told Kershner that, no matter how hard he tried, he couldn't get Maxey to open up about what sorts of beatings, if any, he had received during their time at the orphanage.

Bill and Bevan have taken on that trait on as well. Neither has much to say about the way their parents counseled them in matters of race, because both took pains to keep their fights to themselves. "It was something you try to handle yourself," Bill recalls.

It has now gone a generation further. Bevan's son, Morgan, a 20-year-old sophomore at the University of Washington, hasn't had many run-ins with hatred. When they have happened, though, he hasn't gone to his dad. "I don't really talk to him about stuff like that," Morgan says. "It's not a thing that needs to be brought up." He says such cases are the exception, not the rule. He believes they represent small-mindedness, not oppression.

Maxey Law under Bill and Bevan has represented a fair number of clients in cases of alleged discrimination, and area lawyers say the office started by Carl Maxey still has a reputation for being the kind of place people of color and other minorities can seek justice.

As to the road forward, the brothers say it is important to continue insisting on and facilitating diversity in law and law enforcement. Bevan believes that if there were more black police, there would be less presumption of guilt leveled at black people. He believes that if there were more black prosecutors — or even one black prosecutor — there wouldn't be such a disproportionate number of black suspects shuttled to the city's gang unit. It's less about black people making different choices about black offenders, and more about proximity creating understanding. "A lot of it has to do with just having the opportunity for people to meet one another and communicate with one another," Bevan says, "which, you know, dispels people's misperceptions."

Bill has taken that task on, working in community and professional development. He serves on the board of the Martin Luther King Jr. Family Outreach Center and is also on a host of boards and funds that promote diversity in the legal field.

Bevan speaks in vague terms of a "time when things calm down" as a time when he can pursue other interests. Politics, maybe. He was a Jesse Jackson delegate to the 1988 Democratic National Convention and really enjoyed it. He is not a politician, but he enjoys the interchange of those ideas. He was drawn to the buzz of people around his father, especially during his 1970 Senate campaign. He still struggles, like his father did, about whether he's making enough of an impact in the community.

"You would always like to do more," Bevan says. But then there is day-to-day life and the fact he and wife Martine are staring down the barrel of three college tuitions.

The thing about having opportunities is that, once you've had them, you want to make sure your kids get them, too.

❖ ❖ ❖

In his later years, Carl Maxey would slip into periods of caustic, sometimes crippling self-doubt, mulling questions of the impact he was able to make. On July 17, 1997, in his bed at the house on F Street, he took his own life.

He had never been diagnosed with anything other than extremely high blood pressure, but that blood pressure eventually pushed him toward retirement. He was visibly bothered by the prospect, and people speculated that he had been unable to cope with losing his livelihood.

Bill Maxey does not believe his father killed himself over the loss of his profession, but over the fear of losing his mind. The medical examiner expressed an opinion that Maxey may have had a series of mini strokes.

Bill doesn't view the suicide as a life-long fighter throwing in the towel. He sees it as the actions of a man who fiercely fought for the power of self-determination wanting to have the last say in how he died.

"I think he'd resolved that, you know, if he saw something change where maybe his ability to control life, so to speak, was going to be hampered or hindered, he was gonna do what he did," Bill says.

Bevan still recalls his father's charisma, his infectious laugh, his toughness — and his anger.

"I didn't grow up in his world and I didn't go through what he did and I think if he was in any way different, I think he would have been beaten down long before he ever got to law school," Bevan says. When you grow up wanting to be a doctor or a lawyer and people tell you to "think about being a janitor or something," Bevan says, "you either fight or flee — and he fought."

As a result of their father's sometimes-monstrous temper, Bevan says he and Bill haven't needed to have one: "I can be different, because I am a different person and I grew up in a different world." Bevan's son, Morgan, and the other grandkids get to be different, too.

Carl Maxey would take comfort in hearing that Morgan is uncomfortable in situations of low diversity. He'd probably smile to hear him say, "I don't just like to see one race of people," and knowing that he has found places of real diversity in Spokane, like the community center where he goes to get a decent game of pickup basketball when he's home. The elder Maxey would probably take greater comfort to hear Morgan's reaction when approached by somebody on campus who sees a 6-foot-8 quarter-black kid and asks, *Are you on the basketball team?* It pisses Morgan off a little, but ultimately he feels more pity than spite. "It's just ignorance," Morgan says. "You're not even talking to the person, you're talking to the skin."

The barriers to equality that remain — opportunities for minorities and the poor, vestigial racism in public institutions like the police department — are the sorts of things the brothers believe will get better if everyone with a mind toward progress is present and pushing, a little bit all the time, to ensure it.

The sheer will of a man like Carl Maxey might never be bottled up in a single individual again, but Bill thinks that a similar effect can be achieved if enough people do the small things they can each day to make their community a more decent, sane and hospitable place.

Bill says those masses have begun to assemble locally. For 20 minutes one afternoon, he rattles off names of people doing good work; he spends another 20 minutes in subsequent phone calls adding to his list. People working toward equality in their own way, helping make his father's work the work of a community.

It is the kind of community Bill and his wife, Shannon, want for their three children, Kara, Nick and Alex. It's the community Bevan and Martine want for Marcus and Mason, their two youngest. It's the community Morgan has already begun to search out for himself.

"There's a lot to do — a lot more to do," Bevan says, "and I know I could do more than what I've done, but I feel thankful and I feel good. I know that I've, I've," — the words stick here, for a moment — "I've tried hard."

And while Bevan says could have done a lot of things differently, he wouldn't change the person he is or the people who raised him. They taught him, above all, that passion and principle can overcome seemingly unassailable barriers. They taught him too, that people will mostly behave decently, if you give them half a chance.

Like everything else, that bottomless sense of duty is partially given, partially earned. And while it takes its toll on his health, Bevan says he wouldn't get rid of it if he could. "Caring is important," he says finally, "I think it helps keep you alive." ■

James Glover, the Father of Spokane.

A Tangled Legacy: James Glover

BY LISA WAANANEN JONES

First published in the *Inlander* on August 7, 2014

As the body of the city's most famous pioneer lay silently at the Masonic Temple in 1921, the remaining old-timers and the next generation of city-shapers paid respects to the man known as the Father of Spokane.

"With the passing of James Glover, the truest pioneer I ever knew is gone," said Joe Daniel, who moved to Spokane before its boom era. "He was a power and a force back in those early days, and he was a friend to everyone who ever knew him."

"He was a man of honor, strictly square in his business transactions and more loyal to his friends than any other man I ever knew," said Edward Pittwood, the city's first dentist.

"He was generous to a fault, and when he had much, he shared liberally with all," said W.C. Gray, who owned Spokane's first hotel. "He thought always of the other person, and had a helping hand always ready to extend. A truly great man has gone with the passing of Jim Glover."

More than 90 years later, in the final minutes of a committee meeting this past April, members of Spokane City Council decided against putting Glover's name on the new plaza beside City Hall. The stone with Glover's name had already been engraved for a dedication the following week, but questions had come up about whether the "Father of Spokane" deserved the honor.

"I found out things about James Glover I'm quite frankly not comfortable with," City Council President Ben Stuckart said. "He divorced his wife; she's buried out at Eastern State Hospital in an unmarked grave. This guy had some sketchy stuff going on in his past. It's not a joke. ... Is that somebody we want to honor as a city?"

Others around the table agreed it would be better to open the plaza without a name and involve the community in selecting a new one. The next Friday, the renovated Huntington Park and plaza opened to the public with live music, speeches and a new stone marker without Glover's name on it.

❖ ❖ ❖

James Nettle Glover was by no means the first person to live in this place, nor was he the first white man to recognize the value of the falls. But he was the first white settler to envision a grand city around the falls and then spend his life making it happen. In his old age, the city boosters proudly said he was the only settler in America who lived to see his land claim turn into a city of 130,000 in less than four decades.

Scrub Glover from the story of Spokane, and the city as we know it ceases to exist. He once owned all the land in Spokane's downtown core, and he spent months in Olympia wooing legislators to establish the county's boundaries. He laid out the downtown streets and gave them their names: Sprague for General J.W. Sprague, the railroad superintendent he dealt with most often; Howard for General Oliver O. Howard, who stopped by while leading troops against the Nez Perce; Stevens for the governor of Washington Territory; Post for local mill owner Frederick Post; and the rest for the presidents.

Other settlers and business partners came and left, and the only other white person to arrive in Spokane so early and stay long enough to be buried was Glover's wife, Susan Tabitha Crump. But she is notably absent in memories of Spokane's early days, an erasure more deliberate than the neglectful omission of many women at the time. Spokane's first Mrs. Glover was deliberately snipped out of history – out of spite, embarrassment and ignorance – many years before she was even dead.

❖ ❖ ❖

In his own telling, Glover arrived in Spokane Falls on a beautiful evening in May of 1873. He'd traveled from Salem, Oregon, by rail, river and saddle with a business partner, Jasper N. Matheny, and they arrived to find a handful of wooden structures among the grass and basalt. At that time the river ran unharnessed over the falls, with many rocks later blasted to make way for industry. Two settlers, J.J. Downing and Seth Scranton, had built a sawmill, and the visitors were directed to an unfinished log cabin to spend the night.

Glover fell asleep to the roar of the falls, and the next morning went to explore.

"I was enchanted — overwhelmed — with the beauty and grandeur of everything I saw," he recalled later. "It lay there just as nature had made it, with nothing to mar its virgin glory. I determined that I would possess it."

By the end of that second day, Glover had worked out a deal to buy the land claim that encompassed all of the falls.

At 36, Glover was taller than most men and assessed the world with intense, blue eyes. Later in life he walked around town as a neatly dressed elder statesman, clean-shaven with a silk top hat and gold-topped cane, but he first came to Spokane with dark hair and a beard, skin darkened by the sun and dust. He returned to Spokane a few months later, in August of 1873, with his 30-year-old wife, a slim woman with high cheekbones. In portraits, her downturned mouth and pulled-back hair give her the appearance of someone strained against an invisible wind. During her lifetime, she was described as having a look of melancholy in her eyes.

Both Glovers had come from Missouri on the Oregon Trail as children. James Glover was 12, and his trip took six months and one day; Susan's family came earlier, when she was 3, and they traveled part of the way with the ill-fated Donner-Reed Party on a grueling nine-month journey.

Glover had worked an assortment of enterprises as a young man — a fruit stand in California, mining in North Idaho, a ferry business in Salem — and said he was drawn to the Spokane area because "Oregon was becoming pretty well filled up by that time."

The land wasn't poised for immediate success. Marcia Downing, one of the few settlers living there when Glover arrived, remembered the stony, unyielding ground many years later: "You couldn't put the end of your little finger down without bruising it."

Glover and his business partners improved the sawmill, but there was no demand for lumber. They opened the first store, but their only customers were the Spokane and Coeur d'Alene Indians who came to trade. Only four families lived in Spokane Falls when it hosted a centennial Fourth of July celebration in 1876 that drew visitors from miles around.

One of Glover's favorite stories to tell about the early days was from the summer of 1877, when fighting between settlers and the Nez Perce put the whole region on edge. Spokane Falls had barely grown in the four years since the Glovers arrived, and news of nearby violence made them aware just how quickly their small settlement could cease to exist.

One day a Nez Perce group set up on the edge of town and drummed through the night for two weeks. Glover watched them from the front of his store as the days passed and became more tense, and finally he called a meeting with some of the older Spokane Indian leaders. It had been less than 20 years since Col. George Wright had come through and slaughtered hundreds of the local tribes' horses, and this was still a painful memory. He asked the men at the meeting if they recalled this, and told them to make the Nez Perce men leave by noon: "I am in close touch with the soldiers – the boys with the brass buttons – and if they aren't gone by noon, I will tell the soldiers to come."

The next day, entirely by chance, an infantry regiment marched into town.

Glover, pleased on multiple counts, lobbied for the soldiers to stay. The military decided to build Fort Coeur d'Alene, later called Fort Sherman, and the added protection drew more settlers to the area.

Around the same time, work resumed on the Northern Pacific Railway, which had been slowed by financial troubles but was routed to come through near Spokane Falls. The city soon had its first school, first hotel and first newspaper, the *Spokan Times*. (The spelling of Spokane was debated, and publisher Francis H. Cook felt strongly that the "e" would lead people to mispronounce the city's name.) The first train pulled into town from the west in 1881, and word got out soon that gold and silver had been found in the mountains of North Idaho. After a slow beginning, Spokane Falls became a boomtown.

For two years during this time, a 14-year-old niece, Lovenia, came from Salem to keep her aunt company while Glover was frequently away on business. The Glovers doted on Lovenia, and the letters she wrote back home are the only record of life in their household. She once saw her uncle turn down the covers and spank her aunt for failing to get out of bed in the morning, and she noted that her uncle did all the hiring of household help, which was unusual at a time when that was typically the wife's dominion.

But contrary to what was said later, Lovenia's letters prove the Glovers did share joyful times – the family exchanging gifts at Christmas, Susan playing organ for a choir practice, the Glovers dancing at a Masonic Lodge dedication in 1884. "You should have seen Uncle and Aunty get around," she wrote. "They were as light on their feet as any of the young folk."

❖ ❖ ❖

Shortly before the Great Fire in August 1889, the Glovers moved into their grand mansion on Eighth Avenue, the first designed by Kirtland Cutter. Their time in the home was brief and troubled. In August of 1891, two years after they moved in, Glover had his attorney draw up "Articles of Separation," a less formal alternative to divorce. The four-page document declared that they would live apart, that all property belonged solely to James Glover, and that he would provide his wife with a carriage, a house in Oregon and $100 a month for the rest of her life. Susan departed for Salem almost immediately.

The following January, Glover filed for divorce. His complaint called the marriage "unfortunate in every respect" and accused his wife of being "wholly impotent, barren and incapable of reproduction." It continues: "This incongeniality which existed between the parties was so extreme that it rendered cohabitation and social intercourse between them repulsive, beyond endurance on the part of either, and in fact impossible."

In April, Glover added a paragraph claiming "cruel treatment," a way to expedite the legal process. His wife's failure to respond was considered by the court an admission of guilt, and a judge approved the divorce on March 31, 1892. The man remembered at his funeral for his kindness and generosity extended no charity to his wife of nearly 24 years.

Two days later, Glover married Esther Emily Leslie, a 33-year-old woman from Maine who worked at an insurance office. With doughy features and small, dark eyes, the second Mrs. Glover was neither a trophy wife nor a vivacious socialite. When she died alone a few years after her husband, her obituary listed no civic affiliations. But their marriage must have been a more tolerable one, and the niece who grew up next door remembered "Uncle Jimmie and Aunt Ett" with admiration and fondness.

At the time he remarried, Glover was a millionaire with the finest home in the city. Within a year, the United States fell into the Panic of 1893, the worst economic depression it had yet endured. Glover's entire real estate and banking fortune evaporated when the First National Bank failed in July, and he and his new wife were forced to move out of the mansion.

In an interview decades later, on the occasion of his 78th birthday, he recalled that time:

"When everything seemed going from us in the early '90s, I saw some of my best friends going to the wall, men who were losing the accumulations of a lifetime, men who were broken with sorrow, and at that time I forbade my family to mention hard times and financial troubles at our home. It was one of the ways I had of sustaining the ordeal."

❖ ❖ ❖

All that was left for the first Mrs. Glover fell apart on July 1, 1899. She had returned to Spokane from Oregon just a few weeks after the divorce was finalized, and she spent the next seven years moving from one downtown apartment to another. She decided to buy a house at 316 S. Ash St., which is now a parking lot near the Grocery Outlet store, and moved her belongings there on July 1, 1899.

She came home that evening to find her piano in the street. All her possessions were outside, as if the house itself had spat them out. The hotel proprietor who sold the house said he'd never received payment from Mrs. Glover and moved on to another buyer. When he heard she'd moved furniture in, he and another man went to remove it.

Susan wandered down the block to the home of the McCreas, where she sat on the front steps, inconsolable, until they called the police. The *Spokesman-Review* reported: "Officer Beals found Mrs. Glover sitting on the steps. He tried to induce her to go home, offering to accompany her. She refused. Then the officer said he would send for a carriage and have someone in citizen's clothes go home with her. She violently replied that she did not want to go home, or anywhere, and that she would allow no one to lay a hand on her. When the patrol wagon arrived, Mrs. Glover refused to enter it. The officers lifted her bodily into the patrol. The crazed woman was placed in a cell in the women's department of the county jail."

A hearing was held, at which her former husband and other witnesses testified against her. Physicians filled out a form assessing her condition:

Is there suicidal, homicidal or incendiary disposition? No
Is there a disposition to injure others? No
Is this the first attack? Yes
In what way is the accused dangerous to be at large? unable to take care of her self

The news that she had been declared insane and committed to the asylum at Medical Lake warranted a single sentence in the *Chronicle* on July 4, 1899, between items about a young lady's sightseeing trip to Lake Coeur d'Alene and two sisters' departure for a summer on the coast. The *Spokesman-Review* noted that, "the woman has given the sheriff's deputies considerable trouble since her incarceration Sunday."

❖ ❖ ❖

She never told the story, so we don't know what Susan Glover felt when she first laid eyes on the falls. No one made speeches in her honor or interviewed her about Spokane's early days. We don't know whether she agreed that life in the mansion on Eighth Avenue was "impossible," or at what point she stopped fighting the officials tasked with delivering her to the mental hospital.

At the time she was committed, Eastern State Hospital was called the Eastern Washington Hospital for the Insane, and it was meant to be a self-sufficient community with a dairy, bakery, smokehouse and pleasant grounds overlooking Medical Lake. The standard of care had moved from prison-like restraints, the hospital superintendent said in 1900, to modern methods of "kindness, tact, amusements, exercise, rest of the mind and body, and the proper administration of medicine where the mental or physical health require it."

But there was no treatment for "melancholia" or other mental illnesses, and no expectation that patients would get better. People with all manner of problems – depression, schizophrenia, learning disabilities, alcoholism, erratic behavior – were put into the custody of the mental asylum with the intention that they remain apart from society. In those early decades, the vast majority of patients arrived at Eastern State Hospital on a court order, and few ever left.

Susan gets no mention in most histories of Spokane, but her name is recorded in a handful of written memories of the city's earliest holidays and in a long family history written by one of Glover's nieces and filed with the Oregon Historical Society: "He married Susan Crump, an attractive and highly esteemed woman who from an illness fell into spells of despondency and eventually became completely deranged so that she had to be confined for many years before her death."

The daughter of the niece who once lived with the Glovers in early days of Spokane Falls recalled her mother mentioning an infant, and speculated in correspondence in the 1970s that the "illness" may have been a miscarriage or stillbirth.

Barbara Cochran, who researched the Glovers for historic portraits published posthumously as the book *Seven Frontier Women*, found anecdotes that suggest Susan Glover's health may have been a reason the Glovers left Salem in the first place. Existence for the quiet wife of the ambitious James Glover must have been desperately lonely in the early years, Cochran concluded, and then rapidly overwhelming as the city grew up around them.

With the perspective of many decades, the note Susan Glover wrote in an autograph book the Glovers gave their niece for Christmas in 1884 is a poignant plea:

"Long may you live
Happy may you be
And when you think of Spokan
Don't forget your Aunty."

❖ ❖ ❖

Time both conceals and illuminates, and history is filled with great men judged more critically by later generations. When the names of these men grace street signs, parks and public buildings, communities continue to grapple with the best way to live with their history: Is removing a name an act of healing, or an act of forgetting?

After years of protests from parents, a school board in Florida voted this year to rename a high school named for Nathan Bedford Forrest, a Confederate general who was also an early leader in the Ku Klux Klan.

In Canada, a plan to install a plaque honoring Dr. Helen MacMurchy – a leading public health champion in the early 20th century – was scrapped at the last minute after it came to light that she was also a promoter of eugenics.

In New York, a street called Corbin Place became the topic of controversy in 2007 after a new book revealed that its namesake, 19th-century developer Austin Corbin, was an outspoken anti-Semite. To avoid a costly name change, the city council voted to rename the street for Margaret Cochran Corbin, a Revolutionary War heroine who took her husband's place in battle when he was killed.

Whatever Glover's faults, they do not fall on the scale of mass oppression and systematic injustice. He was not a killer or a slaveholder. There's no evidence he was more prejudiced than most white men of the time. The charges against him are far more intimate, and in that way more timeless – when a wealthy man leaves his mentally ill wife with nothing, there is no context of era or culture that can explain it.

Glover avoided serious scrutiny in his lifetime and died with his reputation intact. But in keeping his first wife out of sight – and out of history – Glover ended up jeopardizing the honored place he worked so purposefully to attain in Spokane's story of itself. Depending how harshly you judge his actions, it's either pitiful or justice that what he determined to forget has come to define his official legacy in the city he cared so much about.

Historian Tony Bamonte, who with his wife edited and further researched Cochran's book, considers Glover a domineering man who used his power to banish his wife when she became an inconvenience.

"His motive was to get rid of her," Bamonte says. "And not just to get rid of her, but to get her off the streets where people wouldn't know that she was having all these troubles and that he was leaving her penniless. And she didn't deserve that."

Throughout his life, Bamonte says, Glover told the story of Spokane in a way that embellished his efforts and marginalized the people who helped him along the way. He helped perpetuate the rumor – taught in local schools for many years – that the two settlers who preceded him, Scranton and Downing, were "horse thieves" in trouble with the law. (Scranton was accused, but found not guilty.) Glover downplayed the influence of others who promoted Spokane in the region, and suggested that business partners who abandoned the settlement in the early years left for lack of dedication and character, rather than practical concerns like money and medical care. Bamonte has no doubt that Glover pulled the necessary strings to make sure his first wife would not return to interfere with the image he was creating of himself.

Glover is a key player in Spokane history, Bamonte says, but it's important that the full story be remembered when his name comes up.

"I think the true story needs to come out," he says. "I think people need to know who he was and what he stood for, and how he manipulated things and how he sought his own recognition. … He did some things that are not acceptable today, and there's a reason they're not acceptable."

❖ ❖ ❖

Forty-eight years after he first arrived in Spokane, James Glover knew death was near. His legs no longer held him, and he refused to go to bed because he did not believe he would get up again. He'd had Kirtland Cutter design a modest, cottage-style home in West Central in 1909, and from there, day and night, he looked out from his chair on the tree-covered hills to the west of Spokane.

On Oct. 11, 1921, as Glover kept vigil over the city he founded, his first wife died at Eastern State Hospital just shy of 80. No family or birth year was listed on her death certificate, and she was buried in the hospital cemetery in a grave marked No. 746.

Five weeks later, on the morning of Nov. 18, Glover died quietly at his home. For a year and a half he had stayed in his chair, and his family finally convinced him to go to bed. He died two days later.

At the meeting after his death, the Spokane City Council passed a resolution honoring Glover's service to the city:

"He died in the fullness of years, honored by his fellow citizens, and leaves behind him in the city he helped to found a monument to perpetuate his name more enduring than modeled bronze or sculptured stone."

Glover Field, the ledge of grass beside the river in Peaceful Valley, was once lined with stands as the city's finest athletic stadium. Before that, it was a significant gathering place for the native people of Spokane, and the city has agreed to let the tribe rename the field in a way that recognizes the site's longer history.

It's not a deliberate ousting of Glover, and few people living in the city today even know the field was named for him. But once, on an autumn day nearly a century ago, a thousand people came to the field and cheered as a granite monument was unveiled to formally dedicate Glover Field as Glover himself looked on. The Chamber of Commerce and the Advertising Club – the new generation of city promoters – had made occasion to honor him at several events when it became clear that time was running out. But this was the greatest honor, and the Advertising Club announced plans to erect a full statue on the granite base so that Glover's figure could forever look east toward the falls. The *Chronicle* reported that the crowd chanted – "Glover, Glover, speech" – and the old man addressed the crowd with a tear in his eye: "Fellow citizens, I am always glad to meet with you."

The statue never materialized, and half a century later the base stood hidden in tangles of grass, its plaque gone and its granite edges chipped away. The Ad Club suggested it be moved to the grounds of Expo '74, now Riverfront Park, but parks officials deemed it inappropriately "tombstone-appearing."

Though most of the names Glover bestowed on Spokane's streets are still used today, he never named a street or any other landmark for himself. Glover Middle School was named for him before it opened in 1958, and will be his only civic presence once Glover Field is renamed.

In 1931, a decade after Glover's death, it was proposed that the recently rebuilt Grand Avenue be renamed Glover Way. No one liked the idea. "Absolutely not!" one man commented in the *Chronicle*. "Grand Boulevard is the grandest name we could have for a street so fine. I'm not a bit strong for this idea of shaking off all the old names which have meant so much to Spokane." A smaller portion of Cliff Drive was briefly considered, and then the idea was dropped.

Today the Glover Field monument still exists in Peaceful Valley. The lowest tier of the concrete base is perched in the original place on the hillside along Main, covered in matted leaves and littered with punctured cans. The rest of the monument stands in a pale patch of grass beside the community center, a pillar of anonymous granite without any plaque or sign to identify the man it once honored. ∎

The approximate location in Riverside State Park of the homestead of
Jaco Finlay, the first white settler in what would become Washington state.

The Wanderer: Jaco Finlay

BY JACK NISBET

First published in the *Inlander* on December 12, 1996

L ate this past summer on a Sunday afternoon, I visited the Spokane House Interpretive Center at Nine Mile. One of the rooms inside was, surprisingly, filled with people. The light in there was dim, and the August heat pressed close until someone cracked a side door in search of a refreshing breeze. The sunlight that immediately blazed through the opening flashed off an elderly gentleman nodding comfortably in his chair. A cluster of women gathered around a musket in a glass case, and children of descending age splayed out around the corner on a cool concrete floor.

As I spoke with a couple of local people from Long Lake, a lady wobbled up with a walking cane and introduced herself as Lucille Otter of Ronan, Montana. Lucille's recent hip surgery had not prevented her from joining a few family members for a drive over Lookout Pass to pay their respects to a relative, Jaco Finlay. In fact, an awful lot of the crowd that day claimed to be direct descendants of Finlay, a local legend who lived at the Spokane House trading post from the moment it was built.

Perhaps more than any single Canadian fur trader, Jaco Finlay left his mark on the Inland Northwest. He had at least three wives, including a Spokane woman whose name was rendered as "Teskwentichina" on her daughter's wedding certificate; he fathered 18 known children – many of whom lived out their lives in the region. Finlay and some of his sons appear on the pay lists of many of the early fur trade districts and expeditions. When Catholic and Congregationalist missionaries first entered the area in the late-1830s, they found Finlay children farming and trapping the land, and hired them as hunters and guides.

As the pace of settlement increased, the Finlay presence crops up in connection with everything from the first gold strike in southeastern British Columbia to the introduction of ring-necked pheasants to the Flathead Valley. There are Finlay descendants to be found in small towns from Polson to Ephrata, and in larger cities from Missoula to Portland; there are Finlays on the Colville, Spokane, Salish-Kootenai and Kalispel reservations.

❖ ❖ ❖

Jaco Finlay traveled a circuitous path before he finally settled along the Spokane River. The son of a French fur agent and a Chippewa woman, he was born Jacques Raphael Finlay in 1768 at his father's trade house near the forks of the Saskatchewan River on the Canadian Prairies. His name surfaced briefly in post journals from the region in 1794 and '96. On a pay sheet for the North West Fur Company in 1799, Finlay was listed under the column of "Proprietors, Clerks, etc." at an annual wage of "1200 livres." It was one of the highest rates on the chart, exactly equal to that of another clerk named David Thompson – an Englishman only two years younger than Finlay who had recently joined the Nor'Westers after 13 years' service with the rival Hudson's Bay Company. Over the next 13 years, the paths of these two men would cross and recross, and because Thompson left behind a wealth of written field journals and Finlay did not, almost all the printed knowledge about him comes to us through the eyes of David Thompson, in the form of brief appearances in his journal notebooks.

By 1804, Thompson had been named as a partner in the North West Company, fully privileged to share in the annual profits. Finlay was on the company list as Jacques Raphael, still holding his 1799 position of commissioned clerk. Finlay continued to work from the western Prairies to the east slope of the Rocky Mountains, in what is now the province of Alberta.

At the North West Company's 1806 annual gathering, several

of the more ambitious partners planned a corporate expansion for the following spring. Beginning at Rocky Mountain House (a trading post on the upper Saskatchewan River), a party would cross over to the west side of the Rockies and establish a new post on the Columbia River. David Thompson, who combined the skills of surveyor and trader and had been on two previous attempts to cross the Continental Divide, was named to lead the expedition. Jaco Finlay's years in the local trade, together with his knowledge of the Blackfeet and Kootenai peoples who lived on either side of the mountains, made him the logical choice as chief scout for the expedition.

David Thompson kept the journal at Rocky Mountain House that fall, and his entries include inventory, equipment and tobacco sent over the mountains to Finlay and some men who were apparently helping him widen an established Kootenai trail across the Divide. On Nov. 19, Finlay arrived at Rocky Mountain House; four days later, after a heavy snowstorm, he "went off for the Mountains" again. Through the dead of winter Jaco's name did not appear in the journal, but at the end of February, 1807, on a day when Thompson recorded a temperature of -30 degrees Fahrenheit, he also noted that he had sent off "sugar flour & spirits for Jaco." At mid-morning on March 25, "Jaco arrived with his woman + 2 children from the mountain." The weather was beginning to break, and for the next month, despite many flurries of snow, Finlay and various members of his family moved back and forth between the trading post and the trail.

In June of 1807, David Thompson's party of 19 people – counting a Scottish clerk named Finan McDonald, several French-Canadian voyageurs and family members that included Thompson's own half-Cree wife and their three children – struggled across what is now called Howse Pass and descended the west slope of the Rockies. They struck the Columbia River near Golden, B.C., then built canoes and paddled upstream on the river to establish Kootanae House near the present town of Invermere. But Jaco's name did not appear again until David Thompson sent a report back to the company partners that September, and in it the party commander was not very complimentary of Finlay's work as a trailblazer.

"From what has been said of the road on the Portage, it is clearly seen that Jaco Finlay with the Men engaged last Summer to clear the Portage Road, has done a mere nothing... and it is the opinion of every Man with me, as well as mine that Jaco Finlay ought to lose at least half his wages for having so much neglected the Duty for which he was so expressly engaged at 150L per year, beside a Piece of Tobacco & Sugar, & a Clerk's equipment."

Not earning your tobacco and sugar were grave offenses in David Thompson's eyes, but he must have maintained some contact with Finlay during that winter at Kootenae House. In a personal letter to a friend sent off in March of 1808, Thompson admitted that his incomplete knowledge of the country had a lot to do with his problems getting over the trail, and he left open the possibility of working with Finlay again – he was the man, after all, with the most experience and best contacts in the region.

"Jaco has behaved like a scoundrel but all is now over. We were ignorant of the proper season and what is worse that season depends so much on the quantity of snow in the mountains, that one may have a good passage one year in June and the next year as late as July."

In the same letter, Jaco's name also appeared in reference to an eastern Salteaux Indian who couldn't shoot straight and an estimate of the next season's fur take that Thompson thought was so wildly inflated that "it makes me smile."

❖ ❖ ❖

In the spring of 1808, Jaco Finlay was back on the east side of the Rockies, working as a "free hunter" or independent trapper. As David Thompson passed by on his way to the North West Company summer meeting on Lake Superior, he stopped and camped nearby. He was on good enough terms with Finlay at the time to pick up his furs of the season to carry them east for sale.

For the next three years, as these two men worked their way through what we now call the Inland Northwest, their complex relationship continued – sometimes contentious, although Finlay was asked to do things that only a close companion could accomplish. Thompson, a man of strict habit, always referred to his fellow fur agents as "Mr." and his voyageurs by their French last name. But Finlay, at least in the daily journals, is always "Jaco."

David Thompson arrived back at Kootenae House in the fall of 1808. On a cold, snowy afternoon, he was hanging the door on the post's warehouse when Finlay rode in, accompanied by his family and five

Iroquois trappers. They camped nearby, and, when Thompson's junior agent went to visit them with some rum, the entire group "drank and fought the whole night." Next evening the same thing happened; the day after that, Finlay left part of his family with Thompson at the trade house while the rest of his party moved south to set up their winter traplines.

At the end of January, Finlay dropped by Kootanae House in need of a gun, and apparently talked about the fact that he was roping and breaking some of the wild horses that roamed the hillsides above the Columbia Valley. In his journal Thompson noted that Finlay "has now taken 10 Marrons," a French slang term for something once tame gone wild. Three days later a journal entry read, "Jaco has now 18 taken." Soon afterwards, Thompson, who up to this point had only killed an occasional wild horse as food, lit out after a herd of marrons himself, chasing them all over the countryside on three of his own best horses. After capturing one of the mustangs, he wrote an enthusiastic description of the technique involved in breaking such a spirited animal to a bridle.

Fur trade journals were rarely a place to reveal personal emotions, but in late April of 1808, as he was trying to doctor the sick wife of one of his voyageurs, Thompson's entry read, "passed a sad night with Lussier's wife who is dying." When the woman passed away the next day, the trader was at a loss as to how to take care of the four young children she had left behind, "the youngest only 6 Months old, which much distresses me." But as Thompson traveled north a week later, preparing to move east again with the year's furpacks, he found the logical solution to his problem: "In the evening came to Jaco & family with whom we left the children of Lussier's deceased woman."

On this same visit, Thompson apparently hired Finlay to build two canoes and lay in some meat for his men – canoe framing and effective hunting were two essential skills that always came with Finlay. The fact that Thompson could trust Finlay with the care of four recently orphaned children, as well as with the transportation and sustenance for his entire party, did not, however, keep him from criticizing Finlay's boatbuilding skills:

"May 23… Jaco got the other canoe down & gummed – they are both badly made in the Bottom & not likely to last any time without being quickly repaired."

When David Thompson returned from his summer meetings

in August of 1809, the first bit of news he heard was that a band of
Blackfeet raiders had slipped over the mountains and stolen most of
Finlay's personal possessions, including his prized string of Kootenai
horses. Thompson's party found Finlay and his family two days later
at the very top of the Continental Divide at Howse Pass, elevation
5,000 feet, badly in need of help. Horses and provisions changed hands,
and the Finlays turned around to accompany the Nor'Westers to the
Columbia River. Finlay hovered around Thompson's party for several
days, spearing salmon as they moved south. Then Finlay separated from
the group, perhaps returning to his family, while Thompson followed
the Kootenai River south and west to what is now Bonners Ferry, Idaho.
From there he followed a native road south to Pend Oreille Lake and
explored its outlet river west to the area around what is now Cusick,
Washington.

The explorer returned to Pend Oreille Lake in November, then staked
out a plan to build a new trading post he called Saleesh House near
modern Thompson Falls, Montana. There, Thompson and his men fell
on hard times hunting and became so weak with hunger that, even with
winter closing in, they could not accomplish much work on the post.
Finlay and his wife chose that moment to reappear, carrying "2 parcels
of dried Meat traded & of his own 28 Beaver Tails about 40 lbs of Bear
Meat 21 dried beavers & 3 pieces of dried Meat." While many early fur
trade parties west of the Rockies spent their time fighting hunger, Jaco
Finlay, moving on his own through territory and tribal groups that he
was much more familiar with, usually seemed to be well supplied.

❖ ❖ ❖

The Finlay family flitted around the edges of Saleesh House that
winter, with Jaco occasionally providing a mule deer or two to the
company people for food. When he brought one in on March 28, David
Thompson "…engaged him in his old Capacity of Clerk & Interpreter."
A few weeks later, "…having given Jaco his summer orders," Thompson
began his annual trek east to report to the company partners; meanwhile,
Finlay moved west along the Pend Oreille River, then down from
Calispell Lake along a trail that led to the wedge of land formed by the
confluence of the Spokane and Little Spokane rivers. This was the site of

an important village of the Upper Spokane people, *n tcmatsi'n*, and there were other villages on both sides of the river close by. The salmon and steelhead fishery at the spot attracted a wide variety of visitors, and made a natural location for a new trade house.

Finlay's "summer orders" apparently were to supervise the building of the first Spokane House that summer. Agent Finan McDonald joined him there later in the year, driven west from Saleesh House by Blackfoot threats. David Thompson did not see Spokane House until he had completed an arduous winter crossing of the Northern Rockies and a long detour through Montana looking for Mr. McDonald. He finally arrived at the post a full year after it was built, in June 1811, and his journal entry for the day marked the first appearance of Spokane House in written history: "Thank Heaven for our good safe journey, here we found Jaco etc with about 40 Spokane families."

Thompson remained in the Northwest for just one more year – a whirlwind of activity that saw him pass through Spokane House no less than five different times. The trading post, manned by Finlay, formed a hub for both explorations and fur transport; the center for messages sent, horses ordered, new men left off, old hands redeployed. On at least two occasions when Thompson sent letters ahead for Finlay to meet him with fresh horses, the two missed connections on the trail.

In the spring of 1812, Thompson stopped at Spokane House for the final time. His pack horses were laden with furs gathered in the Flathead Valley, and when Finlay's winter trade was added in, they amounted to four tons of pelts. Thompson's plan was to move the cargo north, into the Colville Valley. There he would build four cedar-framed canoes, carry them to Kettle Falls, load them with the furpacks, launch them upstream into the Columbia, and paddle north to cross the Rockies for one last time. As Thompson laid out the frames side by side near the modern city of Colville, Finlay joined him in a kind of canoe-building bake-off.

For eight days in April, Thompson's journal entries recorded the meticulous measurements and handiwork of serious craftsmanship, resulting in the completion of two lap-sided cedar plank canoes overseen by him and two traditional birchbark vessels supervised by Finlay. Each evening Thompson recorded the steady advancement on his own two boats, then determined the progress of his employee, competitor,

peer and possible friend. At every phase of the process, Finlay lagged
a little bit behind. As Thompson began to split out oars for his almost-
completed boats, his journal entry read, "Jaco's second canoe the side
seam sewed only."

❖ ❖ ❖

David Thompson left within the week for Montreal, never to return to
the West. Jaco Finlay stayed on, dropping out of the fur journals again for
some time, but apparently continuing to live in the vicinity of Spokane
House. When Finan McDonald, a Scot, retired back to the same village
as Thompson near Montreal in 1825, Finlay again stayed put: he was
a half-breed, and belonged much more to the West than to "lower"
Canada.

By that time, the Hudson's Bay Company had come to dominate
the fur business, and in 1826 they moved their local base of operations
to Fort Colville. After stripping the various buildings around Spokane
House, they left its shell to Finlay as his personal home. Over the next
two years, Finlay was visited there by several early travelers through the
region. When the botanist David Douglas damaged his musket, he was
directed to Finlay as the only person within several hundred miles who
might be able to repair the damaged firearm.

Douglas' visit took place in early May of 1826, when Finlay was 58.
The botanist wrote that Finlay apologized for his meager hospitality, as
they had been short of food for some weeks – the only meal he could
offer consisted of traditional Salish cakes of beaten black lichen. In spite
of the fact that Douglas had some trouble understanding his brand of
French, Finlay did provide him with details concerning the color of local
currant berries and a certain brownish-gray mountain sheep that lived in
the mountains to the north. Finlay promised to collect some currant seeds
when they ripened later in the summer, as well as some curious lilies, and
hoped he might bag one of the *mouton gris* for the naturalist during his fall
hunt. The proprietor of Spokane House also "obligingly put my gun in
good order," and provided his son James to guide Douglas south, into the
uncharted Blue Mountains.

When Douglas and James returned to Spokane House in early
August, after a very successful plant hunt, Finlay was able to provide

them with more proper fare: "We found old Mr. Finlay who gave us an abundance of fine fresh salmon from his barrier, placed in a small branch of the main river."

Jaco Finlay died at Spokane House in September 1828. According to legend, Finlay was buried under the south bastion of the stockade. A 1950s' archeological dig uncovered human remains near the spot. Also found were fragments of a pair of spectacles and five tobacco pipes. One made of clay had what looked to be the initial "J" carved into the bowl, perhaps even "JF." The remains were determined to Jaco's, and he was reinterred, complete with a proper marker, in 1976.

❖ ❖ ❖

At Spokane House on that Sunday afternoon this past summer, the Finlay people knew who they were, and several could trace their lineage back to Finlay through a family tree supposedly drawn by Father DeSmet himself. Most of them had a noticeable pride in their roots and understood that their heritage bridged not only the two centuries of time between Finlay and the present, but the split between cultures that has shaped the history of the West.

Finlay left behind no written record of himself, and no known artistic likenesses of him were made; for information, we have to rely on family lore and the words of David Thompson, a man who sometimes was at odds with the way Finlay lived. Yet, for all that we do not know about him, Finlay obviously fit into this place, and among these people. An awful lot of his descendants – by some estimates numbering in the high thousands – still fit in just as comfortably.

As her niece and a couple of cousins walked out to inspect the grounds around Spokane House, Lucille Otter remained inside the interpretive center. She talked about ranch doings in the Mission Valley, and the progress of the nursing program at the Salish-Kootenai College on the reservation. Then she noticed two baskets of roots in a display case beside the cash register. The baskets, although of different styles, were both beautifully crafted, and Lucille bent over to study the weave. One contained the familiar round black bulbs of camas lily.

"That one looks like Nez Perce, don't you think?" asked Louise. The other, more open at the top, was filled with longer whitish roots identified as "Indian carrots," and she wasn't sure about them. She played around with some of the plants she was familiar with, letting musical Salish words play off her lips.

"Oh well," she said. "We'll just have to remember to look for them next spring."

It seems almost as if Jaco is still out there himself, searching for lilies and mountain sheep, nibbling on currants as he moves through the hills. The Finlays among us make it seem like a reasonable bet that we will actually make it to next spring, and that it will be fun to get out in the greenery and have a look around. ■

Special thanks to Mr. David Courchane for sharing his genealogical detective work on the Finlay family.

Details of portraits of Meriwether Lewis and William Clark by Alonzo Victor Lewis. Gifts from Lewis and Clark High School's first graduating class of 1912, they still hang in the auditorium.

YOUNG KWAK PHOTOS

Into the Unknown: Lewis and Clark

BY ROBERT CARRIKER

First published as a serial in the *Inlander*,
August 18, 2005 to June 29, 2006

The Lewis and Clark Expedition is rightly called America's most perfect 19th-century exploring expedition. For 863 days between 1804 and 1806, the Corps of Discovery paddled, walked or rode horses for nearly 8,000 miles in the Louisiana Purchase and the Oregon Country. In more than 750,000 words, their journals describe the Missouri, Clearwater, Snake and Columbia rivers. William Clark, the expedition cartographer, mapped the rivers and their tributaries; he also established the location of four mountain passes he or Lewis used to cross the Continental Divide. Meriwether Lewis, the expedition naturalist, noted and accurately described 44 mammals, 12 fishes, 15 reptiles and 51 birds that were new to science. The party consisted of 45 men when it left Illinois in May 1804, but it had downsized to 32 adults and one infant when it departed Fort Mandan in April 1805. Upon their return to St. Louis, in September 1806, Lewis and Clark changed American attitudes about Western geography, Native Americans, botany, zoology, linguistics, medicine and economic opportunities on the frontier.

Today, the observations of the men of the Corps of Discovery are still very relevant. It sounds strange, but reading the 200-year-old journals – in which spelling and grammar are often an adventure all their own – seems to bring out a "detective" gene in armchair historians. After reading certain passages, people instinctively want to dig beneath the obvious and ponder, question, seek additional information and sometimes even observe the sites for themselves. For example, after reading journal entries that describe Palouse Canyon, the rocky course of the Snake River, the Wallula Gap and the Columbia River Gorge, many readers familiar with Pacific Northwest geology realize that Lewis and Clark are describing the effects of the post-Ice Age floods that sculpted the landscape of Washington some 13,000 years ago.

The beauty of the Lewis and Clark journals is that the writers described not only what they saw and understood, but also what they saw and did not understand. Passages remain today just waiting to be figured out and enhanced. Thus, in 2005, people can read the captain's words from 1805 and, using the vast store of knowledge that has been uncovered over the past two centuries, expand on those journal entries, making them personal, seeing the landmarks with fresh eyes.

When they began their journey up the Missouri River on May 14, 1804, Lewis and Clark had the benefit of maps and information that Lewis had coaxed out of experienced fur traders in St. Louis; one map they copied of the Great Bend of the Missouri River was made in 1798 by David Thompson, a fur trapper with the North West Company. Later, as the Corps of Discovery pushed, pulled and poled its keelboat and two pirogues on the Missouri, itinerant fur men joined them several times on the upriver journey as guides. During the long winter of 163 days with the Mandan Indians in present-day North Dakota, Lewis and Clark assembled quite a bit of information from the natives about the character of the Missouri River. Thus, when they resumed their trek westward on April 7, 1805, the leaders of the Corps of Discovery had some idea of what to expect.

Information supplied by the Indians, however, took the Corps of Discovery only as far as the Great Falls of the Missouri. After that, they were on their own. Lewis and Clark, therefore, had to make their own decisions when the Missouri split into Three Forks and when the Rocky Mountains seemingly blocked their movement west.

The "evidence" in the Lewis and Clark detective story becomes more difficult to decipher once the expedition crosses the Continental Divide into present-day Idaho. Their route is no longer straightforward, as in "just follow the Missouri River." Even more challenging are relations with the

Native Americans, for three Western tribes had not yet made contact with Euro-Americans. Once across the Continental Divide, Lewis and Clark needed experienced guides more than ever to facilitate their journey. The same is true for 21st-century armchair travelers. Employing a guide is a practice, I suspect, that Lewis and Clark would recommend, because the route of the Corps of Discovery across Idaho and Washington is filled with surprises and some misunderstood moments.

In the coming installments, readers will be guided along the Lewis and Clark Trail across Washington and Idaho – over Lemhi, Lost Trail and Lolo passes on horseback, then down the Clearwater, Snake and Columbia rivers in canoes to the Pacific Ocean.

We pick up the trail on Meriwether Lewis's 31st birthday, 200 years ago, with present-day Idaho stretching out in front of the Corps of Discovery.

❖ ❖ ❖

THE CORPS OF DISCOVERY IN MODERN-DAY

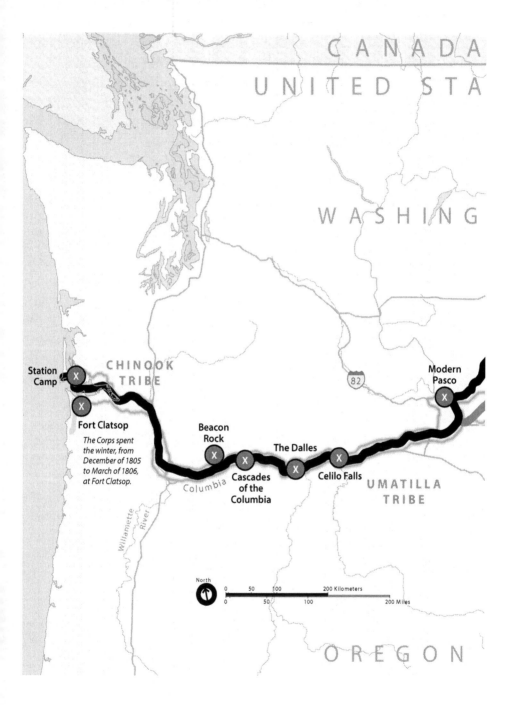

CANADA
UNITED STA
WASHING

Station
Camp

CHINOOK
TRIBE

82

Modern
Pasco

Fort Clatsop
*The Corps spent
the winter, from
December of 1805
to March of 1806,
at Fort Clatsop.*

Beacon
Rock

The Dalles

Cascades
of the
Columbia

Celilo Falls

UMATILLA
TRIBE

Columbia

Willamette River

North

| 0 | 50 | 100 | 200 Kilometers |

| 0 | 50 | 100 | 200 Miles |

OREGON

IDAHO AND WASHINGTON

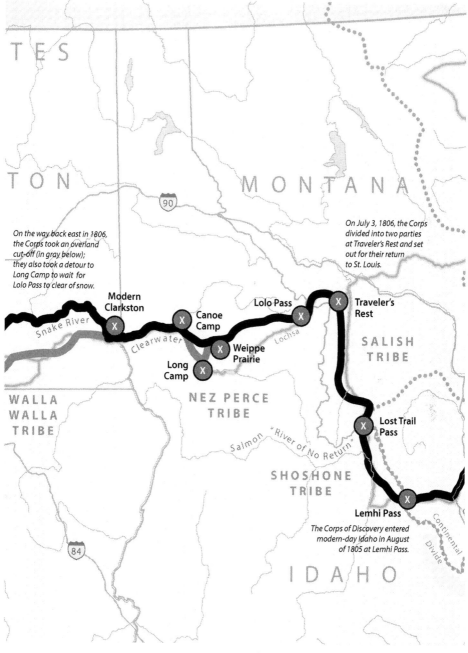

On the way back east in 1806, the Corps took an overland cut-off (in gray below); they also took a detour to Long Camp to wait for Lolo Pass to clear of snow.

On July 3, 1806, the Corps divided into two parties at Traveler's Rest and set out for their return to St. Louis.

Modern Clarkston

Canoe Camp

Lolo Pass

Traveler's Rest

Snake River

Clearwater

Lochsa

SALISH TRIBE

Weippe Prairie

Long Camp

NEZ PERCE TRIBE

WALLA WALLA TRIBE

Salmon "River of No Return"

Lost Trail Pass

SHOSHONE TRIBE

Lemhi Pass

Continental Divide

The Corps of Discovery entered modern-day Idaho in August of 1805 at Lemhi Pass.

IDAHO

CREATED FROM A NATIONAL PARK SERVICE MAP (nps.gov)

Across the Divide

AUGUST 18-24, 1805

Meriwether Lewis deserved a celebration on his birthday. For the past 10 days — ever since he and three trusted men had set out on an independent command from the rest of the Corps of Discovery on the morning of Aug. 9, 1805 — Lewis had significantly advanced the immediate goals of the expedition.

But the introspective Lewis found little in his life to be proud of on Aug. 18, 1805. That evening he wrote in his journal, "This day I completed my thirty first year, and conceived that I had in all human probability now existed about half the period which I am to remain in this Sublunary world. I reflected that I had as yet done little, very little indeed, to further the hapiness of the human race, or to advance the information of the succeeding generation."

Lewis incorrectly minimized his personal achievements. Take his most recent days, for example. On Aug. 12 — 455 days after the Corps of Discovery departed from their winter camp in Illinois — Lewis and his companions became the first citizens of the United States to pass over the Continental Divide when they followed an Indian trail across Lemhi Pass (at 7,323 feet of elevation) that sits between present-day Montana and Idaho.

The following afternoon, Lewis courageously introduced himself to "a party of about 60 warriors mounted on excellent horses who came in nearly full speed," and other Shoshone villagers who lived alongside the Lemhi River. Later, Lewis parleyed with the tribal chief by using "the common language of jesticulation or signs which seems to be universally understood by all the Nations." Dinner that evening included salmon, eliciting from Lewis the comment that "this was the first salmon I had seen and perfectly convinced me that we were on the waters of the Pacific Ocean."

Ultimately Lewis persuaded some Shoshone to return with him to the eastern side of Lemhi Pass, where they met up with William Clark and the main body of the Corps, who were several days behind Lewis. Together Lewis and Clark organized a great council at which the explorers promised the Shoshone headmen future deliveries of firearms if the Indian chiefs, in turn, agreed to furnish the visitors with horses for the transport of Corps' equipment. The achievements of Lewis had been, in truth, monumental, not of "very little" consequence. He truly merited a happy birthday, whether he believed so or not.

For six days following his birthday, Lewis remained on the east side of Lemhi Pass with a contingent of Shoshone tribesmen and some of his own men. His major task was secretly to bury, or cache, the expedition canoes and extraneous supplies. When he ascended Lemhi Pass for the first time, Lewis saw an unsettling vista of mountains stretching west to the horizon: "I discovered immence ranges of high mountains still to the West of us with their tops partially covered with snow."

He had half-expected to see the Pacific Ocean in the distance, but such was not the case. Mountains required horses, not canoes, and the premium placed upon baggage space mandated that some items of the Corps be left behind, hopefully to be picked up on the return journey. To that end, Lewis laid up the expedition canoes in a pond by sinking them with stones, "hoping by this means to guard against both the effects of high water, and that of the fire," which the condition of the landscape suggested to him must be frequent in this vicinity. Overnight temperatures on Aug. 21-22 dipped to 19 degrees and 22 degrees respectively, complicating the operation by forming "ice 1/4 of an inch thick on the water which stood in the vessels."

At times, Lewis occupied himself in camp by observing the social values, physical appearance and habits of the Shoshone people. If Lewis still doubted his ability "to advance the information of the succeeding generation," his extensive and systematic reporting in this area has put that idea to rest for modern scientists. Ethnographers consider Lewis's observations of the Shoshone among the most complete cultural records written during the entire 19th century. He reviewed the tribe's clothing, weapons, hunting techniques, recipes, treatment of women and the elderly, games and gambling.

Meantime, Clark and 13 members of the expedition, including Sacagawea, the Shoshone Indian woman who, with her husband and baby, had joined the expedition during the winter in present-day North Dakota, proceeded over Lemhi Pass for the first time, leaving Lewis to hide the canoes and catch up.

Once across the divide, Clark conferred with the Shoshone leaders about Western geography. Almost immediately, he decided to field-test one possible route, the one which the Indians said would connect to other rivers and ultimately would lead to the "great water" – the Pacific Ocean. With only an Indian to guide him, Clark set out on Aug. 20 to appraise the situation personally. Clark traveled alongside it for 52 miles. In the end, he noted that the hillsides were "like the Side of a tree Streight up" and he agreed with Sergeant Patrick Gass that, "The water is so rapid and the bed of the river so rocky, that going by water appeared impracticable; and the mountains so amazingly high, steep and rocky, that it seemed impossible to go along the river by land."

Clark named it after his partner, calling it the Lewis River. But the name did not stick, and today that river across Idaho, distinguished by foaming rapids and deep canyons, is known as the Salmon.

AUGUST 25-31, 1805

As Meriwether Lewis crossed Lemhi Pass for his third and final time, on Aug. 25 and 26, he came in close contact with the Shoshone Indians who were assisting him. He observed, among other things, that because the Shoshone "possess an abundance of horses, their women are seldom compelled like those in other parts of the continent to carry burthens on their backs." The women "have their children with equal convenience," he added. "One of the women who had been assisting in the transportation of the baggage halted at a little run about a mile behind us, and sent on the two pack horses which she had been conducting by one of her female friends. I enquired of Cameahwait the cause of her detention, and was informed by him in an unconcerned manner that she had halted to bring fourth a child and would soon overtake us; in about an hour the woman arrived with her newborn babe and passed us on her way to camp apparently as well as she ever was."

William Clark, having earlier crossed to the Shoshone camp on the Lemhi River, spent several days in late August examining the Salmon River. According to the Shoshone leader, Camheahwait, the river would eventually join other rivers that ended at "the great lake where the white men lived," but the passage would be difficult. Clark reconnoitered the Salmon River for several days to see conditions firsthand. In the end, he came to the conclusion that the rapids of the river were too treacherous for travel by canoe and the canyon walls were too steep to follow on shore.

Clark reunited with Lewis at the Shoshone camp on Aug. 28. He did not, however, return empty-handed. Accompanying him was Old Toby, whose services he had secured. Shoshone geographers had earlier indicated to both Lewis and Clark that a second way to get to the great lake was to use the "very bad" road of "the Pierced nosed Indians" across mountains. Swooping Eagle, who the explorers always referred to as Old Toby, knew the road of the Nez Perce through the Bitterroot Mountains and he agreed to assist the explorers as a guide.

Sergeant John Ordway felt hopeful when he learned that Old Toby predicted that in "about 15 days we could go to where the tide came up and Salt water." Private Joseph Whitehouse harbored fears: "the Natives tells us that we cannot find the ocean by going a west course for Some of them who are old men has been on that a Season or more to find the ocean but could not find it, and that their was troublesome tribes of Indians to pass. that they had no horses but would rob and Steal all they could and eat them as they had nothing as it were to eat. the country verry mountaineous and no game."

Twenty-nine horses was "not a Sufficint number for each of our Party to have one, which is our wish," but it was all Meriwether Lewis could barter from the Shoshone. William Clark characterized the herd as "indifferent, maney Sore backs and others not acustomed to pack." Nevertheless, the Corps resumed their westward movement on the afternoon of Aug. 30 after a respite of 19 agreeable days with Sacagawea's people – the Shoshone Indians. They proceeded 12 miles the first day out, and on the last day of the month they picked up the pace enough to cover 22 miles.

SEPTEMBER 1-7, 1805

Having made the decision to continue their journey west by following trails through the mountains, rather than launching canoes on the turbulent Salmon, the expedition departed the village of the Shoshone Indians at the end of August. Their route was in the direction of present-day Salmon, Idaho, and from there they began to ascend, for the second time, the Continental Divide. Ultimately, on Sept. 3, the Corps of Discovery – 31 men, one woman, one baby and a dog – would pull themselves, 29 horses and approximately two tons of equipment over the crest of today's Lost Trail Pass and back into modern Montana.

The murky route used by the expedition might be clearer to historians today if Meriwether Lewis had continued to write in his journal. For reasons unknown, however, he ceased writing a daily record on Aug. 26 and, except for a few short stretches that total 10 days, he would not resume his comments until January 1, 1806. While the route may be slightly in doubt, other journalists on the trip leave no question as to the severity of the trail experience.

Private Joseph Whitehouse probably best reflected the feelings of the enlisted men when he wrote in his journal for Sept. 1 that, "we descended a Mountain nearly as Steep as the roof of a house." The next day the trail hugged a flooded creek, which the men called "dismal Swamp, and it is a lonesom rough part of the Country." Sergeant Patrick Gass considered the journey "fatiguing almost beyond description." One part of the trail was so rocky, lamented Whitehouse, that several of the horses "fell over backward with their loads; and rolled down to the foot of those hills, [and] we were obliged to carry the loads of our horses, on our backs up many of the hills, & then load them again." Snow and sleet started to pelt the men at 3 pm on Sept. 3. After a modest dinner, writes Sergeant John Ordway, "we lay down wet hungry and cold." The temperature dropped to 19 degrees overnight.

In the morning, Lewis and Clark led the men "6 miles on a Direct Course over a high Snow mountain," which may have been Saddle Mountain. If so, it would have taken the expedition above 8,000 feet in elevation. Happily, at the conclusion of that difficult march, Old Toby, their Shoshone guide, recognized a creek and they began their descent into the Bitterroot Valley.

At the bottom of Lost Trail Pass, the expedition entered a Flathead (Oot-la-shoot, or Salish) village of 33 lodges with an estimated 400 people and 500 horses. These Indians had likely never before seen a white man, but they nevertheless welcomed the Corps. Oral history says that a Flathead warrior observed the Corps as they struggled down the mountainside and reported back to the camp that the black face of York, Clark's African American manservant, might be a sign of war, though their casual manner said otherwise. The villagers took a chance and met the visitors in peace, giving them some berries and roots. The tribesmen had no meat to offer because they were, in fact, on their way to join the Shoshone for a buffalo hunt at the Three Forks of the Missouri.

The Salish language of the Indians puzzled the Euro-Americans. Lewis wrote down as many vocabulary words as he could. Ordway detected a lisp, but also a burr-sound rolling off the native tongue. He thought it might be a speech impediment. Or that the village might possibly be the legendary "Welsh Indians," a mythological tribe that supposedly left Wales in 1170 and disappeared into a mysterious, unnamed continent. William Clark knew that popular legend, too, but for his part he thought that if there was a "lost" tribe, it was the Mandans on the Missouri River. Still, he agreed that the Salish speech pattern, which he described as a throaty, gurgling sound, was difficult to understand. As a result, when Clark called a formal council to meet with the Flatheads, he devised a complex translation system that used five interpreters: Clark spoke in English to Francois Labieche, who then relayed it to Toussaint Charbonneau in French. Charbonneau, in turn, communicated the message to his wife, Sacagawea, in Hidatsa, so that she could repeat it in her native language, Shoshone, to a Shoshone boy who was a prisoner of the Flatheads, but fluent in their language.

On Sept. 6, the Flatheads headed south, then east, to hunt buffalo, and the Corps of Discovery rode north up the Bitterroot River Valley. Clark anxiously eyed the mountain range to the west. The Shoshone had earlier informed him that a gap through the mountains would make itself evident. But when? And would Old Toby recognize it in the maze of mountains?

SEPTEMBER 8-14, 1805

Moving north along the Bitterroot River in present-day Montana, the men of the Lewis and Clark Expedition felt uneasy. It wasn't the rain and hail, or even the unpredictable success of the hunters. For a time, there was an unfounded concern that the 11 horses and three colts purchased from the Flathead Indians a few days earlier might bolt from the expedition horse herd during the night and instinctively return to their home. What bothered the Corps of Discovery most was the glistening snow on the mountains to the west of them. If they hoped to place their feet on the shores of the Pacific Ocean, they would ultimately have to cross those white peaks. The Shoshone Indians had told them exactly that nearly a month earlier. Would Old Toby, their Shoshone guide, know the trail to the pass? Presumably. But as creeks turned into salmon-free rivers, Lewis and Clark asked questions about the sources of the watercourses, and most times Old Toby "could not inform us." Hopefully, he would have broader knowledge of the mountains.

On Sept. 9, Clark records that "our guide informes that we should leave the river at this place and the weather appearing settled and fair I determined to halt the next day rest our horses and take some scelestial Observations. we call this Creek Travellers rest." They had reached the present-day junction of U.S. Highways 12 and 93, south of Missoula, and the approach to Khusahna Ishkit, or – as it has subsequently come to be known in history – the Lolo Trail. This passageway had been used by the Nez Perce Indians to cross the Bitterroot Mountains since at least the 1730s.

During the day of rest, while Lewis and Clark calculated longitude and latitude, the crew sewed moccasins and the hunters took to the field. In the evening, one of the hunters, John Colter, returned to camp with three Indians. Clark thought them Flatheads, but their knowledge of the trail across the mountains, and the statement by one of the men that he lived on the "plains below the mountains on the columbia river," encourages most readers of the journals to believe them to be Nez Perce tribesmen. The Indians said they were seeking the recovery of 23 horses stolen by raiders. Two of the Indians departed the camp of the explorers after sunset, but the third volunteered to remain with the Corps as a trail guide.

The passage to Lolo Pass began in the late afternoon of Sept. 11 and accomplished a meager seven miles. The Nez Perce guide "thought proper to leave us" that evening, according to Clark. The Corps made an earlier start on the following morning, but rough terrain extended the day into night as, "Some of our Party did not git up [to camp] until 10 oClock P.M." On the third day out from Traveler's Rest, Lewis and some men delayed to recover stray horses, so Clark's forward unit was the first to reach the Lolo Hot Springs in present-day Missoula County. Clark "found this water nearly boiling hot" and "I put my finger in the water, [and] at first I could not bare it in a Second." That evening camp was made in an extensive meadow on the west side of Lolo Pass, bringing the Corps once again back to modern Idaho.

On Sept. 14, the Corps marched "9 miles over a high mountain steep & almost inaxcessible [with] much falling timber which fatigues our men & horses exceedingly." It need not have been so strenuous. Unfortunately,

Old Toby missed a junction and followed the wrong trail coming off Lolo Pass. Instead of following the main trail going to the ridge of the mountains, he led the expedition down a footpath to a fishing creek at the headwaters of the Lochsa River.

That night, the expedition camped at the present site of the USFS Powell Ranger Station. Sergeant Patrick Gass used a biblical reference to lament that "none of the hunters killed any thing except 2 or 3 pheasants; on which, without a miracle it was impossible to feed 30 hungry men and upwards, besides some Indians." Meantime, Lewis passed out some portable soup to the men, an unappealing concoction of flour, cornmeal, sugar, coffee, dried apples and lard of which he had purchased 193 pounds for $289.50 in Philadelphia just for emergencies such as this. Gass asserts that "Some of the men did not relish this soup, and agreed to kill a colt; which they immediately did, and set about roasting it; and which appeared to me to be good eating." Clark named the adjacent watercourse Killed Colt Creek on his map.

After dinner, Sergeant John Ordway took refuge in his tent from the thunder, hail and rain. Even so, he could still see fearsome "high Mountains covered with Snow and timber." Soon Lewis and Clark would come to understand that they had strayed from the traditional trail and that it would be necessary for them to climb from the river to the ridge of those mountains just to regain it.

SEPTEMBER 15-21, 1805

Old Toby, the Shoshone elder recruited by Meriwether Lewis and William Clark to serve as their guide across the mountain passes of the Continental Divide, proved to be exceptionally trustworthy. During the two weeks it took the Corps of Discovery to cross Lost Trail Pass and proceed down the Bitterroot River Valley, he demonstrated near total recall of the trail. But then Old Toby made two mistakes.

The first misreading of the trail, on Sept. 13, forced the party to move three miles out of their way before they recovered. The second error, on Sept. 14, had greater ramifications. After crossing Lolo Pass (elevation 5,233 feet), Old Toby missed a fork in the road and led the expedition downhill to the headwaters of today's boulder-strewn Lochsa River. They should have kept to the main trail that straddled the ridges above the river.

It took only four tough miles of travel on Sept. 15 for William Clark to recognize the mistake. Fortunately the explorers located a seldom-used Indian trail that zigzagged its way back to the ridge above them. The narrow, ill-defined trail showed few marks of traffic and for good reason. It consisted of approximately 10 miles of "high Steep ruged Mountain winding in every direction" as it rose about 3,500 feet in elevation. Two horses gave out after they "Sliped and roled down Steep hills which hurt them verry much." When the men made camp that evening, they had triumphantly returned to the main trail. But they also slept amid patches of snow.

Proceeding along the Lolo Trail tested the mettle of the Lewis and Clark Expedition as never before. The road kept to the ridge that separates the Lochsa drainage from that of the North Fork Clearwater. At an elevation approaching 7,000 feet, snow accumulated to 10 inches, simultaneously obscuring the trail, tiring the packhorses, chasing away deer and elk, and freezing the hands and feet of the men. Clark admitted, "I have been wet and as cold in every part as I ever was in my life, indeed I was at one time fearfull my feet would freeze in the thin mockersons which I wore."

Several years after the event, Clark remembered that, "The want of provisions together with the dificuely of passing those emence mountains dampened the Spirits of the party." In an attempt to uplift the mood of the Corps, he split the party on Sept. 18, taking with him six hunters whose objective was to bag game and leave it for the slower main party. That afternoon, Clark climbed to a ridge and could see salvation in the distance. The next day, Lewis saw it, too: "when the ridge terminated and we to our inexpressable joy discovered a large tract of Prairie country lying to the S.W." He added, "this plain appeared to be about 60 Miles distant, but our guide assured us that we should reach it's borders tomorrow. the appearance of this country, our only hope for subsistance greatly revived the sperits of the party already reduced and much weakened for the want of food." Gass spoke for the enlisted men when he wrote in his journal, "there was much joy and rejoicing among the corps, as happens among passengers at sea, who have experienced a dangerous and protracted voyage, when they first discover land on the long looked for coast."

On Sept. 20, Clark's cadre broke out of the mountains and entered

Weippe Prairie. Three miles into this "leavel rich open Plain" he encountered members of the NeMeePoo or Nez Perce Tribe. His arrival, he said, "raised great Confusion" among a people who may have heard rumors about Euro-Americans, but had not yet been visited by one. "Those people treated us well," writes Clark, and they gave the men buffalo meat along with "roots, dried roots made in bread, roots boiled, one Sammon, Berries of red haws some dried." He found it all "tolerably good" until he became "verry unwell all the evening from eateing the fish & roots too freely." The next afternoon, his hosts led Clark into the gorge of the Clearwater River to meet Chief Twisted Hair. At the end of the strenuous journey, Clark confided to his journal: "I am verry Sick to day and puke which relive me."

Lewis and the lagging main party, meantime, still struggled in the mountains on Sept. 20 and 21. One evening, they "dined sumptiously" on food left for them by Clark's hunters. The next night, they scrounged together a meal made from a few pheasants and a coyote, "which together with the ballance of our horse beef and some crawfish… make one more hearty meal, not knowing where the next was to be found."

SEPTEMBER 22-28, 1805

On Sept. 22, Meriwether Lewis and the bulk of the Corps of Discovery walked off the Lolo Trail and into the same Nez Perce camp of 18 lodges on Weippe Prairie that had given food and shelter to William Clark and his six hunters just two days earlier. Lewis, who had all but stopped writing in his journal some weeks before, celebrated the moment: "the pleasure I now felt in having tryumphed over the rocky Mountains and decending once more to a level and fertile country where there was every rational hope of finding a comfortable subsistence for myself and party can be more readily conceived than expressed." But when William Clark encountered his reassembled exploring party, he was shocked that "our party weacke and much reduced in flesh as well as Strength." Clark cautioned the men about "the Consequences of eateing too much &c."

But his warning came too late. The men of the Corps of Discovery, whose normal daily diet consisted almost exclusively of red meat, had already eaten heartily at the Nez Perce buffet of berries, roots and salmon. Clark saw Lewis become so weak that he was "Scercely able to ride on a jentle horse" and "Several men so unwell that they were Compelled to lie on the Side of the road for Some time." Clark rummaged through the expedition medicine chest, but no pills, salts or tonic brought from Philadelphia could relieve the men's distress. Private Joseph Whitehouse lamented that, "Several of the men Sick with the Relax, caused by a suddin change of diet and water as well as the climate." Even a week later Clark lamented that, "Our men nearly all Complaining of ther bowels, a heaviness at the Stomack & Lax."

In spite of the illness in camp, there was work to be done. First on Clark's to-do list was convening a cartography conference with the Nez Perce. There being no interpreter when he interviewed Twisted Hair, "we were Compelled to converse alltogether by Signs." Drawing on a white elk skin with charcoal, Twisted Hair traced the westward flow of the Clearwater River, conveying as best he could the "Situation of Indians" ahead and noting two major tributaries. He recorded the distances as "2 Sleeps" and "5 Sleeps" beyond.

Next there was the matter of constructing canoes. While on the Lolo Trail, Lewis saw trees that he estimated to be "large enough to form eligant perogues [dugout canoes] of at least 45 feet in length." Clark had no intention of returning to the mountains for suitable trees, so, taking Twisted Hair and his two sons with him, he scouted along the Clearwater River in a hunt for "trees Calculated to build Canoes." He found his so-called Canoe Camp opposite the mouth of the North Fork of the Clearwater, not far from today's Orofino, Idaho. The site held several large, straight ponderosa pine trees, each with a minimum of knots. Best of all, they could be felled in close proximity to the river and, upon completion as dugouts, could easily be shoved into the water. Beginning Sept. 27, "all the men able to work comenced building 5 Canoes, Several taken Sick at work."

Shaping dugout canoes – essentially hollowed-out logs – with an adz and ax is labor-intensive, a fact Clark had learned earlier in the spring. At both Fort Mandan and the Great Falls of the Missouri River, members of the expedition built a total of eight dugout canoes. From this experience, Clark knew that "our axes are Small & badly Calculated to build Canoes of the large Pine." Happily, Nez Perce leaders offered good advice to the carpenters of the Corps. Instead of chopping deep into the log with axes, Twisted Hair urged the explorers to flatten the topside of the tree and then blanket it with hot coals. When the wood charred sufficiently, it could be easily chipped out. The recommended process took more time but less work – an important consideration when many of the explorers felt ill. Clark wisely followed the instructions of his Nez Perce mentor, and work on the canoes began in earnest.

SEPTEMBER 29-OCTOBER 5, 1805

"Men Sick as usial, all The men that are able to at work, at the Canoes." Clark's summary of conditions at Canoe Camp on Sept. 29 may be awkwardly phrased, but it is, nevertheless, an accurate statement. Ever since their arrival at the Nez Perce camps on Sept. 20 and 22, a majority of the members of the Corps of Discovery – Clark estimated three-fourths – suffered distress in the bowels and stomach. Perhaps it was the change in diet from red meat to roots and salmon. Perhaps it was the adjustment from rarefied mountain air to the heat of the Clearwater River bottom. Perhaps it was just sheer exhaustion from the Lolo Trail experience. No matter what the cause, the result was that the duty roster of available hands to form five dugout canoes varied from day to day.

The first two canoes were finished and launched on Oct. 5. It would have been helpful if the carpenters could have tested the balance of the log by floating it in the Clearwater River before they began the work of shaping it, but that does not seem to have been the case. Luck, however, favored the Corps, and Clark approved the finished products, in spite of the fact that "one proved a little leakey."

With the canoes coming along, it was time to make provisions for the expedition horses. Lewis and Clark planned to retrace their steps back to St. Louis from the Pacific Ocean in the spring of 1806, so they would need horses again for the eastward journey across the Lolo Trail. On the same day as the first canoes were completed, they began collecting the 38 horses belonging to the Corps of Discovery. For purposes of future identification each animal had its mane cropped before it received a brand on the near fore shoulder: "U.S. Capt. M. Lewis." (The branding iron was found near The Dalles in the early 1890s and today is a proud possession of the Oregon Historical Society in Portland.) With those tasks completed, Clark delivered the horses to two brothers and one son of Chief Twisted Hair and "to each of those men I gave a Knife & Some Small articles &c." Clark received their promise "to be attentive to our horses untill we Should return."

With the canoes and the horses provided for, the evening of Oct. 5 should have given the captains of the expedition a feeling of satisfaction. Unfortunately, it was not so. "Nothing to eate except dried fish & roots," moaned Clark, inasmuch as of late "our hunters with every diligence Could kill nothing." As a result, "Capt. Lewis & myself eate a Supper of roots boiled, which Swelled us in Such a manner that we were Scercely able to breath for Several hours." They would have, naturally, preferred venison, but "the hills high and ruged and woods too dry to hunt the deer which is the only game in our neighbourhood." Several days earlier, when the hunters returned with just a small coyote, the enlisted men butchered a horse "and we eat the meat as earnest as though it had been the best meat in the world," proclaimed Sergeant John Ordway. On another evening, Ordway reports that some of the party purchased a fat dog for supper. In future months, it has been estimated, the expedition would purchase approximately 250 dogs as a food source.

During all of these work assignments, the Nez Perce tribesmen proved to be excellent partners with the Corps of Discovery. Lewis and Clark referred to them as Chopunnish, which they understood to be the tribal word for "Pierced Noses." Later, French-Canadian fur traders translated the "Pierced Noses" into Nez Perce. The villages of the nation – probably the most numerous and powerful of all Pacific Northwest tribes at this time – followed a seasonal cycle in their search across the present-day states of Washington, Oregon and Idaho for roots, wild vegetables, berries, salmon and big game. Except for the single instance when Clark "displeased an Indian by refuseing to let him have a pice of Tobacco," relations between the two cultures were cordial.

Clark anticipated that the remaining three canoes would be completed very soon. Next on the agenda would be to bury the packsaddles, plus whatever supplies were being left behind. Then there was the delicate matter of asking for Nez Perce guides. On Sept. 21, Clark made his first inquiries about the route to the west – and at that time, an Indian told him about a "falls below which the white men lived from whome they got white beeds cloth &c. &c." That information had simmered within Clark for more than two weeks. He greatly desired to have a Nez Perce show him the way.

OCTOBER 6-12, 1805

As William Clark had hoped, the five dugout canoes constructed by his men near present-day Orofino, Idaho, entered the Clearwater River on the evening of Oct. 6. In the morning, the canoes were loaded and launched.

Thus far in their expedition – going on 18 months at this point – the Corps of Discovery had not paddled with the current of a river. Previously they had to push, pull or pole against the current. Now the Clearwater current caught the canoes and forced them into 10 "danjerous" rapids. Fortunately, Clark reported only one accident: "the Canoe in which I was Struck a rock and Sprung a leak in the 3rd rapid." That night, Clark ordered the canoes unloaded, examined and mended with pine resin. And well he should have, for on Oct. 8, the Clearwater challenged the explorers with 15 more rapids. Again, only one "axident": "one canoe in which Serjt. Gass was Stearing and was nearle turning over, She Sprung a leak or Split open on one Side and [the] Bottom filled with water & Sunk on the rapid, the men, Several of which Could not Swim hung on to the Canoe." Clark unloaded the other canoes and, with the assistance of Indians, got the men and equipment out of their "doleful Situation."

The event alarmed the men, but that afternoon an unexpected silver lining presented itself. When the Corps had departed their canoe camp, they looked for but could not make contact with Twisted Hair and Tetoharsky, the Nez Perce men who had promised to accompany the expedition down river. When it became necessary, on Oct. 8, to expose their wet equipment to the sun, Clark visited an Indian camp and located Twisted Hair and Tetoharsky. "We took them on board," Clark explained, "after the Serimony of Smokeing."

Almost as if on cue, the following day Old Toby and his son, the reliable Shoshone guides who had traveled with the Lewis and Clark Expedition since late in August, "left us without our knowledge." Lewis and Clark were disappointed that their companions had not seen fit to allow a proper farewell. The captains urged Twisted Hair to send a horseman after Old Toby and bring him back to receive his pay and some presents, but the chief declined, explaining frankly that the Nez Perce "would take his things from him before he passed their camps."

It took a full day to dry the expedition equipment, after which the Corps resumed their westward journey on Oct. 10. About 5 pm, as the canoeists approached their 60th mile on the Clearwater, a large southerly fork about 250 yards wide came into view. They Corps had found the spot where the Clearwater joins the Snake River, at present-day Lewiston, Idaho. The Snake is a twisting stream of more than one thousand miles with scores of tributaries.

The first camp of the Lewis and Clark Expedition in present Washington state was located about a mile from the confluence of the Clearwater and Snake rivers. Clark sensed that he had just entered the influences of a new geographic region, so that evening he penned a complimentary essay in his journal about the character, appearance and amusements of the Nez Perce Tribe. His thoughts were interrupted when a rare disagreement among the men broke out between Toussaint Charbonneau, the interpreter, and the brothers Joseph and Reuben Fields. Possibly the rift had to do with a jest about the "diet extremely bad haveing nothing but roots and dried fish to eate."

The hungriest of the men had to wait until the next day to fill their stomachs. Six miles down the Snake River, the expedition stopped at a village "and took brackfast, we purchased all the fish we could and Seven dogs." Fifteen miles farther, they stopped again, this time trading for roots, five dogs and dried fish. Otherwise everyone's attention remained focused on the turbulent river. In 30 miles on Oct. 11, the canoes ran nine rapids. On Oct. 12, the explorers duplicated that feat in similarly swift water.

OCTOBER 13-19, 1805

The unrestricted Snake River flowed with such velocity through present-day Washington state that by Oct. 14, Sergeant John Ordway, the third in command of the Corps of Discovery, wished he could portage the canoes around the worst rapids. Especially after "the canoe I had charge of ran fast on a rock in the middle of the river... we attempeted to git hir off but the waves dashed over hir So that She filled with water. we held hir untill one of the other canoes was unloaded and came to our assistance... She went off of a sudden & left myself and three more standing on the rock half leg deep in the rapid water. untill a canoe came to our assistance."

But Meriwether Lewis and William Clark decided against portages because the autumn was already "So far advanced and time precious with us." In a race against winter, the Corps of Discovery needed to quickly connect with the Columbia River and after that continue on to the Pacific Ocean.

Sergeant Patrick Gass thought the rapids brought an element of beauty to the landscape, "by interposing variety and scenes of romantick grandeur where there is so much uniformity in the appearance of the country." The country, he explained, "on both sides is high dry prairie plains without a stick of timber." Gass qualified his comment by adding: "This river in general is very handsome, except at the rapids, where it is risking both life and property to pass."

When the Nez Perce guides indicated to Lewis and Clark that the Snake would soon merge with an even greater river, the captains urged Twisted Hair and Tetoharsky to move ahead and announce their approach to any villagers. As a result, on Oct. 16 several Indians intercepted the expedition, arriving in "great haste" from a "Point" just ahead. The captains smoked with the Indians and gave them presents to take back to the "Point" as a sort of peace offering. The Indians then "Set out in a run & continued to go as fast as They Could run as far as we Could See them." The men of the expedition hurried behind them as far as "the big forks," which today we know as Sacagawea State Park in Pasco, Washington – the spot where the Snake River enters the Columbia River.

Native Americans and Euro-Americans celebrated together that evening. The Corps of Discovery marveled at their own accomplishment of having reached the Columbia River after 195 days on a trail from their winter encampment at Fort Mandan, around the Great Falls of the Missouri, over three mountain passes, and now surviving a wild canoe ride of half a hundred rapids on the Clearwater and Snake rivers. The Indians exhibited their joy at being hosts by forming a half-circle around the visitors, "Singing and beeting on their drum Stick and keeping time to the music."

President Thomas Jefferson had specifically requested that Lewis collect information about the Columbia River. Therefore, on Oct. 17-18, Lewis and Clark took elaborate longitude and latitude readings, they estimated the width of the rivers ("Distance across the Columbia 960 3/4 yds water, Distance across the Ki-moo-e-nim [Snake] 575 yds water"), and commented in their journals on the language and customs of several Indian nations. Clark also made a brief side trip up the Columbia, proceeding to a viewpoint of the Yakima River.

The Columbia, Lewis and Clark found, was "Crouded with Salmon," and so clear that a fish "may be Seen at the deabth of 15 or 20 feet" with "great numbers of Salmon dead on the Shores, floating on the water and in the Bottoms." Clark estimated he "must have seen 3 or 400 dead and maney living." Neither Lewis nor Clark understood that Pacific salmon are anadromous, meaning they are born in freshwater streams, stay in their upriver habitat for several months, then migrate to the ocean in the spring where they spend most of their adult life before returning to fresh water to spawn and die.

Late in the afternoon of Oct. 18, the expedition resumed travel, this time on the Columbia River. Every man in the expedition knew the Pacific Ocean lay in front of him, to the west. But how far away was it? The men got their first hint later that day. From a height of land, Clark viewed in the distance a snow-covered mountain. The next day he saw another far-off mountain, which he ventured might be Mount St. Helens. Clark knew that William Broughton of the British navy had named Mount Hood and Mount St. Helens in 1792 from a turnaround point in the Columbia about 125 miles upstream from the Pacific Ocean. Clark surmised that if he could see what Broughton had named, then the Pacific Ocean was not far away. (The reality is that Clark viewed Mount Hood on one day and Mount Adams on the other.)

OCTOBER 20-26, 1805

The Corps of Discovery seldom lacked for company during their journey down the Columbia River. As they awoke on the morning of Oct. 20, for example, approximately 200 Umatilla Indians greeted the explorers at their camp near modern Boardman, Oregon. The previous morning, something similar had taken place 36 miles upstream with Walla Walla tribesmen. These experiences made William Clark appreciate another attribute of Sacagawea, the Indian woman who, with her husband and baby, traveled with the Corps of Discovery as an interpreter. Her presence demonstrated to people, he said, "our friendly intentions, as no woman ever accompanies a war party of Indians in this quarter."

Private Joseph Collins, meantime, demonstrated to Clark an additional skill when, on Oct. 21, he concocted a brew that Clark considered "excellent beer." Collins simply used old bread he had acquired at the Nez Perce camps nearly a month earlier. The bread was prepared from camas, an edible, starchy bulb that flourishes in Pacific

Northwest meadows during the spring and summer. For more than two weeks it had been "frequently wet molded & Sowered &c." But it could still produce a satisfying liquid after being squeezed and filtered through mosquito netting. Clark was so impressed he even noted the location on his map.

After approximately 120 miles of swift but manageable water on the Columbia, the Corps of Discovery entered a stretch of river crowded with major obstacles to navigation. Just downstream from present-day Wishram, Washington, the canoes of the Corps of Discovery halted before the first of the obstructions, Wyam, or Celilo Falls. Lewis and Clark had missed the fall salmon run on the river, an event that made this location a magnet for several thousand people from a variety of regional tribes, so they never fully realized its significance until their return journey in 1806. What they did comprehend immediately was the danger and labor that would be required to pass across the falls.

The carrying of goods around the falls commenced on Oct. 22, with the heaviest articles being carried on Indian horses – except for the canoes, which were too bulky. After two men of the expedition located the spot used by the Indians to take their canoes through several narrow channels, so too did the Corps of Discovery beginning the next morning. Sergeant Patrick Gass described the scene: "for three miles down, the river is so confined by rocks (being not more than 70 yards wide) that it cannot discharge the water, as fast as it comes over the falls, until what is deficient in breadth is made up in depth. About the great pitch the appearance of the place is terrifying, with vast rocks, and the river below the pitch, foaming through different channels." Nevertheless, by 3 pm all the canoes had made it safely through the turbulent waters and were safe in camp. The maneuverability of the expedition canoes concerned Lewis, so that evening he exchanged the expedition's smallest canoe for a native one in consideration of a "Hatchet & few trinkets." He believed the canoe to be "neeter made than any I have ever Seen and Calculated to ride the waves, and carry emence burthens."

Just three miles beyond Celilo Falls, an obstruction later named the Short Narrows of The Dalles halted the progress of the Lewis and Clark Expedition again. Clark estimated the width of the channel at 45 yards. Two others in the party thought it closer to 20 yards wide. After a quarter-mile, it widened to 200 yards. Portage was impossible.

"I deturmined to pass through this place notwithstanding the horrid appearance of this agitated gut swelling, boiling & whorling in every direction," proclaimed Clark. When the men of the expedition got through successfully, despite the raging waters, Clark sheepishly added an aside to his journal entry: "from the top of the rock [it] did not appear as bad as when I was in it … we passed Safe to the astonishment of all the Inds."

The next day, the Corps confronted yet a third barrier in the Columbia: the Long Narrows of The Dalles. But by now the men of the expedition had a routine for passing such dangerous places, so except for one canoe that nearly filled with water when it was being lined through by elkskin ropes, there was no damage. Clark "felt my Self extreamly gratified and pleased."

But also sad, because a day earlier Twisted Hair and Tetoharsky, the Nez Perce guides, asked permission of Lewis and Clark to return to their homelands, saying they could be of no further service. They knew nothing of the river below Celilo Falls and, besides, "the nation below had expressed hostile intentions… perticularly as They had been at war with each other." The captains requested that the two Nez Perce stay with them through the Narrows, which they did. Then Twisted Hair and Tetoharsky purchased horses, turned them to the east, and began their journey home.

OCTOBER 27-NOVEMBER 2, 1805

From Oct. 22-26, navigating the Columbia River had been exceedingly difficult for the members of the Lewis and Clark Expedition. Three major obstructions in the river – Celilo Falls, the Short Narrows and the Long Narrows – tested the resolve of the party. Happily, a job well done earned everyone a day of rest on Oct. 27. Hunters filled the larder with four deer, a grouse and a squirrel. Meriwether Lewis jotted down some vocabulary words uttered by Indians. William Clark, meantime, inquired as to why "all the Bands flatten the heads of the female Children, and maney of the male children also."

Clark had first noticed the Indian practice of head-flattening on Oct. 17 when the expedition spent two days at the confluence of the Snake and Columbia rivers. The desire, it seemed to him, was to compress the head "so as to form a Streight line from the nose to the Crown of the head." Eleven days later, while at rest, Sergeant Patrick Gass laid the groundwork for several decades of historical confusion when he wrote in his journal, "We suppose them to be a band of the Flathead nation, as all their heads are compressed into the same form." He explained that, "This singular and deforming operation is performed in infancy in the following manner. A piece of board is placed against the back of the head extending from the shoulders some distance above it; another shorter piece extends from the eye brows to the top of the first, and they are then bound together with thongs or cords made of skins, so as to press back the forehead, make the head rise at the top, and force it out above the ears."

Gass meant that the natives he observed near present-day The Dalles practiced skull shaping. Clearly, by his description, Gass is describing a head that is flat on the backside. He was not saying that the Indians he observed were members of the Flathead Tribe, a Salish-speaking group in Montana that Lewis and Clark had met during the first week of September. The Flathead Tribe of Montana denies that their ancestors flattened their heads and they suggest the origin of the name relates to sign language where they are identified by pressing both sides of the head with the flat of the hands. Their heads are flat on top, not reshaped to form a crown. Gass published his journal in 1807, a year after the return of the expedition to St. Louis and seven years before the journals of Lewis and Clark reached print, so his comment was misinterpreted for many years. Clark maintained his interest in the practice for several more days, noting that, "This amongst those people is considered as a great mark of buty." On Nov. 1, he even made a drawing of the process.

That same day, the expedition passed through the river's fourth, and final, natural obstruction, the "Great Shute," or the Cascades of the Columbia. The men managed the feat by laboriously walking the "baggage over the Portage of 940 yards, after which we got the 4 large Canoes over by Slipping them over the rocks on poles placed across from one rock to another." At the end of the Cascades stood "a remarkable high detached rock... about 800 feet high and 400 paces around," a conspicuous landmark protected today in Beacon Rock State Park near Skamania, Washington.

Now on the western side of the Cascade Mountains, the environment of the Columbia River influenced the Lewis and Clark Expedition in new ways. For example, the Cascades form a climatic barrier wherein the temperature moderates and rainfall increases. The annual average rainfall at The Dalles is 12 inches; at the Cascades of the Columbia, it exceeds 70 inches annually. Consequently, forests grow tall and close, and wild creatures find protection and multiply. Additionally, Clark spotted a harbor seal – he thought it a sea otter and tried to shoot it – which seemed to support his belief that since he could not see any more rapids for a long distance, the now calm river "had everry appearance of being effected by the tide." It is true. While the tide of the Pacific Ocean flows only 20 miles into the estuary of the Columbia River, the effects of tidewater can be felt at Beacon Rock, which is 140 miles deep into the river.

Even as the environment had changed, so too did the attitude of the Indians. For some time Lewis and Clark had noticed machine-made clothing and industrial-quality pots at the Indian villages, an indication that they had entered the trade zone of "Boston men" who frequented the mouth of the Columbia River. Lewis and Clark continued to trade with the Indians for nuts, berries, dried fish, dogs, baskets and rain hats, but suddenly the natives "are high with what they have to Sell, and Say the white people below Give them great Prices for what they Sell to them."

NOVEMBER 3-9, 1805

The behavior of the Columbia River changed abruptly at Beacon Rock. In disbelief, Meriwether Lewis and William Clark watched the river on which they had logged 183 turbulent miles suddenly turn docile. Clark recognized that the Corps of Discovery now floated on Pacific Ocean tidewater. "The River got more Smooth, the current gentle wide and Strait," is the way Sergeant John Ordway described the change. Presumably the river's modification foretold the nearness of the Pacific Ocean. That idea gained support on Nov. 3, when, according to Private Joseph Whitehouse, "towards evening we met Several Indians in a canoe who were going up the River. they Signed to us that in two Sleeps we Should See the Ocean vessels and white people &c. &c."

Each succeeding day brought additional evidence to the Corps of Discovery that the Pacific Ocean lay just ahead. They saw Indians dressed in sailor's jackets, overalls or blue and scarlet manufactured blankets. Some carried muskets and used tin flasks to hold their powder. At least one native could curse in English. Most of the Indians seemed unafraid of the Euro-

Americans, not assigning to their visitors any special status, as had the more remote tribes of the Rocky Mountains. In fact, on Nov. 4, while taking a meal, Clark found the Indians "assumeing and disagreeable," especially after "those fellows Stold my pipe Tomahawk." While searching in vain for the pipe tomahawk – one of two dozen trade items with a hollow stem and a pipe bowl attached to the back of a tomahawk blade – Clark discovered that the Indians had also secreted an expedition member's coat under the root of a tree. It was with a sense of relief, then, that Clark looked around his camp the next evening and noticed that, "This is the first night which we have been entirely clear of Indians since our arrival on the waters of the Columbia River." A further comment by Clark may explain why: "we are all wet Cold and disagreeable … I saw 17 Snakes today."

Islands hampered easy passage on the river and, at times, blocked views of the shore. Thus, the Corps of Discovery missed seeing the Willamette River, a major tributary of the Columbia, because they were on the wrong side of Sauvie Island, which is 15 miles long and four miles wide. (They would "discover" the river on their return journey in 1806.) Clark found the Columbia "So Cut with Islands" on Nov. 7 that he hired "an Indian to pilot us into the main chanel [after] one of our Canoes Seperated from us this morning in the fog."

That evening, after 34 miles on the water, the fog lifted and Clark proudly wrote in his journal: "Great joy in camp we are in View of the Ocian, this great Pacific Octean which we been So long anxious to See. and the roreing or noise made by the waves brakeing on the rockey Shores (as I Suppose) May be heard disticly."

The expedition was, at this point, approximately 28 miles from the breaking surf of the Pacific Ocean. Leaning into their paddles the next morning, the men of the Corps of Discovery forced their dugout canoes toward the ocean against both tide and wind. But the Columbia is eight miles wide at Grays Bay, and the river's ocean-like swells soon overwhelmed the explorers. Several in the party became sea sick. "We thought it imprudent to proceed," writes Clark. The refuge Clark chose on the beach, however, proved to be untenable, "in as much, as we have not leavel land Sufficient for an encampment and for our baggage to lie Cleare of the tide, the High hills jutting in So Close and Steep that we cannot retreat back, and the water of the river too Salt to be used, added to this the waves are increasing to Such a hight that we cannot move from this place, in this Situation we are compelled to form our camp between the hite of the Ebb and flood tides, and rase our baggage on logs."

As anxious as the members of the party were to abandon that spot, the Corps of Discovery had no choice but to hunker down on Nov. 9 and stay put. A bad situation got worse at 2 pm when rain, driven sideways by wind, pounded the camp, and the floodtide pushed driftwood ashore. It was only "with every exertion and the Strictest attention by every individual of the party [that it] was Scercely Sufficient to Save our Canoes from being crushed by those monsterous trees maney of them nearly 200 feet long and from 4 to 7 feet through," reports Clark. In spite of everything, Clark believed that the members of his command remained "chearful and anxious to See further into the Ocian."

NOVEMBER 10-16, 1805

Tempestuous weather at the mouth of the Columbia River marooned the Lewis and Clark Expedition in a makeshift camp for two days in November of 1805. Fortunately, on Nov. 10, the wind and waves subsided, so the expedition members loaded their canoes and resumed their interrupted journey. By hugging the Washington shore, paddling from cove to cove, the Corps of Discovery managed to log 10 miles in salty water.

A morning of progress energized the expedition members, but every mile they advanced put them that much closer to the pounding ocean surf with its unrelenting rhythm of rising and falling. When the waves increased in size and strength beyond the point of prudence, Meriwether Lewis and William Clark called a retreat and the canoes made an about turn. Two miles later, they took refuge in a small indentation in the coastline. "Here we scarcely had room to lie between the rocks and water," complained Sergeant Patrick Gass, "but we made shift to do it among some drift wood that had been beat up by the tide." After a delay of only a few hours, the expedition launched their five canoes again, but for the second time that day, they had to retreat, this time to a "small holler." The rain continued for the seventh consecutive day.

River swells kept the Corps of Discovery in camp on Nov. 11. An exasperated Clark lamented, "we are truly unfortunate to be compelled to be 4 days nearly in the same place at a time that our days are precious to us." Perhaps hunters could look for game in the forest. Alas, they returned to say that the hills were "So high & Steep, & thick with undergrowth and fallen Timber" that foot travel was as impossible as canoe travel. That afternoon, "at a time when the wind was verry high and waves tremendous five Indians Came down in a Canoe loaded with fish." The natives sold salmon and roots, and then they departed. Their route, writes Clark, took them straight across the river, "which is about 5 miles wide through the highest Sees I ever Saw a Small vestle ride." It is certain, he added in admiration, "they are the best canoe navigators I ever Saw."

Unable to move again the next day, Clark assessed the condition of the men, their rotting clothes, the lack of food and the frightening thunder and lightening. "Our Situation is dangerous," he concluded. At least by the end of the day, the members of the expedition were able to move their camp around a point of land to a more sheltered location. They proceeded on foot and left the canoes behind.

Isolated for a second and third day in what Sergeant John Ordway called a "disagreeable harbour," the Corps of Discovery eventually pulled their canoes to camp. That modest accomplishment, however, was offset by the expedition's third and fourth failed attempts to pass around "Point Distress," a protrusion in the shoreline that had stymied the expedition since Nov. 10. Today it is known as Point Ellice, the location where the 4.1-mile Astoria-to-Megler Bridge anchors itself to the Washington shore. On the evening of Nov. 14, the Corps of Discovery occupied three separate camps on the Columbia shoreline.

"About 3 oClock" on Nov. 15, "the wind luled, and the river became calm, I had the canoes loaded in great haste and Set Out, from this dismal nitch... proceeded on passed the blustering point." Miraculously, a "butifull Sand beech" stretched out before Clark's men, and beyond that lay a commanding view of the Pacific Ocean. Goal accomplished. Destination reached. The sounds of the ocean that evening soothed the party to sleep.

In the light of morning on Nov. 16, the enlisted men of the Lewis and Clark Expedition understood what their captains had recognized the day prior. "We are now in plain view of the Pacific Ocean, the waves rolling, & the surf roaring very loud," marveled Private Joseph Whitehouse. Gass sounded even more excited: "We are now at the end of our voyage, which has been completely accomplished."

Some historians have decreed that Lewis and Clark's most severe challenge on their 8,000-mile journey had taken place two months before, on the Lolo Trail in the Bitterroot Mountains in September. Most historians in Washington state, however, take a different view, citing journal passages written during mid-November of 1805.

NOVEMBER 17-23, 1805

Between Nov. 8 and 15, Meriwether Lewis and William Clark measured their forward progress along the estuary of the Columbia River not by miles but by sheer effort. Eight days of struggle against the elements – a river current that clashed with tidewater amid wind-driven rain – yielded the Corps of Discovery a net advance of only 13 miles. But it was enough distance to take them across Point Ellice, their final obstacle. On a sandy beach in Washington, roughly 15 miles from Pacific Ocean breakers, and in clear sight of landmarks at the mouth of the Columbia River, Lewis and Clark congratulated themselves for having reached the goal set for them by President Thomas Jefferson.

Lewis and Clark felt compelled to verify their accomplishment. To that end, Clark busied himself with a sextant, taking astronomical calculations and drawing a preliminary map. The sergeants saw to the task of establishing, and securing, a camp that would be the home of the expedition for, as it turned out, the next 10 days. Clark ultimately named the place "Station Camp," and so it is known today in the Lewis and Clark National Historic Park. On Nov. 17, Clark "Sent out 6 men to kill deer & fowls." He also received a one-eyed chief of the Chinooks – a tribe Clark estimated to be "about 400 Souls" – who came to pay an official visit to the newcomers. Later, when Meriwether Lewis returned from a reconnaissance to Cape Disappointment, a mariner's landmark from the 1780s whose name reflects the frustration of attempting to pilot a ship across the bar of the Columbia River, Clark volunteered to take "all the men who wished to See more of the Ocean to Get ready to Set out with me on tomorrow day light." Eleven men turned out, including York, Clark's manservant.

While William Clark is best known in history for his accomplishments as a cartographer, during this three-day journey he revealed an equally strong intellectual attraction to natural history. He noted, for example, the backbone of a beached whale, probably a gray whale since scientists tell us that approximately 800 of those marine mammals die on Pacific beaches each year. Clark also described "a Curious flat fish Shaped like a turtle" and sketched it in such a realistic fashion that today ichthyologists recognize it as a starry flounder. When one of the men downed a "Buzzard," Clark penned such a competent description of the bird that ornithologists agree that Clark examined a California condor. And before Clark's mini-expedition returned to Station Camp, he took the time to inspect a deer brought in by one of the hunters. The deer of the Pacific Coast, he concluded, "differ materially from our Common deer in [as] much as they are much darker deeper bodied Shorter ledged [with] horns equally branched from the beem the top of the tail black to the end [and] Eyes larger and do not lope but jump." An awkward description, yes, but still accurate enough to enlighten scholars who subsequently named the Columbian black-tailed deer a subspecies heretofore unknown to science. Clark's only academic misstep was an inexact description of a 10-foot-long dead sturgeon.

The most poignant episode to take place at Station Camp involved Sacagawea, the young Indian woman who joined the expedition at Fort Mandan in the spring of 1805 with her husband and 55-day old son. Sacagawea was, in all respects, a valuable and uncomplaining auxiliary member of the otherwise all-male Corps of Discovery. One afternoon – the date is either Nov. 20, 22 or 23 because, oddly, four expedition journalists who reported the event cannot agree when it took place – some Chinooks visited Station Camp and Meriwether Lewis took a strong liking to an Indian robe made from sea otter skins. Lewis offered a blanket, even a coat, in exchange, but the Chinook man held out for blue beads, of which Lewis, unfortunately, had none. Lewis had purchased nearly 50 pounds of multicolored trade beads in Philadelphia, but he had no way of knowing at the time that the Indians would exhaust his supply of prized blue beads first. Clark joined the negotiations when he judged the robe "more butifull than any fur I had ever Seen." He upped the ante to two blankets, but the owner said he would not take even five. Finally, according to Clark, "we at length precured it for a belt of blue beeds which the Squar – wife of our interpreter Shabono wore around her waste." Did the captains ask Sacagawea for her belt or did they order it taken off? Did she volunteer for the good of the expedition? No one says.

All we know is that on another day Clark reports, "we gave the Squar a Coate of Blue Cloth for the belt of Blue Beeds we gave for the Sea otter Skins."

NOVEMBER 24-30, 1805

On the tenth day of their stay at Station Camp on the north shore of the Columbia River, Meriwether Lewis and William Clark asked themselves this question: What now? They had reached the Pacific Ocean by traveling the Missouri and Columbia rivers, thereby fulfilling President Thomas Jefferson's major requirement for their expedition. Several passages had also been located across the Continental Divide. Sure, they would return to St. Louis and Washington, D.C., but not until the spring of 1806. Vast experience on the trail caused them to believe that snowstorms had already choked closed the high elevation passes at Lolo and Lemhi.

"Being now determined to go into Winter quarters as Soon as possible," Clark writes, the captains quickly focused on their new task. In June of 1805, when at the confluence of the Missouri and Marias rivers, Lewis and Clark had evaluated two possible routes by asking the men for their opinion. On Nov. 24, the captains once again convened a meeting of expedition members to seek advice. "At night," recounts Sergeant Patrick Gass, "the party were consulted by the Commanding Officers as to the place most proper for winter quarters." Private Joseph Whitehouse similarly used the word "consult" in his journal entry. Sergeant John Ordway characterized the event only slightly different, writing that the officers drew conclusions from "the oppinion of the party." Currently it is fashionable to use the word "vote" for what took place that evening, but casting votes, as we understand it today, is not supported by any journal entry.

Three sergeants were the first to answer the captains. Privates, interpreters and York, Clark's manservant, followed. Toussaint Charbonneau declined to offer an opinion. Sacagawea, however, made known her preference for "a place where there is plenty of Potas," a reference to wapato roots, a tuber that grew upstream around the confluence of the Willamette and Columbia rivers and could help sustain the Corps through the winter. It is not clear from Clark's tally if Sacagawea – on this occasion referred to as "Janey" – was asked her opinion or if she just spoke up spontaneously.

The sergeants all held the same view: cross the Columbia to the south bank and seek a place to build a fort, all the while monitoring the disposition of the Indians and the likelihood of finding herds of elk, a necessity for both food and clothing. Only one man disagreed with the sergeants. Clark added more good reasons to stay near the coast. First, a Euro-American trading vessel just might arrive at the mouth of the Columbia River. Second, salt, an essential item for preserving meat, can be boiled from ocean water. And lastly, the coast range of mountains on the southern shore would provide protection from the constantly blowing wind.

It having been agreed that the southern shore should be explored, the captain's follow-up question asked the men to indicate their secondary preference should the first choice prove to be undesirable. This time three possibilities emerged from the meeting. Six men urged the captains to immediately begin the journey east, but stop and spend the winter near Celilo Falls. Nine men also wished to paddle up river right away, but they thought the Sandy River – opposite where Camas, Washington, is today – might be the most hospitable spot. Thirteen men suggested what Clark recorded as "lookout" or "up," shorthand terms that remain undeciphered today. (If a person wishes to check the opinion of individual explorers, the tally is in Clark's journal entry. Note that Clark made a mathematical miscalculation in his summary statement, one that has been adjusted for this telling.)

Fortified by their evening discussion, the Lewis and Clark Expedition broke camp on Nov. 25 and returned to their canoes. Unfortunately, the "Wind being high rendered it impossible for us to Cross the river from our Camp, [so] we deturmind to proceed on up where it was narrow." In the vicinity of Pillar Rock – roughly 28 miles from the Pacific Ocean – numerous islands clog the Columbia, thus making passage across the river a series of easy hops. The Corps of Discovery spent their final night on the north shore of the Columbia under cloudy skies, although there was enough visibility to see Mt. St. Helens in the distance. On the morning of Nov. 26, the expedition canoes passed lazily among Columbia River islands and inlets until they reached the shores of present-day Oregon.

On the Oregon side of the Columbia River, the Corps of Discovery built and occupied Fort Clatsop, making it their official headquarters. Lewis and Clark would not return to Washington state until late in March of 1806.

❖ ❖ ❖

Heading Back Home

MARCH 23-29, 1806

Meriwether Lewis, usually the more expressive of the two men who led the Corps of Discovery, noted a momentous event on March 23, with an uncharacteristic economy of words: "at 1 P.M. we bid a final adieu to Fort Clatsop." Lewis's co-commander, William Clark, displayed considerably more sentiment: "at this place we had wintered and remained from the 7th of Decr. 1805 to this day and have lived as well as we had any right to expect, and we can Say that we were never one day without 3 meals of Some kind." Several of the enlisted men on the expedition furnished additional details. Sergeant John Ordway, the third in command, proudly noted that his men had kept the larder full at this outpost on the southern shore of the Columbia River notwithstanding "rain which has fallen almost constantly." Another sergeant, Patrick Gass, estimated that during the winter the party kept the pantry stocked by killing 155 elk along with 20 deer. According to Private Joseph Whitehouse, the downed animals furnished not only meat but also the leather for 338 pairs of moccasins. The men would need that much footwear, he added, in order to return an estimated 4,134 miles "to the place from whence we took our departure," meaning the confluence of the Missouri and Mississippi rivers.

Paddling five canoes against the current of the mighty Columbia River – sometimes against a "Stiff breese from the S.W. which raised Considerable Swells" – sapped the strength of the expedition men. Inasmuch as they had spent the winter ashore, the men need not have felt embarrassed at being a little out of shape, but another episode probably did shame them. Earlier, on March 17, as the captains made final preparations for the journey back to Missouri, Lewis bought a canoe from the Clatsop Indians at a price that required him to give up his uniform coat plus a quantity of tobacco. He confided to his journal that "we yet want another canoe, and as the Clatsops will not sell us one at a price which we can afford to give we will take one from them in lue of the six Elk which they stole from us in the winter." Clark concurred. The following day, Ordway reports, "4 men went over to the prarie near the coast to take a canoe which belonged to the Clatsop Indians, as we are in want of it." Two men concealed the canoe near the fort until it was time to depart on March 23. But on the afternoon of March 24, when the expedition got lost among some islands, "an Indian perceiving pursued overtook us and put us in the wright channel." Unexpectedly, the Indian recognized his canoe in the flotilla manned by the Corps of Discovery. Oops! Lewis writes that the man "consented very willingly to take an Elk's skin" for the canoe after which he immediately departed. Is receiving an elk skin a fair trade for a handcrafted canoe? Not usually. In this instance, a lone man stood before 31 other men, each of them possessing a rifle.

As had been the case on the westward journey, the men of the expedition favored daily meals of meat to fuel their hard-working bodies. Hunters took to the field daily, but ultimately elk disappeared from the dinner menu. Deer flesh could not satisfy, remarked Clark, as it "is too poore for the men to subsist on and work as hard as is necessary." On March 26, the hunters returned to camp, having killed three eagles and a large goose. Dogs could be acquired from the natives, but that usually required offering tobacco, a commodity valued as much by the buyers of canines as the sellers. After such bargains, the chewers of tobacco among the men substituted bark from wild crabapple trees; they found it bitter but agreeable. The smokers in the group adjusted by peeling the inner bark from the red willow tree and mixing it with dried leaves. Sometimes fish, roots and fruit were the only foods available. Lewis and Clark preferred sturgeon among the fish; the flesh of harbor seals they also found a worthy substitute for elk meat. Wapato, dug in marshes along the river, became the vegetable of choice, it being a "species of small white tuberous roots about 2 inches in length and as thick as a man's finger; these are eaten raw, are crisp, milkey, and agreeably flavored." It was not yet berry season in the Pacific Northwest, but the expedition did manage to trade with the Indians for some dried raspberries. Lewis thought them "reather acid tho' pleasantly flavored."

Near present Longview, Washington, William Clark sought to honor his sister Frances by placing her nickname on a shallow valley, labeling it "Fanny's Valley" on his map – a fortunate revision, because, in his journal, he had referred to the site as "Fanny's bottom."

MARCH 30-APRIL 5, 1806

Paddling five canoes against the relentless current of the unrestrained Columbia River exhausted the men of the Corps of Discovery. Their fatigue can partly be explained by the failure of the expedition hunters to regularly procure protein-rich elk meat for meals. Extreme weariness in the men can also be attributed to the design of the expedition canoes. Most of the canoes had been crafted half a year earlier in present-day Idaho, and while they performed adequately the previous fall going downstream on the Snake and Columbia rivers, the vessels now seemed clumsy and unmanageable. On March 30, 1806, when the expedition landed in the vicinity of present Vancouver, Washington, Sergeant Patrick Gass mused that "The natives of this country ought to have the credit of making the finest canoes, perhaps in the world, both as to service and beauty." Captain Meriwether Lewis also envied the native canoes, and on April 1, he purchased one, paying with 36 feet of strung colored beads. But the man "shortly after returned and canceled the bargain, took his canoe and returned the beads." Alas, "this is frequently the case in their method of traiding and is deemed fair by them," observed a dejected Lewis.

Increasingly, certain practices of the Indians annoyed both Lewis and Clark. Lewis disapproved, for example, of the "very singular custom" among one tribe of "baithing themselves allover with urine every morning." Clark decried the "leather breech clout" worn by the women of another tribe as "indesant." Described as being the width of "a Common pocket Handkercheif or Something Smaller and longer," in Clark's view it "bearly covers the *Mons venus*, to which it is drawn So close that the whole Shape is plainly perseived." (Writers in the Jeffersonian era commonly used Latin for sensitive terms because it was thought that only the most educated among the populace would have an interest in science – and besides, in this case, the matter concerned the female body.)

Nine days after leaving Fort Clatsop, the Corps of Discovery reached present Washougal, Washington. Here they planned to delay for a day or two to "kill Some meat to last us through the Western Mountains." That arrangement, however, underwent revision when "three Indians encamped near us and visited our fire we entered into a kind of a Conversation by signs, of the Country and Situation of the rivers." New information at that meeting greatly surprised – and dismayed – Clark, the expedition's geographer. Apparently the Corps of Discovery had failed to notice a considerable tributary that entered the Columbia several miles below their present camp. "This information if true will render it necessary to examine the river below," Clark confided to his journal, for the description by the Indians made it sound as if the river had its source in California. The next morning "this information was corroborated by that of sundry other indians who visited us." On April 2, another party of eight natives arrived at the expedition camp and they too confirmed the existence of the river, one man even drawing a map using charcoal and a mat. To resolve the mystery of the river, which the Indians called Mult-no-mah, Clark organized a small party of six enlisted men plus an Indian guide.

Clark's party, traveling in a single canoe, encountered their first Indian village later that afternoon. The captain entered a house and offered to trade for food with the inhabitants. He found them "Sulkey and they positively refused to Sell any." Vexed, Clark took a piece of rope impregnated with gunpowder – the sort of fuse that might be used with a cannon – out of his pocket and slyly placed it in the fire where it "burned vehemently." Simultaneously, Clark pulled out his compass and, using a magnet, caused the needle to spin wildly. Clark's magical combination generated uncommon apprehension among the natives, some of whom rushed forward with a full amount of wapato roots, placing them at Clark's feet. At this point, Clark later told Lewis, the natives "appeared Somewhat passified and I left them."

Entering the Willamette River, Clark confirmed the veracity of the Indian report of an overlooked river. He continued about six miles up the river until, on April 3, he became "perfectly Satisfied of the Size and magnitude of this great river" and ordered his men to reverse course. All went well on the return journey until Clark's small unit visited the home village of their Indian pilot. There the father of their guide introduced them to "a woman who was badly marked with the Small Pox and made Signs that they all died with the disorder which marked her face... from the age of this woman this Distructive disorder I judge must have been about 28 or 30 years past." That evening Clark rejoined Lewis at the main camp. He had many stories to tell at the campfire.

APRIL 6-12, 1806

After breakfast on April 6, the Corps of Discovery broke camp near
present Washougal, loaded their five canoes with the bounty from
six days of uninterrupted hunting, and set a course in the direction of
Beacon Rock. As the small flotilla proceeded east, expedition hunters
prowled the shore looking for game. Huntsmen, Meriwether Lewis
noted, "killed three Elk this morning and wounded two others so badly
that they expected to get them." Even though the canoes had progressed
only 10 miles, Lewis called a halt for the day so that butchers among the
men could carve the carcasses into thin strips and begin the process of
smoking it into jerky. The elk, thought Lewis, would provide sufficient
stores of dried meat to take the expedition to the land of the Nez Perce,
"provided we can obtain a few dogs horses and roots by the way."

The downside to this windfall of meat, in the eyes of Lewis, was that
"we found some indians with our hunters when we arrived; these people
are constantly hanging about us." Late that night, "the centinel detected
an old indian man attempting to creep into camp in order to pilfer" a
spoon. According to Lewis, the sentry "gave the fellow a few stripes
with a switch and sent him off." Lewis, William Clark, and a number of
the enlisted men found the near-constant company of Columbia River
Indians on the return journey stifling in the extreme. On April 9, about
a mile below Beacon Rock, John Colter, one of the expedition stalwarts,
"observed the tomehawk in one of the lodges which had been stolen
from us on the 4th of November last as we decended this river; the
natives attempted to wrest the tomahawk from him but he retained it."
Lewis blamed some "illy disposed" Indians. Later that day, when stopped
at another Indian village, Lewis characterized the inhabitants as "great
rogues" and obliged his men "to keep them at a proper distance from
our baggage." Portaging the canoes around the rapids and falls of the
Columbia River only brought the two cultures into closer contact. Near
the Cascades of the Columbia two Indians stole a dog from John Shields,
the expedition blacksmith, after which they "pushed him out of the road."
Shields, Lewis continues, "had nothing to defend himself with except a
large knife which he drew with an intention of putting one or both of
them to death before they could get themselves in readiness to use their

arrows, but discovering his design they declined the combat and instantly fled through the woods."

That same afternoon, "villains" of the same tribe stole Seaman, Lewis's Newfoundland dog. As soon as he heard the news, Lewis dispatched "three men in pursuit of the thieves with orders if they made the least resistence or difficulty in surrendering the dog to fire on them." After two miles of pursuit, the expedition patrol came within sight of the bandits but, happily, bloodshed was averted because the Indians "left the dog and fled." Meantime, another Indian grabbed an ax from the expedition stores, only to have one of the expedition members wrestle it back. Fed up, Lewis ordered his sentinels to keep the Indians out of camp. And Clark informed the Indians by signs that if they "insulted our men or Stold our property we Should Certainly put them to death." Finally, Lewis complained to the village headman. It was his hope "that the friendly interposition of this chief may prevent our being compelled to use some violence with these people; our men seem well disposed to kill a few of them." He added, to no one in particular, "I am convinced that no other consideration but our number at this moment protects us."

Amid all of these distractions, the Corps of Discovery steadily conquered the free flowing, swollen Columbia River, mile by mile. Lewis believed the rapids to be much worse than when they passed through them the previous fall, mainly because "the water appears to be upwards of 20 feet higher than when we decended the river." When possible, the expedition portaged supplies around the rapids. Bulky canoes, however, had to be lined through, sometimes with unintended results. One canoe, for example, turned broadside in the current on April 12 "and the exertions of every man was not Sufficient to hold her. the men were Compelled to let go the rope and both the Canoe and rope went with the Stream." The ramification of such a loss was great, for "the loss of this Canoe I fear," wrote Clark, "Compell us to purchase another at an extravigent price." Opening negotiations for a canoe would only bring the leaders of the expedition into closer association with the Columbia River natives – considering recent events, not a good prospect.

APRIL 13-19, 1806

The loss of a canoe at the Cascades of the Columbia on April 12 forced Meriwether Lewis and William Clark to redistribute the expedition crew and supplies into four remaining watercraft. This, however, "rendered our vessels extreemly inconvenient to mannage and in short reather unsafe in the event of high winds." Lewis responded the next day when he gave two robes and four elk skins for two small Indian canoes.

Early in the afternoon of April 14, near present White Salmon, Washington, Lewis and Clark paused at a small village where, to their surprise, they found "some good horses of which we saw ten or a douzen. these are the fist horses we have met with since we left this neighbourhood last fall." Lewis predicted that the villagers would not value the animals highly because "they reside immediately on the river and the country is too thickly timbered to admit them to run the game with horses." Perhaps the expedition could purchase horses and continue their journey overland?

After mulling the idea overnight, at first light on April 15, Lewis tested the market: "accordingly we exposed some articles in exchange for horses the natives were unwilling to barter." Within hours, the expedition stopped at another village. The inhabitants exhibited several horses, but they "would not take the articles which we had in exchange for them." The Indians wanted an "eye-dag" knife, a dagger with a hole in it suitable to insert a rope looped around the wrist. At this point, the Corps of Discovery had been on the trail for one month shy of two years, and their supply of trade items had fallen woefully low. At any rate, that particular item came to the Pacific Northwest with Boston-based sailors, and Lewis and Clark had no access to it when they purchased their stores in Philadelphia. Later that day, after establishing camp at present The Dalles, a group of Indians stopped for a visit and Lewis and Clark once again broached the topic of horses. Tomorrow, they were told, cross the river and there will be trade.

Negotiating for horses, especially when one party has little to offer, can be a long-drawn-out exercise. And so it was for William Clark, the expedition's designated bargainer. On April 16, Clark crossed the Columbia with 11 men: nine to assist with the merchandise plus two interpreters, George Drouillard and Toussaint Charbonneau. Once ashore, the men split up, going to two villages. Unfortunately, Indians at both villages delayed the greater part of the day without trading a single horse. It might have ended there, except a crippled great chief appeared and told Clark if he would come "to his Town his people would trade." Clark agreed, reaching the village at sunset. "I saw great numbers of horses," he wrote. He wanted a dozen of them.

Trade efforts turned sour on April 17. "I made a bargain with the Chief who has more horses than all the village besides for 2 horses. Soon after he Canseled his bargin, and we again bargined for 3 horses, they were brought forward, and only one fit for Service, the others had Such intolerable backs as to render them entirely unfit." Clark packed up to leave, but an Indian came forward to sell two horses and another man sold a third. Charbonneau "purchased a verry fine Mare." Clark decided to stay one more night and continue trading in the morning, after which he would move east. He so informed Lewis by a note, adding that he hoped Lewis would bring the main party and meet him. Lewis dispatched a note back to Clark, urging him to double the price heretofore offered for horses and, if possible, obtain as many as five. He reasoned that delay is "expensive to us inasmuch as we will be compelled to purchase both fuel and food of the Indians, and might the better enable them to execute any hostile design."

Lewis and Clark reunited at 3 pm on April 18. Clark still had only four horses, though he had once again been "tanteerlised with the expectation of purchaseing morre imediately." Four horses were not the hoped-for five, but they were enough to transport some of the supplies, so Lewis ordered the men to cut up two of the canoes for firewood. On April 19, happily, a breakthrough took place. Unexpectedly, Clark "purchased 4 horses at the town & Capt Lewis purchased one." Why the sudden success? Because in desperation, the captains authorized the trading of iron kettles, an item prized higher by the Indians than common elk skins, cloth or ribbons. One can understand then, why Lewis, when one of the men "was negligent in his attention to his horse and suffered it to ramble off," reprimanded him "more severely for this piece of negligence than had been usual with me."

APRIL 20-26, 1806

The Corps of Discovery needed horses. Paddling canoes against the current of the Columbia River — overfull with spring runoff — was a difficult task by itself, but it became impossibly arduous once the expedition reached the The Dalles, a series of foaming rapids. Then the canoes became a liability. Transferring the loads to horses was an option, but Indians would sell them only reluctantly and then for a steep price. Such was the reality of geographic determinism. Twice yearly runs of migrating salmon leaped over boulders at The Dalles, creating a fishing opportunity that lured members of 10 or more tribes to the river's edge. In addition to netting salmon, tribesmen traded among themselves. Wolf hides, cedar bark baskets, elk teeth jewelry and a hundred other items changed hands a dozen times or more. Lewis and Clark considered The Dalles "the Great Mart of all this Country," and for good reason. These Indians loved the challenge of a good barter. Frustrated by their independence, Meriwether Lewis characterized the Indians as "poor, dirty, proud, haughty, inhospitable, parsimonious and faithless in every rispect."

By April 20, the expedition had acquired only eight horses. The number fluctuated. For example, Lewis learned that "one horse which I had purchased and paid for yesterday and which could not be found... I was now informed had been gambled away by the rascal who had sold it to me and had been taken away by a man of another nation." William Clark attempted to make up for the loss, admitting that he used "even false Statements to enduce those pore devils to Sell me horses."

Trade negotiations hit a snag after the natives pilfered six tomahawks and a knife from the party. Lewis warned the Indians that if he "caught them attempting to purloin any article from us I would beat them severely." Conversation ended at that point as the natives "went off in reather a bad humour." In the morning, Lewis noticed that the Indians made away with yet another tomahawk overnight, and he actually caught a fellow stealing an iron socket from a canoe pole. Sergeant Patrick Gass wrote in his journal that one theft by an Indian "so irritated Captain Lewis that he struck him; which was the first act of the kind, that had happened during the expedition. The Indians, however, did not resent it, otherwise it is probable we would have had a skirmish with them." For the second time, Lewis spoke directly to the tribesmen, saying that next time he "would shoot the first of them that attempted to steal an article from us. that we were not affraid to fight them, that I had it in my power at that moment to kill them all and set fire to their houses, but it was not my wish to treat them with severity provided they would let my property alone." Fortunately, they soon did.

Once the Corps ventured beyond the narrow confines of the Columbia River at Celilo Falls, the landscape flattened out and opened up. More and more Indian villages contained horses, many with owners willing to sell. "It astonished me to see the order of their horses at this season of the year," remarked Lewis. "I did not see a single horse which could be deemed poor and many of them were as fat as seals."

Soon the expedition had enough animals to pack the supplies. As Lewis and Clark acquired more horses, the captains divided the men into two groups, allowing them to alternate with each other: one day riding horses, the next day walking. It took only one day, noted Gass, before "The men in general complain of their feet being sore; and the officers have to go on foot to permit some of them to ride."

With the canoes now being extraneous, two were disposed of in mid-April, three more were detached on April 21, and the final two were sold on April 24. Deciding to abandon the canoes and continue their journey on overland trails involved risk. The wisdom of Lewis and Clark's action, however, can be seen in a comparison of miles traveled. In the week between April 14, when they first saw horses on the return journey, and April 20, when the Corps of Discovery had maneuvered through The Dalles, the expedition canoes traveled a total of 27 miles. On April 25, after the Corps of Discovery had divested themselves of all canoes, they made 20 miles on a trail that paralleled the Columbia River. The next day they increased their distance to 28 miles. That evening they made camp in present Plymouth, Washington, opposite present Umatilla, Oregon, and adjacent to what would become McNary Lock and Dam. Each day brought them closer to St. Louis and the conclusion of their remarkable journey.

APRIL 27-MAY 3, 1806

Having disposed of their canoes earlier in the month, after April 26 the Corps of Discovery traveled east by horse and on foot following a trail on the north bank of the Columbia River. A Nez Perce man, returning to his home in the Clearwater Valley, served as their volunteer guide.

On the afternoon of April 27, the Lewis and Clark Expedition entered a village of the Walla Walla Indians about 15 miles below where the Snake River merges with the Columbia River. Meriwether Lewis and William Clark knew the "Wallahwallahs" slightly, inasmuch as the expedition had spent a night with the tribe in mid-October of 1805 during their westward journey. Chief Yellippit, who presided over the 15 lodges, invited the expedition to remain with his people for three or

four days, assuring them, said Lewis, that "we should be furnished with
a plenty of such food as they had themselves; and some horses to assist
us on our journey." In addition, the Indians revealed to the captains
that opposite their village, at the mouth of the Walla Walla River, a trail
began that continued uninterrupted to the merge of the Clearwater River
and the Snake River. According to the Indians, the road abounded with
deer for food and grass for the horses. Clark calculated that such a path
"would Shorten the rout at least 80 miles." Actually, the shortcut would
save the expedition approximately 155 miles, but 80 seemed enough to
excite the interest of the captains.

Buoyed by the prospect of saving time, Lewis and Clark eagerly
arose on April 28. Good things began to happen early. In the morning,
Yellippit "brought a very eligant white horse to our camp and presented
him to Capt. C." Clark reciprocated by offering his sword, 100 rifle balls,
plus powder. The chief also allowed the expedition to borrow canoes,
which they used to ride herd on their horses as they swam them from the
north bank of the Columbia to the south side. Good fortune continued
when, upon reaching the south bank, "we found a Shoshone woman,
prisoner among these people by means of whome and Sahcahgarweah
we found the means of conversing with the Wollahwollahs." One source
of conversation was about Indians who requested medical assistance:
"one had his knee contracted by the rheumatism, another with a broken
arm &c." Clark, who acted as the expedition's medical officer, placed
the broken arm in a splint and sling and did what he could to relieve
the pain of the other man. Additional tribesmen sought relief from sore
eyes. Clark thought the constantly blowing sand on the plains most
likely caused the disorder. He had no remedy other than "Some eye
water" from the expedition medicine chest. The busy day ended with a
spectacular dance. The fiddlers among the expedition members "played
and the men amused themselves with dancing about an hour. we then
requested the Indians to dance which they very Cheerfully Complyed
with; ... the whole assemblage of indians about 350 men women and
Children Sung and danced at the Same time."

The following day, a cadre of expedition men, joined by Walla
Walla Indians, transported baggage across the Columbia. Clark,
meanwhile, continued to practice medicine and, by skillful trading, the
expedition horse herd increased to 23 young animals. With preparations

complete, on April 30 the Corps of Discovery, assisted by a Walla Walla guide, resumed their journey to St. Louis by following the short cut recommended by Yellippit. The Nez Perce volunteer guide continued on as well.

A fork in the road on May 1 created a rift between the Walla Walla guide and the Nez Perce man. One branch would have "plenty of wood water and only one hill" and the other would not. Contradictory opinions "perplexed us a little" admitted Clark. "Some words took place between these two men," after which, according to Clark, the Walla Walla Indian mounted his horse and rode off. This unsettled both Lewis and Clark so they dispatched a man to go after the guide and inform him "we believed what he said." When the guide returned, the Nez Perce man separated himself from the unit. Strangely, on the morning of May 3 the Walla Walla guide "reather abruptly" detached himself from the expedition. However, in a constantly changing cast of characters on the shortcut road, that afternoon the Corps of Discovery met up with Bighorn, a Nez Perce chief, and 10 of his men. Clark recognized Bighorn as a man who had traveled a portion of the Snake River with them in the fall of 1805, and "I believe was very instremental in precureing us a hospital and friendly reception among the nativs." Surely he would lead the Corps of Discovery the rest of the way to the Clearwater River.

MAY 4-10, 1806

Using a shortcut trail from the Columbia River to the Clearwater River in late April and early May proved to be more difficult than expected for the Corps of Discovery. Nevertheless, the Lewis and Clark Expedition pushed on. Because of information provided to them on May 3 by a friendly Nez Perce chief, Lewis and Clark knew that they had only to surmount one more hill and then follow a creek downhill to reach the Snake River at a point not far from its merge with the Clearwater River.

May 4 dawned "cold and disagreeable," but it could not dampen the spirits of the expedition. The hill – Alpowa Summit above present Clarkston, Washington, at 2,785 feet of elevation – turned out to be "most parts rocky and abrupt" and difficult for the horses. Even so, eight miles down the hill, the expedition arrived at a lodge of six families living on the banks of the Snake River: "we obtained a few large cakes of half cured bread made of a root which resembles the sweet potatoe, with these we made some soope and took breakfast." Sergeant Patrick Gass viewed this meal as "a scanty allowance for thirty odd hungry men." Another eight miles up the Snake River, Lewis and Clark knew from experience gained the previous fall that the Clearwater River joined the Snake River and beyond that lay the homeland of the Nez Perce Indians. Taking the advice of the local Indians, the expedition crossed to the north side of the Snake River and made its way east toward the Clearwater. They established their final camp in Washington just west of present-day Clarkston.

Small settlements of Nez Perce families lined the Clearwater River at irregular intervals. As they proceeded down the river on May 5, the Corps of Discovery several times stopped and asked for food. The inquiry brought two different sets of responses during the next several days. In the best cases, Lewis and Clark learned that when they provided medical attention to the natives, the Nez Perce, in return, would offer food. It turned out that when, in the fall of 1805, Clark had spent time with the Nez Perce, "I gave an Indian man some Volitile liniment to rub his knee and thye for a pain of which he complained, the fellow soon after recovered and have never seased to extol the virtue of our medicines." A second man also sang the praises of Clark: "as we decended last fall I met with a man, who could not walk with a tumure on his thye... I gave this man a jentle pirge cleaned & dressed his sore and left him some casteel soap to wash the sore which soon got well. this man also assigned the restoration of his leg to me. those two cures has raised my reputation and given thos nativs an exolted oppinion of my skill as a phician." Inasmuch as the Indians paid for the care, Clark continues, "in our present situation I think it pardonable to continue this deception for they will not give us any provisions without compensation in merchendize, and our stock is now reduced to a mear handfull." He adds that, "We take care to give them no article which can possibly injure them, and in maney cases can administer & give such medicine & sirgical aid as will effectually restore in simple cases &c."

Gass shows that he adapted quickly to his new neighbors with this reflection: "All the Indians from the Rocky Mountains to the falls of Columbia are an honest, ingenuous, and well-disposed people; but from the falls to the sea-coast, and along it, they are a rascally, thieving set." Lewis perhaps needed to make these distinctions, too. One evening at dinner, Lewis reports, "an indian fellow verry impertinently threw a poor half starved puppy nearly into my plait by way of derision for our eating dogs and laughed very heartily at his own impertinence; I was so provoked at his insolence that I caught the puppy and thew it with great violence at him and struk him in the breast and face, siezed my tomahawk and shewed him by signs if he repeated his insolence I would tommahawk him, the fellow withdrew apparently much mortifyed."

Getting along with the Nez Perce would be imperative for the Corps of Discovery because the Indians informed Lewis "that the snow is yet so deep on the mountains that we shall not be able to pass them untill the next full moon or about the first of June; others set the time at still a more distant period." Clark considered this "unwelcom inteligence to men confined to a diet of horsebeef and roots, and who are as anxious as we are to return to the fat plains of the Missouri and thence to our native homes."

MAY 11-17, 1806

When the Lewis and Clark Expedition transitioned from the Snake River to the Clearwater River at today's Clarkston on May 5, they entered the traditional homeland of the Nez Perce Tribe. Each day through May 13, the Corps of Discovery traveled in an easterly direction until, as Sergeant John Ordway put it, "we are now as near the Mountains as we can git untill Such times as the Snow is nearly gone off the mountains as we are too eairly to cross."

During their wanderings across the Nez Perce territory, Lewis and Clark took every opportunity to meet with tribal leaders. From May 10 to May 12, for example, the expedition camped with Broken Arm, one of the four great chiefs of the Nez Perce. Later, the other headmen of the tribe – Cut Nose, Red Grizzly Bear and the One-Eyed Chief – joined the conversation. The chiefs asked the explorers, "Why are you here in our country?" To that query, Lewis spoke eloquently about how the United States government wished to establish trading houses among the Western tribes. But, he cautioned the Indian leaders, trade will come only after tribes have made peace with each other. The meeting ended with what historians have irreverently called "The Lewis and Clark Traveling Show," a practiced routine to awe the Indians they counseled with along the trail: "we amused ourselves with shewing them the power of magnetism, the spye glass, compass, watch, air-gun and sundry other articles equally novel and incomprehensible to them."

The next morning, the Indian leaders met among themselves "with rispect to the subjects on which we had spoken to them yesterday." William Clark understood the result was favorable and that the Nez Perce "had only one heart and one tongue on this Subject." Broken Arm used a unique tribal protocol to bring finality to the discussion. The chief "thickended the soope in the kettles and baskets of all his people," using flour pounded from dried wild vegetables. Then he invited all men who would "abide by the decrees of the council to come and eat." He asked those "as would not be so bound to shew themselves by not partaking of the feast." One of the expedition men maneuvered close enough to observe the proceedings and he told Meriwether Lewis that "there was not a dissenting voice" and "all swallowed their objections if any they had, very cheerfully with their mush."

At this point, the Indian leaders invited Lewis and Clark into their tent. The headmen wanted to inform the captains not only of their decision to cooperate with the Great Father, but also "that there were many of their people waiting in great pain at the moment for the aid of our medicine." According to Lewis, "it was agreed between Capt. C. and myself that he should attend the sick as he was their favorite physician while I would [stay] here and answer the Chiefs." So it was that Clark became "closely employed" with about "40 grown persons" in need of medicine; Lewis spent his afternoon responding to the chiefs and "smoking the pipe."

The Corps of Discovery moved into a "permanent camp" on May 14. Lewis thought the chosen site "a very eligible spot for defence." In addition, "we are in the vicinity of the best hunting grounds from indian information, are convenient to the salmon which we expect daily and have an excellent pasture for our horses. In short," he concluded, "as we are compelled to reside a while in this neighbourhood I feel perfectly satisfyed with our position." Here the Corps of Discovery would remain until June 10, a period of 28 days. Expedition journals confer no name on this camp, the third-longest used by the Corps of Discovery. In the 20th century, historians coined the term "Camp Choipunnish" for the site, though today the location near present Kamiah, Idaho, is commonly called Long Camp.

Set free to pasture, the stallions – "stone horses" in the terminology of the times and a reference to the male testicles – became unruly. Lewis attempted to trade the stallions to the Indians for "mears or geldings but they will not exchange altho' we offer 2 for one." There remained two solutions to the problem. Sergeant Ordway documented one: "we eat several of our stud horses as they have been troublesome to us." The alternate solution was to castrate the stallions. George Drouillard, the expedition's man of all trades, gelded two of the animals but yielded to an Indian who offered to perform the task in the Nez Perce way. The Indian method produced less swelling in the horses, though it let more blood. Lewis thought the Indian practice ineffective, yet on subsequent days the animals treated by the Indian recovered easily while one of Drouillard's horses died in pain. Later, Lewis admitted that "the indian method of gelding is preferable to that practiced by ourselves."

MAY 18-24, 1806

As soon as Meriwether Lewis and William Clark established Long Camp, the home of the Lewis and Clark Expedition from May 14 to June 10, they listed among the site's advantages the likelihood of good hunting. On their first evening at the new location, the men of the Corps of Discovery enjoyed a feast of grizzly bear shoulders and hams that were pit-roasted Indian-style beneath pine boughs. In the days ahead, the camp cooks added pheasants, grouse, owls, sand hill cranes and squirrels to the menu. Hunting deer was possible, but it involved considerable travel to the uplands and it could exhaust the horses. Moreover, expedition hunters could not keep up with the Indians. Sergeant Patrick Gass admitted, "These Indians are the most active horsemen I ever saw: they will gallop their horses over precipices, that I should not think of riding over at all." Lewis agreed: "it is astonishing to see these people ride down those steep hills which they do at full speed."

While it is true that not all members of the Corps of Discovery appreciated the taste and health benefits of eating fresh salmon, it was a food source that could not be overlooked. Shortly after establishing Long Camp, Lewis and Clark noticed Indians erecting a fishing stand near them, "no doubt to be in readiness for the salmon, the arrival of which they are so ardently wishing as well as ourselves." Nothing. Another time, George Drouillard killed an eagle which had residue of a salmon in its talons, "the latter altho' it was of itself not valuable was an agreeable sight as it gave us reason to hope that the salmon would shortly be with us." Still nothing.

The Indian woman who accompanied the expedition had, on several occasions, pointed out edible plants to Lewis and Clark, and she did so again at Long Camp. "Sahcargarmeah gathered a quantity of the roots of a specis of fennel," writes Lewis, "which we found very agreeable food, the flavor of this root is not unlike annis seed." This "mush of roots," he added, "we find adds much to the comfort of our diet," because it served as an antidote to the flatulence that came with eating either cous, a member of the carrot family, or the starchy bulbs of camas. Clark confirmed that the plants assembled by Sacagawea were "paleatiable and nurishing food," noting that "The men who were complaining of the head ake and Cholicks yesterday and last night are much better to day." As a result, the captains urged Sacagawea to accumulate a "store of the fennel roots for the Rocky mountains," a task that she began on May 18.

Sacagawea served a dual purpose during her search for natural foods. She identified and gathered plants familiar to her. More important, she avoided harmful flora. Lewis writes in his journal: "we would make the men collect these roots themselves but there are several speceis of hemlock which are so much like the cows that it is difficult to discriminate them from the cows and we are affraid that they might poison themselves." Hemlock, like cous a member of the carrot family, is a toxic herb.

Meantime, Clark's medical practice continued to pay dividends. Grateful Indians frequently offered Clark a colt in exchange for his medical expertise, and in time his price for consultation became fully accepted by both parties. "Horsebeef" gradually replaced dog meat in the men's diet. Only as a last resort would Lewis and Clark trade an item from their supplies for food. According to Lewis, "brass buttons is an article of which these people are tolerably fond." In fact, on May 21, he "divided the remnant of our store of merchandize among our party with a view that each should purchase therewith a parsel of roots and bread from the natives as his stores for the rocky mountains for there seems but little probability that we shall be enabled to make any dryed meat for that purpose and we cannot as yet form any just idea what resource the fish will furnish us." Lewis estimated that "each man's stock in trade amounts to no more than one awl, one Knitting pin, a half an ounce of vermillion, two nedles, a few scanes of thead and about a yard of ribbon; a slender stock indeed with which to lay in a store of provision for that dreary wilderness."

The "dreary wilderness" that Lewis had in mind was, of course, the Bitterroot Mountains. For now the expedition played a waiting game. When the water in the Clearwater River rose higher, it would be a doubly good sign: first, that the spring salmon run would soon begin, and second, that the snows were melting in the mountains. Until then, William Clark could only look longingly at "that icy barier which seperates me from my friends and Country."

MAY 25-31, 1806

During his stay at Long Camp on the Clearwater River, William Clark grew steadily more confident in his role as a frontier physician. Indians assembled each day at Clark's tent-turned-clinic where his patient load often exceeded 40 persons. On May 24, Clark faced his most vexing case, an Indian man who had, over a period of three years, "lost the use of all his limbs and his fingers are Contracted. We are at a loss to deturmine what to do for this unfortunate man." In the morning, Meriwether Lewis informed Clark that he was "confident that this would be an excellent subject for electricity" – a reference to Benjamin Franklin's early experiments with the use of voltage to treat paralysis. He had to admit, however, with "much regret that I have not in my power to supply it." Clark proscribed a program of "Sefere Swetts" for the man. Happily, after three treatments in which the man sat in an enclosed 4-foot-deep hole lined with heated rocks, the "sick Chief is fast on the recovery, he can bear his weight on his legs, and has acquired a considerable portion of strength."

"One of our men Saw a Salmon in the river to day," Clark reported on May 26, "and two others eat of Salmon at the near Village." After nearly a month of waiting for the spring salmon run to begin, that welcome prospect seemed finally near. Rather than wait, the captains decided to be pro-active and on May 27 ordered Sergeant John Ordway to cut across the plains to today's Salmon River where he would "precure Some Salmon on that river, and return tomorrow if possible." Ordway would, in fact, be absent for a week, not returning to camp until June 2.

Relying on his three Indian guides, Ordway, accompanied by privates Peter Weiser and Robert Frazier, followed today's Lawyer Creek going west. They spent their first night in an Indian village waiting out a thunderstorm before continuing on in the morning. Ordway is appreciated by historians for being the only member among seven journalists to write an entry for each of the 863 days of travel by the Corps of Discovery. Unfortunately, Ordway lacked a descriptive writing style with the result that his route is not always clear. It is certain, however, that his small party reached a powerful river on May 28 after an arduous trip down steep bluffs. They saw a bighorn mountain sheep and 14 deer, but no salmon. Ordway believed he was only on a fork, though he almost certainly had reached the main Salmon River.

Being unsuccessful in locating salmon, Ordway led his group up and over a height of land — today's Wapshilla Ridge — after which a trail took them down, according to Ordway, "the worst hills we ever saw a rode made down." This time the watercourse he intercepted was the Snake River. Again, because of imprecise statements, Ordway could have come down by Cottonwood Creek, by Cave Gulch, or even by China Garden Creek. In any case, at the moment Ordway could not comprehend that by having climbed over Wapshilla Ridge his expedition had moved from the Salmon River to the Snake River. He had been only nine miles from the confluence of the two rivers — a point approximately 50 miles upstream from today's Clarkston — but he didn't know it. Only on the return trip to Long Camp would it become evident to Ordway that he had visited two rivers, one a tributary of the other. Entering an Indian camp on the Snake River, the headman welcomed the travelers to his lodge. Dinner consisted of a roasted salmon so large that the famished men could not eat even one-quarter of the fish.

The next day, May 30, Ordway and his men waited patiently while Indians snared salmon with dip nets "in the whorls & eddys" of the river. When Clark took Ordway's report about his experience, the captain wrote in his journal that at the fishery "there is a very considerable rapid, nearly as Great from the information of Sergt. Ordway as the Great falls of the Columbia," meaning Celilo Falls. That afternoon, Ordway "purchased as many Salmon as we thought was necessary to take home and hung them up." Alas, on the morning of May 31, Ordway awoke to discover that "Some of the young Indians Stole Some of our fish and went away in the night." Ordway renegotiated for 17 more salmon and, leaving the guide behind, "followed back the same road we went on."

Once again, Ordway crossed Wapshilla Ridge, returning to the Salmon River. Almost immediately the hazy map of the Nez Perce country that Ordway had imagined in his mind's eye became clear.

JUNE 1-7, 1806

"We begin to feel some anxiety with rispect to Sergt. Ordway and party who were sent... for salmon, we have received no intelligence of them since they set out." Both Meriwether Lewis and William Clark were worried as they penned identical feelings in their journals on June 1. When they sent Ordway into the field on May 27, they anticipated that he and his men would return the next day. But Ordway did not immediately return to camp. In his search for salmon, Ordway crossed plains, descended steep bluffs and climbed rocky roads that took his party to the Salmon and the Snake rivers. Happily, about noon on June 2, Ordway's small party returned to Long Camp near present Kamiah, Idaho.

Ordway had much geographic information to share, but the captains seemed just as interested in the 17 salmon he laid before them. Lewis thought "these fish were as fat as any I ever saw; sufficiently so to cook themselves without the addition of grease; those which were sound were extreemly delicious; their flesh is of a fine rose colour." The Corps of Discovery needed food, and Ordway's success provided hope that the long anticipated spring salmon run on the Clearwater River would soon begin. Lewis lamented, "having exhausted all our merchandize we are obliged to have recourse to every subterfuge in order to prepare in the most ample manner in our power to meet that wretched portion of our journy, the Rocky Mountain, where hungar and cold in their most rigorous forms assail the waried traveller; not any of us have yet forgotten our sufferings in those mountains in September last, and I think it probable we never shall."

Increasingly, as May turned into June, all thoughts of the Lewis and Clark Expedition turned toward the mountains and, beyond that "icy barrier," to home. As soon as the snow sufficiently melted to clear the Lolo Trail, they would break camp and resume their eastward march. Clark monitored the increased flow of the Clearwater River. According to the Indians, when the water in the river subsided – meaning the spring melt was complete – then the mountains would be passable. Lewis, meantime, chose to measure the rise in air temperature, doing so with not only a thermometer, but also by counting the number of blankets he needed to sleep comfortably. On June 2, he needed "one blanket only," a very good sign. Clark recorded a 15-inch drop in water level on the Clearwater on June 4; the next morning Lewis was equally pleased to find no frost on the ground. The measuring sticks of Lewis and Clark may have been unscientific, but their calculations offered hope to the men of the expedition.

Meantime, Lewis learned on June 3 that "today the Indians dispatched an express over the mountains to travellers rest," a meadow about 10 miles south of today's Missoula. Did this mean the Lolo Trail was open to travel? Certainly, thought Lewis, if the mountains were "practicable for this express we thought it probable that we could also pass." Upon inquiry, however, their Indian informants said no. Several creeks were still too high to by swum by horses, they cautioned, and the road remained slippery in the extreme. Besides, it was too early for grass in higher elevations, and the horses would go hungry for three days. The chiefs, reports Clark, "inform us that we may pass Conveniently in twelve or fourteen days."

Not so, the captains resolved. Together they made plans to wrap things up at Long Camp by June 10 and move closer to the Lolo Trail. After a few days hunting in the vicinity of "quawmash flatts" – today's Weippe Prairie – they would "attempt the Mountains about the Middle of this month." Laying in a stock of meat was critical inasmuch as Lewis now admitted that, "I begin to lose all hope of any dependance on the Salmon as this river will not fall sufficiently to take them before we shall leave it."

Final preparations for closing Long Camp took many forms. Men built a sturdy corral for the horses – about 65 of them – because "many of them have become so wild that we cannot take them without the assistance of the Indians who are extreemly dextrous in throwing a rope and taking them with a noose about the neck." Gradually, Clark closed down his medical practice, though not for Jean Baptiste Charbonneau, Sacagawea's infant son, who suffered from high fever and tonsillitis. Clark also hurriedly quizzed the Nez Perce about their names for rivers east of the Rockies. He wanted to know the depth of Nez Perce geographic knowledge since the expedition would rely on their information when crossing the Lolo Trail.

JUNE 8-14, 1806

When Meriwether Lewis and William Clark made their decision on June 3 to abandon Long Camp on the Clearwater River in favor of a new camp at Weippe Prairie, it raised the spirits of the party. For an intense week, the Corps of Discovery packed camp supplies, repaired equipment, rounded up their horses and began to dismantle the camp that had been their home for nearly a month. By June 8, the men could relax. "Several foot races were run this evening between the indians and our men," reports Lewis, "the indians are very active; one of them proved as fleet as Drewer and R. Fields, our swiftest runners." After the races, "the men divided themselves into two teams and played prison base," a popular roughhouse game of catch and rescue. Lewis encouraged the games because "those who are not hunters have had so little to do that they are getting reather lazy and slothful." After dark, as a sort of cool-down to the exercise, "we had the violin played and danced for the amusement of ourselves and the indians." The next evening the men did more of the same, but added a game of "pitching quites," meaning quoits, a game much like today's horseshoes.

Clark appreciated that "our party exolted with the idea of once more proceeding on towards their friends and Country." Too bad, then, that one of the Indians informed him that "we could not cross the mountains untill the full of the next moon, or about the 1st of July... this information is disagreeable to us." The plan of Lewis and Clark had been to begin the Lolo Trail in the middle of June, not two weeks later. "The river has been falling for several days and is now lower by near six feet than it has been; this we view as a strong evidence that the great body of snow has left the mountains... a few days will dry the roads and will also improve the grass." Accordingly, on June 10 the Corps of Discovery took their leave of Long Camp and pointed themselves in the direction of Weippe Prairie, the spot where the Lewis and Clark Expedition had first met the Nez Perce in the fall of 1805.

The 12-mile trek to the eastern edge of "quawmash flatts" went smoothly enough, writes Lewis, inasmuch as each man rode a horse and led another lightly packed animal. Feeling confident that his command was now "perfectly equiped for the mountains," Lewis

allowed himself the luxury of returning to his role as the expedition's
botanist. Among the trees identified by Lewis were several species
of fir, the Engelmann spruce, Ponderosa pine, mountain larch and
the alder. In the undergrowth, he observed chokecherry, redroot,
serviceberry, gooseberry, poison sumac and poison ivy. His collection
included a specimen of syringa, now the state flower of Idaho; scientists
subsequently referenced the Corps' leader when they named the plant
Philadelphus lewisi.

Weippe Prairie abounded in camas, an edible plant with onion-sized
bulbs that the Indians commonly roasted, or dried and pounded into
flour. Sergeant Patrick Gass, who estimated the prairie at 2,000 acres,
comments that the camas "looks beautiful, being in full bloom with
flowers of a pale blue colour." Lewis agreed, adding that "the quawmash
is now in blume and from the colour of its bloom at a short distance it
resembles lakes of fine clear water, so complete is this deseption that on
first sight I could have swoarn it was water." Beautiful as the sight may
have been, Clark did not forget that "this root is palateable but disagrees
with us in every shape we have ever used it. … when we first arrived
at the Chopunnish last fall at this place our men who were half Starved
made So free a use of this root that it made them all Sick for Several days
after."

William Clark confessed his concerns about returning to the Lolo
Trail when he wrote his journal entry for June 14. In the morning, the
expedition would move in earnest, he scribbled, "over those snowey
tremendious mountains which has detained us near five weeks in this
neighbourhood waiting for the Snows to melt." He could not help but
"Shudder with the expectation," knowing from past experience the
"great dificuelties in passing those Mountains, from the debth of snow."
Meriwether Lewis penned a similar entry: "I am still apprehensive
that the snow and want of food for our horses will prove a serious
imbarrassment to us." Still, "every body seems anxious to be in motion,
convinced that we have not now any time to delay if the calculation is to
reach the United States this season."

JUNE 15-21, 1806

Faced with the challenge of crossing the Lolo Trail for the second time in
10 months, Meriwether Lewis mused on June 14: "this I am detirmined

to accomplish if within the compass of human power." June 15 tested his resolve. The horses straggled off overnight and collecting all 66 of them delayed the start until 10 am. A hard rain fell throughout much of the day. The single-file line of men on horseback forded swollen creeks, then pushed upward through broken country where "the fallen timber in addition to the slippry roads made our march slow and extreemly laborious." Still, the Corps of Discovery did not halt for the night until they had logged 22 miles.

The expedition got an early start on June 16 and they needed every bit of daylight to put 15 miles between camps. After midday the trail passed through "large quatities of snow yet undisolved," some of it three feet deep. Lewis bemoaned, "appearances in this comparatively low region augers but unfavorably with rispect to the practibility of passing the mountains, however we determined to proceed." Fortunately, the combination of cooler temperatures in the higher elevation with the setting of the sun allowed the snow to become "Sufficently firm to bear our horses, otherwise it would have been impossible for us to proceed as it lay in emince masses in Some places 8 or ten feet deep." The expedition camped on Hungry Creek. Clark described it as "Small at this place but is deep and runs a perfect torrent; the water is perfectly transparent and as Cold as ice." The next day, to his dismay, he would respect the accuracy of his description.

Hungry Creek is, arguably, the most isolated and untouched section of trail associated with the Lewis and Clark Expedition. It was unkind to the Corps of Discovery and it remains a challenge to 21st-century hikers and trail riders. Almost immediately on June 17, Hungry Creek exasperated the Corps of Discovery: "We found it difficult and dangerous to pass the creek in consequence of its debth and rapidity; we avoided two other passes of the creek," Lewis explains, "by ascending a very steep rocky and difficult hill." Ultimately the party pulled itself out of the creek drainage by scaling the high ridge overlooking today's Lochsa River. At this higher elevation the snow overwhelmed them.

Sergeant Patrick Gass records that, "When we got about half way up the mountain the ground was entirely covered with snow three feet deep; and as we ascended, it still became deeper, until we arrived at the top, where it was twelve or fifteen feet deep." Gass continues: "We therefore halted to determine what was best to be done, as it appeared not only imprudent but highly dangerous to proceed without a guide of any kind. After remaining about two hours we conluded it would be most adviseable to go back to some place where there was food for our horses. We therefore hung up our loading on poles, tied to and extended between trees, covered it all safe with deer skins, and turned back melancholy and disappointed. At this time it began to rain; and we proceeded down to Hungry creek again." Lewis adds the perspective of a leader: "here was winter with all it's rigors; the air was cold, my hands and feet were benumbed... if we proceeded and should get bewildered in these mountains the certainty was that we should loose all our horses and consequently our baggage instruments perhaps our papers and thus eminently wrisk the loss of the discoveries which we had already made if we should be so fortunate as to escape with life." He concluded that, "under these circumstances we conceived it madnes in this stage of the expedition to proceed." Clark labeled the retreat a "retrograde march" in his journal.

The observation of Gass that the expedition needed a guide was not lost on the officers. In the morning, Lewis and Clark sent two men back to the Nez Perce village to offer a rifle to anyone who would serve as a guide. Meantime, the rest of the expedition sullenly retraced their steps down the mountain they had conquered only the day before. One man fell from his horse and cut a vein on the inner side of his leg requiring Lewis to quickly apply a tourniquet. A bit farther on, John Colter's horse tripped crossing Hungry Creek "and himself and horse were driven down the Creek a considerable distance roleing over each other among the rocks." The camp they made that evening, June 18, is where they would continue to stay through June 21. It was only two miles distant from where the expedition had camped on June 15, their first day of easterly travel on the Lolo Trail.

JUNE 22-28, 1806

Their brief eastward passage along the Lolo Trail having ended in failure on June 17, the Lewis and Clark Expedition grimly retraced their steps down the ridge overlooking today's Lochsa River. The temporary camp they established on June 18 served them well until June 21. At that point, the captains wished to know if George Drouillard and George Shannon, the two men they had sent back to the Nez Perce village to locate a guide, had been successful. So the expedition retreated all the way back to Weippe Prairie, the place where they had camped earlier from June 10-15. On the way down, the expedition met two mounted Nez Perce men heading up the mountain. Meriwether Lewis arranged for these men to halt and wait for two days while the Euro-American explorers reassembled and returned.

It took some time for the Corps of Discovery to reconstitute itself. Not until June 23 did Drouillard and Shannon rejoin the main camp, bringing three Nez Perce men of "good Charrector" with them. Meantime, expedition hunters stalked deer and bear in the forest, being often out of contact with the main camp. Lewis complicated matters by ordering a sergeant and five privates to return to the two Indians who were marking time on the Lolo Trail. Reassure them the Corps of Discovery was coming back, Lewis instructed his sergeant, but if the Indians refused to delay any longer, then two privates should stay back and the others should "accompany the Indians by whatever rout they might take to travellers rest and blaize the trees well as they proceeded."

The expedition began its second attempt at crossing the Bitterroot Range of mountains on the morning of June 24. About noon, the expedition reunited with two of the privates earlier sent on temporary duty. The rest of their detachment, plus the two Indian men, were reeled in by day's end. That evening, the five Nez Perce guides prayed for good weather by setting fir trees on fire, a ritual William Clark found entertaining. The trees "when Set on fire create a very Sudden and emmence blaize from bottom to top of those tail trees," Clark remarks, "they are a boutifull object in this Situation at night. this exhibition remide me of a display of firewoks."

Day after day, the travelers plodded forward through meadows, across creeks, and "along the Steep Sides of tremendious Mountains." On June 26, the expedition reached the spot where snowdrifts had terminated their progress 10 days earlier. Scars on the trees left by staggering pack animals on June 17 confirmed to Clark that the depth of the snow had reached higher than 10 feet. This day, he estimated the snow pack "had sunk to 7 feet tho' perfectly hard and firm." The baggage earlier cached in the trees remained undisturbed, but it took two hours to redistribute it into new packs. Another Nez Perce man joined the party that afternoon. Several times the captains recognized camp locations they had used in

231

mid-September 1805 when the expedition followed the Lolo Trail going west. Even with their earlier experience, however, it would have been difficult – maybe impossible – for the explorers to follow the trail if not for their Indian guides.

That sobering thought hit Clark most directly on June 27 when, "we halted by the request of the Guides a fiew minits on an ellevated point and Smoked a pipe." At first, Clark's thoughts focused on the "extencive view of these Stupendeous Mountains principally Covered with Snow like that on which we Stood." Then he realized, he wrote, that "we were entirely Serounded by those mountains from which to one unacquainted with them it would have Seemed impossible ever to have escaped." Honestly, Clark admitted, "without the assistance of our guides, I doubt much whether we who had once passed them could find our way to Travellers rest… those indians are most admireable pilots." Still, Clark boasted in his journal, he viewed the scene before him as "Sufficient to have dampened the Spirits of any except Such hardy travellers as we have become."

Relentlessly the Corps of Discovery marched on, looking somewhat like a procession. The trails were always snow-covered. "We find the travelling on the Snow not worse than without it," notes Lewis, "as the easy passage it gives us over rocks and fallen timber fully compensate for the inconvenience of sliping, certain it is that we travel considerably faster on the snow than without it." They accomplished 28 miles on June 27 without once "releiveing the horses from their packs or their haveing any food." Consequently, the next day, the expedition traveled only 13 miles "along the dividing ridge over knobs & through deep hollows," but they quit at noon when they reached "an untimbered side of a mountain" sprouting an abundance of grass for the "much fatigued" horses.

JUNE 29-JULY 5, 1806

During five trying days on the Lolo Trail in June, the single-file Lewis and Clark Expedition looked like a solemn procession. Beginning on June 29, however, their progress took on aspects of a triumphant parade.

To begin, just five miles into the day, the Lolo Trail dropped from the heights of the ridge to the river below. "When we descended," notes Meriwether Lewis approvingly, "we bid adieu to the snow." Near the river, the hungry men found, and ate, a deer that an advance party of hunters had killed and hung for them. Two miles farther and they could see, very plainly, the "old road" they had followed in September of 1805. The road took the Corps of Discovery to a vast, grassy field that today is an attachment to the visitor's center at the summit of Lolo Pass on U.S. Highway 12. All of this took place before noon.

Seven miles below the meadow, the expedition reacquainted itself with Lolo Hot Springs, a warm-water oasis they had first encountered on the westward trek. This time, they stopped for the night and enjoyed the resort-like experience. William Clark estimated the temperature in the pools to be about the same as ones he had frequented in Virginia. He bathed for 10 minutes; Lewis timed his repose at 19 minutes. In addition, "both the Men and the indians amused themselves with the use of the bath this evening." Everyone slept that evening in present-day Missoula County, on the eastern side of the Bitterroot Range.

Clark's journal entry for June 30 gets right to the point with his first words: "Descended the mountain to Travellers rest leaving those tremendious mountanes behind us – in passing of which we have experiensed Cold and hunger of which I shall ever remember." One must read the journal of Lewis to realize that it took a full day of travel – 32 miles, in fact – to reach Traveler's Rest a little before sunset. Lewis tells of struggles, including his own mishap when his horse "sliped with both his hinder feet out of the road and fell." His journal entry for the day closes with the comment that "here we Encamped with a view to remain 2 days in order to rest ourselves and horses and make our final arrangements for Seperation." The important word in this statement is "Seperation."

So confident had Lewis and Clark become in their own judgment, and the abilities of the men they led, that on July 1 they unveiled a travel plan that divided the expedition into groups, each led by a captain, but with detached patrols under three sergeants. Everyone was to meet at the junction of the Missouri and Yellowstone rivers, approximately the location of the border between Montana and North Dakota, which was more or less 850 miles distant. From there, they would continue canoeing on the Missouri River to St. Louis. It was a bold plan, the purpose of which was to include in their final report to President Thomas Jefferson additional details by Lewis about an Indian path reputed to link the Lolo Trail with the Great Falls of the Missouri. Additionally, Clark would present new information about the previously unexplored Yellowstone

River. Maybe the "Seperation" was foolhardy, since it put small units of men at risk from hostile tribesmen and treacherous natural elements. No matter – the captains announced their decision and the enlisted men volunteered for one or the other of the patrols.

As arranged, on July 3 the Lewis and Clark Expedition divided. Lewis recorded the moment in his journal: "All arrangements being now compleated for carrying into effect the several scheemes we had planed for execution on our return, we saddled our horses and set out I took leave of my worthy friend and companion Capt. Clark and the party that accompanyed him. I could not avoid feeling much concern on this occasion."

❖ ❖ ❖

From Traveler's Rest, Meriwether Lewis and his men passed through present-day Missoula, followed the Indian's "buffalo road" to Lewis and Clark Pass, and finally reached Great Falls. During a subsequent side trip, Lewis and some of his men came to blows with the Blackfoot Indians, killing two. They returned to the Missouri River and hastily paddled east. William Clark and his men, meantime, followed the expedition's western route in reverse back to the Three Forks of the Missouri. They crossed Bozeman Pass to reach the Yellowstone River, and, on Aug. 3, merged into the Missouri River. Clark moved on, slowly, until Aug. 12 when Lewis caught up to him – a year to the day from when they passed into what is now Idaho.

On Sept. 23, 1806, after some 8,000 miles traveled and 28 months away from home, the Corps of Discovery returned to St. Louis. "We were met by all the village and received a harty welcom," wrote Clark. That day, Lewis wrote to President Thomas Jefferson: "It is with pleasure that I anounce to you the safe arrival of myself and party… In obedience to your orders we have penitrated the Continent of North America to the Pacific Ocean, and sufficiently explored the interior of the country to affirm with confidence that we have discovered the most practicable rout which dose exist across the continent by means of the navigable branches of the Missouri and Columbia Rivers." ■

ALSO IN THIS SERIES

If you enjoyed *Inlander Histories, Volume 2*, you'll also like 2014's *Volume 1*. Featuring stories on Woody Guthrie, May Arkwright Hutton, Expo '74 and the eruption of Mt. St. Helens, visit inlander.com/books to find out where you can buy a copy.

INLANDER BOOKS, SPOKANE, WASHINGTON

ABOUT THE AUTHORS

LUKE BAUMGARTEN was a staff writer and culture editor for the *Inlander* from 2005-12.

SHERI BOGGS was a staff writer and culture editor for the *Inlander* from 1999-2005.

ROBERT CARRIKER was a professor of history at Gonzaga University for five decades; he retired in 2015. He is the author of *Father Peter Jean DeSmet: Jesuit in the West.*

PATRICK HEALD was a freelance writer for the *Inlander* from 1993-95.

E.J. IANNELLI has been a freelance writer for the *Inlander* since 2010.

LISA WAANANEN JONES was the *Inlander*'s web editor from 2012-14.

TED S. McGREGOR JR. is the publisher of the *Inlander.*

IVAN MUNK was a Spokane artist and historian who contributed to the *Inlander* from 1994-2000; Munk passed away in 2006.

HENRY MATTHEWS is an emeritus professor in Architecture at Washington State University and author of *Kirtland Cutter: Architect in the Land of Promise.*

RONALD A. MYERS is a Spokane historian.

JACK NISBET is a naturalist and historian in Spokane. His most recent book is *Ancient Places.*

DAN RICHARDSON was a staff writer for the *Inlander* from 2001-02.

WILLIAM STIMSON is a journalism professor at Eastern Washington University and author of *A View of the Falls.*

JESS WALTER is a Spokane author and National Book Award finalist. His books include *Citizen Vince* and *Beautiful Ruins.*

ROBERT M. WITTER was a freelance writer for the *Inlander* in 1994.

J. WILLIAM T. YOUNGS is a history professor at Eastern Washington University and author of *The Fair and the Falls.*